Field of Blood

GWALLA

[signature]

To: Liz Blair

*Thanks Baby
Your Amazing!!*

*GWALLA Music
2020*

CLIFFORD "GWALLA" EVANS

PAGE PUBLISHING, INC.
Conneaut Lake, PA

First originally published by Page Publishing 2020

ISBN 978-1-64544-816-7 (pbk)
ISBN 978-1-64544-817-4 (digital)

Printed in the United States of America

Chapter One

Back in 1979, in New Orleans, Louisiana, a Creole man named Beaver from the 9th Ward quickly fell in love with a beautiful black woman named Ann, who was raised in the 7th Ward Saint Bernard project. Before the year was out, within a blink of an eye, Ann became pregnant. The couple was excited about the opportunity of adding a new member to their family.

Ann already had two daughters. They called the oldest Bubbles, and they nicknamed the younger daughter Fat. Ann always wanted to have a boy and prayed to God every day that she would be pregnant with a boy.

On August 19, 1980, Ann's prayers were answered. She gave birth to a healthy boy, eight pounds and five ounces. He looked like Beaver, a spitting image of him. The baby boy had light skin with big bubble eyes and a tremendously loud mouth to match his father's. Ann looked at Beaver with a smile of satisfaction.

"Congratulations! You have a Siamese twin."

Beaver looked at her and smiled as he thought to himself, *If I asked for a paternity test, I'll look like a fool.* Beaver was happy to have his first child with Ann, and it was a boy.

Two days after giving birth, Charity Hospital released Ann. By now she was living downtown in the 8th Ward on Saint Roch Street. Ann enjoyed every moment of tending to her newborn. They quickly gave him the nickname Baby Dumpling. For short, they called him Dump.

Bubbles was two years older that Fat. They loved having a baby brother, but after a while, they became resentful, because Ann started to show them less attention. To them, it became obvious that Dump was the prince.

It was crazy how quick one, two, three, four years blew by. Beaver and Ann's relationship had begun to change. Normally, Ann would go to work and come straight home most of the time; she would even beat Beaver home from work. She would cook, clean, and tend to the children. Then Ann's routine started to change. As soon as she got off work and made it home, she would be back out the door before Beaver made home.

Ann and her twin sister, Betty, would always go places only to return home pissy drunk. Fat and Bubbles could tell that their parents started to grow apart. Dump was only four years old, so he was too young to understand, but soon he would be in for a big surprise.

By the age of five, Dump started going to a school close to his mother's side of the family house in the 7th Ward. When he made it home from school, his sisters would take care of him. The house was full of fun, until both parents made it home from work. Then it would be so silent you could hear a pin drop. Beaver and Ann seemed as if they were no longer in love. They both knew that the family would never be the same, and they both made a decision and had no intentions of changing it.

It was the summer of 1986, and Dump's seventh birthday was a week away.

He kept asking Bubbles, "When is my birthday? What will I get?"

Bubbles would smile and say, "It's a secret."

Dump would be so highly upset till he would fold his arms into each other and pout. Bubbles loved getting Dump worked up. Ann spoiled Dump. He could get whatever he desired when he wanted it, but when she or Fat asked for something, Ann always gave them a reason as to why they had to wait.

The next day after Bubbles, Fat, and Dump made it home from school, everything suddenly felt strange. Dump was in his own world, playing with his toys, while Bubbles and Fat were cleaning up. When Beaver and Ann made it home from work, they were both in a good mood. Everything appeared to be okay, although the weather seemed to have gotten hotter and more humid as the night had begun to fall.

Bubbles had decided to open up her bedroom window to cool the room off while she got ready for bed. The room cooled, but for some reason, Bubbles still felt uncomfortable. She tossed and turned, trying to position herself to get comfortable as the cool air blew through the window, making the blue-and-red polka-dot curtains dance lightly through the air. After one too many countless toss and turns, Bubbles decided to close the window.

When she walked to the window, Bubbles noticed a man sitting on the roof of the house next door, looking down into the window at her. Like a deer in headlights, Bubbles stood stuck in place with wide, innocent doe eyes. Her heart beat feverishly, pounding like a bass drum in her ears. She looked closer and realized the man on the roof was naked and was pulling at his private.

At the top of her lungs, Bubbles screamed as she ran into her parents' room to tell them what she saw. Beaver immediately jumped up, running out the front door to search for the man, but he was nowhere to be found.

Beaver walked back into the house, upset, and announced, "Always be sure to keep the windows and doors locked at all times. Pay attention to your surroundings. This neighborhood is not safe."

From that day on, Bubbles and Fat became extremely cautious, paying close attention to everything, and wondering what would happen next. Dump paid no attention to what happened that night. All he could think of was, *My birthday could be tomorrow.*

The next morning, Dump woke up to a brown-and-white puppy with a big red satin bow tied around its neck.

He ran around the house, super excited, yelling, "This has to be my birthday!"

Beaver and Ann were excited that Dump was excited. They allowed him to play with the puppy for a little while before getting ready for school.

Every morning Dump played with his puppy, Do-do, before school while his mother wrote a note to the bus driver giving directions on what busses Dump needed to transfer to and from in order to reach his destination. Dump was only six and thought nothing strange about it, although many passengers often wondered how and why in the world was he so young catching the bus alone.

Early one Saturday morning, Dump decided to give Do-Do a bath. He took the puppy out on the porch then put him in a small tub and began to bathe him making sure to get him sudsy all over. Dump talked to Do-Do while he bathed him as if he could understand every word. Dump was so focused on washing Do-Do that he didn't notice the brown station wagon rolling slowly up the street until something instinctually told him to look up. That was when he noticed the station wagon one door down from in front of his house creeping slowly down the street. As the station wagon got closer to the house, the slower it approached. Dump never took his big bubbled eyes off the spooky-looking wagon as it crawled to a stop in the middle of the street directly in front of Dump's house. Dump's heart began to beat faster and faster as he noticed a man in the station wagon looking at him straight in the eyes.

It was the first time Dump was able to recognize feelings of fear while being alone. Within a fraction of a second, Dump left his puppy full of bubbles in the tub and ran inside the house. The strangest thing about it was that he never told anyone, but it stayed on replay in his mind that whole day. He kept wondering what would've happened if he stayed on the porch. Dump's mentality had begun to evolve.

Dump started to go outside more, making friends and learning how to interact with others in the neighborhood. Little did he know, he would always have issues with getting along with people because of his self-centered characteristics. Ann always treated Dump as if he was second to none, so he acted as he was treated, which kept his sisters envious and resentful of him. Any friends that he interacted with would eventually feel the same way. It wasn't his fault; it was just the way he was trained, and soon enough, he would have to learn how to deal with the repercussions. Time after time, day after day with each friend Dump made, he would eventually have to fight. Dump went from having five friends to understanding that real friends didn't come easy.

One day after Fat, Bubbles, and Dump came home from school, Fat started doing her homework while Bubbles started doing her daily chores of cooking, cleaning, and keeping an eye on Dump and his best friend, Do-Do, who were both making a mess in the house.

After a few hours later, Beaver walked into the house from work early. He came into the house so quietly that the children didn't even know he was home until Bubbles walked into the living room to vacuum. Beaver was sitting quietly on the couch, looking far off into the distance.

"Are you okay?" asked Bubbles.

Startled, Beaver looked at her then put his head down low, but he never responded. Bubbles could tell something heavy was on Beaver's mind. She returned to the kitchen to finish cooking. Bubbles checked on the pot of chili on the stove, giving it a few strong stirs before checking on Dump, who was just as quiet as his dad was.

She opened the door only to find Dump on the floor, sleeping like a baby with Do-Do's head resting on his leg. Before she could close Dump's door, she could hear Fat hollering from her room, "Is the food ready?"

Bubbles answered with an irritated, "No! Give me a minute!"

She walked back into the kitchen to finish cooking when suddenly, the power in the house went out. She went into the living room to ask Beaver if he knew what happened, but he was gone. She opened the front door to see if he was outside, but just like the man that was lurking on the roof of the house next door, Beaver was nowhere in sight.

It was November, and the weather was cold. They all put on their jackets because the temperature dropped in the house quick. Bubbles walked outside to check the fuse box, and when she opened it, all the fuses were gone, just like Beaver. Nothing like this ever happened before. Bubbles didn't understand what was going on. She walked back into the house with a concerned frown.

"Fat, I'm going use the phone next door to call Mom. Keep an eye on Dump."

Bubbles called Ann and told her what was going on. Ann left work and was on her way home. She knew exactly what was going on and why Beaver left, but she didn't expect him to leave the way he did. They easily fell in love fast and were married quick, but it didn't last. It had become obvious that time brought on a change.

Chapter Two

A couple of years passed, and Dump was eight years old. A few things changed, but one thing remained the same: he missed his father and could never understand why he was gone.

Dump, Bubbles, Fat, and his mother, Ann, moved from the 8th Ward to the 9th Ward. Beaver once told them that the area in the 8th Ward wasn't safe, but the 9th Ward was a far cry from being better. It was intense in every aspect. The house that they moved into was a town house right across the street from Dump's new school. He didn't have to catch a bus anymore. He would walk across the street reciting the "Pledge of Allegiance" all the way up till he reached his class.

Ann gave him a key to the house so when he got out of school, he could get inside. His sisters had after school volleyball and majorette practice, while Ann was still at work. Dump began to love his neighborhood. It made his school days go by much faster.

The hood was full of children. After school, they all came outside to play. He was new to the hood, so everybody wanted to meet him. They all came by his door for a minute to play. It went on for a week or two, but he started to get a bad vibe. Since they were different from all the other children in the neighborhood, the boys started a gang.

In elementary school at lunchtime, they all hung together. Every day they hit the yard clapping their hands and stumping their feet like, *stump! Stump! Stump! Stump! Stump! Stump! Stump! Stump! Stump!* From their mouths screaming, "That TSP! Too Short Posse!" over and over again. Strange, but true, the group consisted of twelve boys that were different, yet they were the most popular boys in the school.

Time seemed like it was flying by. Dump was now twelve years old. Fat was fourteen, and Bubbles was sixteen. After school, Dump would make it home first, then Fat, and Bubbles was always last. Ann routinely went to work after she sent them off to school and come home late that evening. After work, Ann would always sit at the kitchen table smoking her cigarettes, drinking beer, and listening to blues music. Every night, Dump would be up late playing *Super Mario* on his Nintendo. He was addicted to playing *Duck Hunt* with the plastic gun. Dump got a kick out of pointing the gun at the TV screen to kill the ducks. Little did he know, that same characteristic from that video game would eventually become a reality in his life. Squeezing a trigger was being engraved in his heart. He had no idea that he was in training, nor did he know what he was in training for.

One day Dump woke up getting ready for school. He was pooped from the night before from playing all those repetitive *Duck Hunt* fights, plus he wasn't feeling well. For a second, he thought he should ask Ann could he stay home, but he knew she would say no.

Dump got ready for school as usual, and on his way out the door, he told his mom, "I love you, Mom! I'll see you later!"

Ann replied, "I love you too, baby!"

As soon as she heard the door close, Ann continued to put on her makeup while praying to God for a financial breakthrough. She thanked God in advance for her blessing.

Dump stood in the parking lot with the rest of the students at school with their right hand over their hearts, left hand raised to the sky, reciting the pledge. As he recited the pledge, he noticed his mother walking up the block to the bus stop on her way to work. He was thinking about the key in his pocket and was ready to use it, knowing no one was home.

After the "Pledge of Allegiance," all the students started entering the school. Dump decided to dip through the crowd then cross the street and go home. It was odd for a fourth-grade student to be cutting class, but to Dump, it seemed ordinary. He thought his mom would never find out. He thought about how much fun he would have. He could do whatever, however, and whenever he wanted to without a problem.

Back to back for three days, Dump did the exact same thing, but on the third night, Ms. Powell, Dump's fourth-grade teacher, called and asked, "Mrs. Evans, why has Cage been missing school?"

Concerned, Ann responded, "Ms. Powell, what do you mean? I've been sending him to school every day."

Ms. Powell replied, "Ms. Evans, he hasn't been present."

Ann resounded, "Okay, thanks, Ms. Powell."

Meanwhile, Dump was upstairs taking a bath. He had no idea his teacher had called. Ann hung up with Ms. Powell and walked upstairs to Dump's room. She took one of the game joysticks and wrapped it around her hand. As soon as Dump started getting out of the tub, Ann bust through the door. Asking no questions, she immediately started whipping Dump while he was still wet.

It caught him off guard. He could tell his mother was enraged. As she was swinging the joystick rapidly against his wet naked body, he could hear the wire inside the joystick breaking like the sound of a whip in the wind. As the wire whapped him profusely, Ann was hollering, "When you don't go to school, I'm gone bust ya ass like this every time," while she held one of Dump's arms in the air and whipping the fuck out of him with the other hand.

Dump was present at school every day after that. That beating scared him, and it never left his mind. At that point, Dump understood the consequences of being guilty.

Chapter Three

Bubbles was now seventeen, turning eighteen. She had graduated high school and was now working. Fat was a junior in high school. For some reason, she was so anxious to graduate, because she had a plan that no one knew about. Dump was now fourteen and a freshman at George Washington Carver Senior High School. There were three dominate hoods that were interesting, relevant, popular, and caustic at the school. One of the neighborhoods they hung around was the Desire Projects. Second hood was the Florida Project. Last but not least was Press Park, Dump's neighborhood. It was where all the TSP BOYS still hung together.

They all grew older but still had the same mind-set. Every chance they got, they showed off, spazzing out, making sure they captured everybody's attention. They had evolved to be a gang that actually grew a bond with one another, but on the cool, they were in competition with one another. They always stuck together when it came to beefing with other hoods, but when they were alone in their own hood, they always had a problem among themselves.

Ann was caught up in still treating Dump as a number one. Dump and his sisters grew even further apart. It was ten times worse than when they were younger. Back then, they had to interact with one another. But now that they were older, all three siblings were in the house together, not saying a word to one another. Dump paid it no mind, but Fat took the situation seriously. In her mind, once she finished school, she was moving away to her father's house. That was her best-kept secret.

Dump was always fresh when he went to school; however, one day he came to school fresher than a pair of Pradas. It was no secret; he was cutting the fuck up, showing out harder than ever. The girls were loving it. On the other hand, not only the dudes from the other hood were hating, but so was his own team. They hated the zone he was in. They didn't care that he was representing the hood. They resented the fact that Dump had become "Today's Hottest Topic." Dump didn't care. He felt like good publicity and bad publicity were all the same.

Later on that day while Dump and his team were all walking home from school, one of his friends named Pook had started making fun of him. The other eight guys that were walking with them started snickering and laughing under their breath.

Dump looked at them and said, "Everything that shine ain't gold."

They stopped laughing. They caught on to what he meant. They knew that they were rocking sideways and were far from keeping it real. Dump and Pook made eye contact and started fighting. The friends found it entertaining because Pook was getting the best of Dump, so they had no intentions of breaking up the fight, but the tables began to turn. Dump started hitting Pook with a few straight punches. Suddenly, the friends decided to come between them and stop the fight.

Once the fight was broken up, Dump jerked away from them and walked off. When he turned his back to them, they let Pook go. Pook ran up from behind Dump and snuck a punch to the back of his head him then took off running in fear because he knew Dump was going to chase him in rage. Dump couldn't catch him because Pook was short, small, and fast. After that day, Dump always had a chip on his shoulders. And from that moment on, the bond of their team started to slowly wither away.

Meanwhile, all the other teams stuck together. The other two 9th Ward hoods were historical projects with hundreds of guys on their teams. However, the guys were broken up into sections. The Desire Project had three sections. Because of the size of the land and project units, it literally was the largest project in America. Each building had six units. Two units on each floor standing three stories high stacked brick on top of brick. All together, it was ten long blocks. The three sections were the "Up Front Boys," the "Benefit Boys," and the "Back Boys." The Benefit Boys were in the middle of the project, so they stayed neutral, and their turf was mutual grounds. The Up Front Boys were all about selling drugs, getting money and stunting. The Back Boys were in too many different things like hustling, robbing, killing, partying, and fighting.

The Florida Project had only two sections: The "Dark Side" and the "Murder Side." Both sides were about selling drugs, doing drugs, and killing. The Desire and Florida Projects had no problem naming the sections different because of their differences, and they had no problem tending to their issues in the public openly.

Press Park had two sides, but under one umbrella. It was a strange situation, but that was how it was. They appeared to be loyal with one another as well as solid, but in actuality, they were undercover slick wilding with their own intentions. Because the other teams were much larger, when the Park Boys were in the streets, they would be one body, one mind, and one sound, which was definitely a smart move in those situations. It was only twenty-seven of them. The other group had fifty to one hundred in each section.

In the summer of 1995, Press Park Boys were one of the 9th Ward's hottest topics. Buku dudes were hating only because the young bucks were too flashy. The girls were loving it though because they were popular. Dump was a part of a group where each member felt like they were the hottest member in the group. On the 4th of July, an artist named Fila Phil from their hood dropped his first album, *Da Hustler*. That added nothing but fuel to the fire, and these boys were hot. They were already well-known in their area, but Fila Phil expanded their reputation. With Dump seeing the excitement of the life of an artist, it inspired him to become an artist. He started to write a lot of raps and tweaking to perform, but he never had the chance because he was knee-deep in the streets dealing with his gang on a day-to-day basis in the bricks.

One day, a dude named Snick came home from serving a juvenile sentence for sexually assaulting another younger boy. Nobody showed that they held it against him because he was a great fighter and a pure bully. He immediately hooked up with another member of the gang, Shit-O. He was also a great fighter who never lost a fight in the hood. Those two hung all day long. Dump was with a few guys shooting dice when the duo Shit-O and Snick showed up. They noticed Dump was fresh dressed in all white, and from his ears to his waist, Dump was rocking a sick ice game. Shit-O started cracking jokes on Dump talking sideways and showing off in front of Snick because he was released. Snick was beside himself, not knowing where Dump's mind-set was at that moment. While the jokes were cracking Dump kept silent, but he wanted to bat the fuck out of Shit-O. Dump was too fresh to entertain the dumb shit. Instead, he cracked a smile and just walked away, sticking a big knot of cash in his pocket. When he made it home, he laid down, thinking to himself, *Tomorrow I'mma beat the fuck out him*, as he dozed off to sleep.

The next morning Dump woke up early with last night on his mind. He thought about nothing else but catching Shit-O walking home from work and beating the breaks off his ass. Shit-O always walked home from work the same way every day, so Dump sat in one place and waited. An hour passed, but he never came.

Still Dump waited patiently but was anxious. Knowing that no one ever beat him, Dump wanted to make a statement, so he waited and waited until he heard Shit-O's voice coming from another direction. It caught him off guard just as he was about to catch Shit-O off guard with his move. Shit-O saw Dump, and they made eye contact. Shit-O caught the vibe and attempted to avoid the situation, so he dipped in the store. Dump waited outside.

When Shit-O came out, Dump asked, "What's up?"

He replied, "What's up with what?"

Dump reminded him, "What's up with that shit you were talking with Snick last night? Let's get it in."

Dump could tell by Shit-O's face that he was shaken.

Shit-O paused then stated, "All right, come on."

Shit-O started walking around the buildings through the cuts. Dump didn't know where he was going or what was on his mind, but he followed him anyway, thinking it was kind of foolish. Shit-O turned the corner. Dump was ten paces behind him. When he turned the corner, he saw Shit-O bending down in front of his older brother swapping shoes and lacing them up. Not only that, the block was packed. Dump had no idea the block was full of people because he sat in one spot for hours. It was obvious that Shit-O needed a crowd to show off. Dump showed character by waiting alone and going at him solo, young man to young man, checking him without a crowd. That was what shook Shit-O. It seemed as if Shit-O needed back up in an effort to try to intimidate Dump.

Shit-O's older brother, Al, was a well-known hit man that would murder an innocent person for an unworthy reason, but Dump's mind was so foolish that he didn't give two fucks. The anticipation and the energy had the crowd going dumb. They all knew in their minds that Dump would lose the fight.

Shit-O finished lacing up his shoes and said, "Come on," while he rushed Dump.

Dump sidestepped him and hit Shit-O with a quick and hard three piece. Shit-O fell back. He shook it off and rushed again. Dump did the same thing. He dipped. *Bang! Bang! Bang!* Shit-O's brother Al started talking shit to Dump, but Dump kept punishing Shit-O's ass while talking shit back to a cold-blooded killer.

Al said, "Bitch, don't play with my brother! He gone blend your ass!"

Dump responded, "Fuck all that. He ain't get a lick yet." Then he hit Shit-O with a quick blend, grabbing him when he got closer. Al looked his brother in the eye and could see he was dazed up.

Al demanded, "Let him go! You better not hit him!"

Dump looked Al in his eyes and could feel his blood bubbling. He pushed Shit-O off, hitting him with a crucial right hook. While he was falling, Al went into rage and charged at Dump, kicking him in his stomach. As Dump was falling, he looked at his so-called closest friend and yelled, "Big Donkey! You see this shit?"

Big-Donkey didn't respond. The brothers kept kicking Dump. Either the kicks were too soft, or the blood in his veins was burning too hot, because he didn't feel a thing. After a few more kicks, Shit-O and Al quickly dipped off.

After that, Dump had that reality sink in again, "There is no such thing as true friends."

Dump's life was bringing on a change, but the principles forever remained the same.

Chapter Four

The day after the fight, Dump wasn't tripping. Even though Shit-O and his brother Al rushed him; he was satisfied, because everybody knew he smashed on their asses. Dump didn't realize at that time, although he won the fight, his homies hated him more. They became even more envious of Dump because none of them ever beat Shit-O, plus they all wanted to see Dump lose just so they could clown him.

It was about noon one evening when Big Donkey and Dump were chilling on the block. Al pulled up in his black Lincoln. Dump looked at Big Donkey and could tell he was nervous 'cause he was feeling uneasy himself. Al rolled down the front passenger door window and told them with a demanding tone, "Get in."

They didn't want to, but because of his reputation, they did. Dump sat in the front passenger seat, and Donkey sat in the back. Al pulled off. The car was quiet. They bent two corners then pulled up on an isolated back street with stolen burned cars on the block. Al pulled to the side then stopped. He looked at Dump with a cold stare, then he looked in the back seat at Donkey and asked," You straight?"

By the tone of his voice, they could tell what was on Al's mind.

Donkey responded promptly, "Fucking right I'm good."

The only thing Dump could think of was, "Why the fuck none of us have a gun?"

He turned back to the front and looked back at Dump and pulled off while telling them, "Don't fuck with my lil brother no more. Y'all leave that shit alone."

Dump looked back at him and nodded. Al dropped Dump and Big Donkey off and burned out. After that day, Shit-O could never look Dump in his eyes, but Al always did. He could tell that Dump wasn't cool with that backstreet play. Dump just wasn't in position to do anything about it. He was still learning the streets.

That night when he went home, he started acting different and Ann could feel that something was up.

She told him, "Oh, Dump, I want you to go to church with me in the morning!"

He agreed, "Okay, cool."

He needed to hear the Word to help him relax and pray. He wanted to be around more positive energy because the last few weeks had been off the wall. He always talked with God, but he didn't have a major relationship with Him like God wanted him to, but sooner or later, that would change.

Early Sunday morning, he woke up from a crazy dream, but he couldn't remember what the dream was about. He started getting dressed for church, but when he finished, he noticed that Ann was still in bed.

He asked, "Mom, are you going to get ready?"

She said, "No, baby. I don't feel good. We can go next Sunday."

He screamed, "Okay!"

Dump decided he would go to church by himself for the first time. When he made it to the church and walked in, members of the congregation began to greet him. They were shocked that he was attending services young and alone. He took a seat on the second row feeling like it was meant for him to be there. Dump prayed, asking God to give him understanding of his Word. His mind was in grief, back and forth about what had been going on in his life. Dump started listening to the preacher preach. The pastor connected with his spirit, giving a message about God speaking to a man named Balaam. The pastor read the Word, saying, "From the book of Numbers chapter 22, starting at verse 12, and the Word of the Lord says, 'And God said to Balaam, "You should not go with them. You should not curse the people, for they are blessed." So Balaam rose in the morning and said to the princes of Balak, "Go back to your land, for the Lord has refused to give me permission to go with you." And the princes of Moab rose and went back to Balak, and said, "Balaam refuses to come with us." Then Balok again sent princes, more numerous and more honorable than they.'"

Then the preacher said, "Now let's skip to verse 20. 'And God come to Balaam at night and said to him, "If the men come to call you, rise and go with them; but only the word I speak to you that you should do." So Balaam rose in the morning, saddled his donkey, and went with the princess of Moab. Their God's anger was aroused because he went, and the Angel of the Lord took His stand in the way as an adversary against him. Now the donkey saw the Angel of the Lord standing in the way with His drawn sword in His hand, and the donkey turned into the field. So Balaam struck the donkey to turn her back onto the road. Then the Angel of the Lord stood in a narrow path between the vineyards with a wall on this side and a wall on that side. And when the donkey saw the Angel of the Lord, she pushed herself against the wall and crushed Balaam's foot against the wall; so he struck her again. Then the Angel of the Lord went further and stood in a narrow place where there was no way to turn either to the right hand or to the left. And when the donkey saw the Angel of the Lord, she lay down under Balaam; so Balaam's anger was aroused, and he struck the donkey with his staff. The Lord opened the mouth of the donkey, and she said to Balaam, "What have I done to you, that you have struck me these three times?" And Balaam said to the donkey, "Because you have abused me. I wish there were a sword in my hand, for now I would kill you!" So the donkey said to Balaam, "Am I not your donkey on which you have ridden, ever since I became yours, to this day? Was I ever disposed to do this to you?" And he said, "No." Then the Lord opened Balaam's eyes, and he saw the Angel of the Lord standing in the way with His drawn sword in His hand; and he bowed his head and fell flat on his face. And the Angel of the Lord said to him, "Why have you struck your donkey these three times? Behold, I have come out against you, because your way is perverse before Me. The donkey saw me and turned aside from Me those three times. If she had not turned aside from Me, surely I would have killed you by now and let her live."'"

After speaking the Word, the pastor's voice went down low to a whisper, but clear. Dump drifted into a trance. From the beginning his ears were open, but at that moment, his vision was open just as the angel of the Lord opened Balaam's eyes.

Dump started to feel God speaking to him as the pastor was saying, "The message slash moral to this story is, don't go like Balaam did, traveling up the wrong road beating the wrong ass. The donkey was not the one who deserved to be beaten. Balaam was the one who disobeyed God's instructions. Therefore, he should've beat himself."

Dump snapped out of it and understood every word. He got up and left service before it was over. In his mind, he heard exactly what he needed to hear. Dump made up his mind not to just act different, but to think different as well. He went home thinking about everything that happened last week.

He said to himself, "I feel like I'm going down the wrong road, but I'm addicted." He positioned himself in his bed on his back, listening to *All Eyes on Me* until he dozed off.

The next morning Dump woke up, and the song "Picture Me Rolling" off the *All Eyes on Me* album was playing on repeat. It was creepy because he never touched the radio before he dozed off, and the album was playing straight through. Once he realized that someone or something touched the radio, he turned it off, got dressed, and left.

As soon as he walked out the door, he had to put his hand over his eyes because the sum was beaming. He decided to walk around to the back of his house. When he goes to the back, he looked down the ally and took a double take. At first he thought he was tripping, but he wasn't. Behind his yard, there was a man lying facedown on the sidewalk, not moving at all. He walked to the front of the house, told Ann what he saw, and she called the police.

When they arrived, they asked Dump, "Did you see or hear anything?"

Dump said, "I don't know what happened. I woke up, saw a body, and called you."

The office replied, "So you're saying that a person was murdered behind your house and you didn't hear, see, or know nothing?"

Dump looked at the officer as the officer was looking at him with a stale face, as if he really had something to do with it. Dump paid it no mind. He walked off, wondering who was the man that was lying on the ground. He thought to himself, "How could I sleep and not hear gunshots?"

The family came to identify the body before the coroner came to pick the body up. The police notified them that the deceased had drugs and a gun on his waistline. Between the deceased's reputation and a gun on his waist not drawn, it was obvious that the murderer was somebody he trusted. He was shot once in the head and two to the body at close range. Dump thought long and hard, trying to figure out who was connected enough to go dumb in his cut and not be exposed. Dump left before they took the body. He was so addicted to chasing the money; murder didn't stop the business. The hood he lived in was full of dope dealers and drug addicts. Dump had reached the point where he wanted to be drafted into the league.

For the last five years Dump had lived right next door to the biggest drug dealers in the neighborhood. It was transparent that it had a tremendous influence on him—so much so that Dump had set up a meeting with the Big Homies, but when he went to the spot to meet with them, only one of the OG's sons showed up.

When he walked in the spot, he greeted Dump, "What's popping, lil homie? What the business is?"

Dump replied, "I'm cooling, Big Homie. I'm trying to run some numbers up."

Big Homie blinked his eyes twice, grinned, then said, "I feel ya, lil homie. Play ya position, and I got cha."

Dump said, "Cool."

He played his position and let a few days blow by.

The summer was almost over, so Ann gave Dump a few hundred dollars to go school shopping. When he hit the block with the gang, the hot topic of the day was that everyone wanted to buy a pair of red Bally Animals for school.

Dump asked, "How much do they cost?"

Choppa answered, "They cost $237. We all gotta get that."

Suddenly, Dump felt like he was obligated to buy the shoes. He felt like if he didn't wear them, he would be out of uniform. Dump took the three hundred dollars and caught a ride to the Canal Place Mall with Big Homie's mother, Ms. Phyllis, and his little brother, O-Head. They walked into Bally's shoe store, which was the most upscale store that he had ever been in. He and O-Head brought the shoes and left.

After leaving the store, Dump was deep in thought, realizing that he was introduced to another feeling of blowing money. The feeling had him high on life, and he was quickly addicted.

That school year, Dump and his team were going to make a statement at Carver Senior High School.

When Ms. Hazel pulled up to the house, Dump got out and went inside. Ann looked at him poking her lips out while pulling her right hand on her hip and asked, "Boy, where is the rest of your stuff? Is that all you have?"

"Yeah, Ma!" Dump replied. "This all I had enough for."

Dump could tell Ann was pissed. "Three hundred dollars and that's all you had enough for?"

"Yeah." Dump assured her.

Ann looked at Dump with a disappointed face and told him, "Boy, you're really starting to act foolish."

Not understanding, Dump asked, "Why do you say that, Ma?"

She just walked off, shaking her head at him. He went to walk up the stairs to his room with his bag, wondering what his mother was thinking. He went into his room and set the bag on the bed. He heard Ann calling him back downstairs.

When he walked up to her, she gave him another hundred dollars and said, "Look, I'm working hard to provide for us. I don't have a million dollars to buy the world. I'm gone all day working, leaving you money and giving you the opportunities to make your own decisions, and you're not making them wisely. I'm telling you! I want you to listen and listen good. Don't grow up acting and living foolishly."

Dump responded, "Okay."

But he actually paid her no mind because he didn't feel as if he was acting foolish. He didn't know it, but what Ann said stuck in his head, bouncing back and forth like last night's murder.

Later that evening, Dump walked out the back door into the yard, then opened the gate, walking out to the murder scene. It was strange. The blood stains were still there as if they didn't clean it at all. They just simply took the body. The fact that the victim was a popular hustler from the hood made the situation more fucked up in Dump's mind. He walked back into the house and told Ann that life was seeming to be unfolding quickly.

She asked, "What do you mean?"

He said, "I heard of lots of murders and know a few killers, but for a killer to kill someone right behind our house makes it feel like situations in life are becoming more graphic and even closer to home."

Ann went in her purse, took out a cigarette, lit it, inhaled, and blew out a thin and long winding cloud of smoke.

She said, "Son, I pray to the Lord for you every day. That's why I talked to you about acting foolish."

He said, "I understand, Mom."

The truth was, he didn't.

As the sun set, Dump was alone to himself rocking solo. He got to a point where he didn't know who to trust anymore. Dump went to his room, grabbed a pack, then went in the backyard and rolled some piff to blow as he relaxed his mind. When he put the gar to his mouth and blazed up, he saw Big Homie rolling up on him as he rolled down his window.

"What's popping, lil homie?"

Dump cracked a smile and said, "You already know, Big Homie. Same shit, just a different day."

Big Homie nodded and said, "Believe that! Come hop in."

As he rolled the dark tinted window back up, Dump put the piff out, walked up to the Rover, and opened up the passenger door to get in, but Al was sitting there. He walked to the back door, popped it open, and sat behind Al, next to another natural-born killer named Aggie, who was sitting behind Big Homie. Dump closed the door and felt the energy. He was in the mist of one of the top dogs and his two hit men. Dump could tell that they just came back from doing some street work, but he asked no questions because it wasn't his business.

Instead, he said, "I been waiting for you, Big Homie."

Big Homie said, "Shit. I told you I got you. Take this slab, and bring me back fifty."

Dump took the slab, looked at it, tucked it in his pocket, and said, "Dig that.

He looked at Aggie and Al, then gave Big Homie dap and exited the vehicle. That moment changed the whole field.

Chapter Five

Dump walked back to the yard, lit up the gar, sat down and said out loud, "It's on nah!"

He hit the gar and a few times then dipped his head in the back door. He saw Ann sitting at the table, smoking her cigarettes, drinking beer, and listening to B. B. King. He could tell a lot was on her mind. Dump and his mom made eye contact but didn't speak. Dump went in the house, walking past Ann and went upstairs. Bubbles just made it home from work, so she did the same thing as Dump and headed straight for the stairs. Fat was by her father's house. She tried her best to stay out of sight, out of mind.

As Dump was walking out of the bathroom, Bubbles was walking into her room.

Dump asked, "Do you know what's bothering Mom?"

Bubbles just looked at him, rolled her eyes, walked in her room, and closed the door. Dump went downstairs and took a seat at the table.

He asked Ann, "Mom, what's going on?"

She just shook her head, putting it down, while tears started to run from her eyes and answered, "Nothing, son. God is going to take care of it."

Dump questioned, "What do you mean nothing? You're crying. Something is wrong. Is there anything I can do to make you feel better?"

Ann replied, "Yes, make better choices, and trust God."

He hugged her, saying, "I love you, Mom."

Dumped walked back to his room.

The next morning Dump woke up early, and the only thing on his mind was moving up from a hundred-dollar slab. It was two weeks before school started, and he had plans to run his money up. Dump knew this tall, slim, dark-skinned Hustler that was a powder addict on the cool named Snoopy that sold rocks out a crack house. Dump knew nothing about chopping rocks, so he had to get at him.

When he left out the house, his first move was running into Snoopy, grinding at the spot. He walked up the block slid through the cut then knocked on the door. Nobody answered, so he walked in and saw Snoopy wasn't there. Dump sat on the couch and hung out for a minute, waiting for the homie to show up.

Meanwhile, he overheard two cluckers talking in the room about how the cops ran in the spot last night then he heard one say, "Man, they took everybody's work but let 'em go free. The game fucked up out here."

As the vicks were walking out the room, Snoopy and Blow were walking in the front door, dying laughing.

Snoopy looked at Dump and said, "Lil nigga, what the fuck you doing in here?"

Dump responded, "I need to learn how to chop up and let somebody test this shit."

Dump pulled the slab out his packet and sat it on the table.

Snoopy grabbed it, then told Blow, "Get the razor!"

Blow tossed a razor to him, then Snoopy got up and took a plate out the dish rack, opened the pack, chopped a dime, passed it to Blow, and said, "Beam up, Scotty! Let me know what it's hitting for."

Blow dipped in the back room where Dump sat at the table. Snoopy started chopping.

He began to explain, "You lay it down like this, and pluck it right here. Then you flip it like this and cut it like that. After you cut it all down, you take the shake, put it in a bag, then give it out as a sample to a vick that always spends money."

Out of the blue, Snoopy and Dump heard a strange sound. It sounded like someone was jumping on the mattress.

Snoopy said, "Dump, go see what the fuck that nigga doing!"

He got up, walked to the door, and opened it. Blow was foaming from the mouth while his body was shaking and bouncing around on the mattress, going into convulsions. Dump heard about people overdosing, but now he was seeing it with his own eyes. It had him thinking, *Damn, Blow about to die from some shit I showed up with.*

Snoopy spazzed out, screaming, "Ma! Oh, Ma! Hurry up! Come get Blow!"

Ma ran into the room and said, "Dump, bring me some ice quick!"

Dump ran to the freezer, grabbed the tray, and sprinted to the room with it. Ma ripped Blow's shirt off and then unbuttoned his pants. After that, she took the ice tray from Dump and started rubbing the cubes on Blow's chest in a circular motion, but he was still shaking while his stomach was jumping.

Ma said, "Snoopy, get the milk!"

He dipped to it. When he came back with it, she was rubbing ice on Blow's nuts. Dump noticed he stopped moving. He looked dead. That made Dump walk out the room. He grabbed his work off the table and walked out the house with his mind boggled. As soon as he shut the door, he heard a fully automatic ringing shots out on the side of the spot. Then two dudes ran right by him through the cut. When Dump walked out the cut to the street, he saw a super wet black Impala burning out with a dude lying face down on the ground, not moving. Dump turned around and walked back in the cut. Snoopy walked out the house and said, "Come on, let's go. Ma shocked him back."

Dump said, "I'mma fuck with you tomorrow, fam. This bitch hot as the fuck."

Snoopy replied, "I know. Lay low young, and stay focused out here."

Dump walked up the block to his house. When he made it home he went to the kitchen, grabbed a plate, went upstairs, turned on the TV, flicked to the news channel, and started chopping down his work.

When Dump finished he had seven rocks and had to pluck three more. He chopped the first one, then he heard the breaking news theme music. The reporter started, "This morning, in the 9th Ward, a man was ambushed on Higgans and Press Street. He was shot nine times in his back with an assault rifle. The victim survived but is in critical condition. If anyone has any information, please contact Crime Stoppers at 522-2222. Your name is not needed, and if provided, it will be kept confidential."

Dump finished bagging, turned the TV off, and dozed off. When he woke up, it was about 1:00 p.m. He went outside and walked up the block by his homie Slob's house. He stashed the dope and knocked on the door. Nobody answered, so he sat on the patio, waiting to see a fiend to give 'em a sample.

Over thirty minutes passed, and Dump didn't see a soul. Shit was like a ghost town. It was too quiet. All he could hear was the birds chirping. At that moment, he saw Slob walking up and said, "What's up?"

Dump rubbed his nose like, "Shit, I'm out here trying to get it."

Slob looked back at him and said, "Bet!" Slob walked inside. Dump could tell Slob was handling some personal business, so he grabbed his dope and burned out. Later that evening he ran across a couple of vicks and made a few pops and for the next two weeks, it was all hustle.

It was the day before school started. Fat came home from her dad's house. This year she was a senior and ready to graduate so she could get away from her mother's side of the family. Her daddy treated her as a princess just as Ann treated Dump as a prince.

On the other hand, Bubbles's father was always missing in action. She always took care of herself with no help as she grew older. It seemed to her as if all Ann provided for her was a roof over her head, accompanied with responsibilities. Little did Fat and Bubbles know Dump actually loved them. He also paid close attention to their resentment toward him.

Chapter Six

It was early Monday morning before school. The Park Boys all met by Slob's house. They were sitting on the patio listening to their homie Fila Phil's hit single "Where My Hustlers At." The song was hot with a banging-ass beat. As it played, Slob was singing it, "Rat-ta-tat! rata-tat-tat trigga! Pass the callico to ah 9ᵗʰ Ward nigga!"

Everybody in the crew started to check out their Ballys, talking about the bright-red color with the red animal shapes in the white shoe soles.

Gug announced, "Today we gone go through that bitch shitting on 'em. I'm gone be turned the fuck up on them bitches and them bitch-ass niggas ya hard me!"

Shit-O said, "Believe that!"

As they began to walk off, Ma came walking through the cut and told them, "I don't fucking believe it. Snoopy was killed last night. Y'all be fucking careful out here."

Dump said, "Hold up. When he got hit at and who did it?"

She said, "I don't know who, but I bet it was somebody from the Desire. I don't know where it happened at."

It was strange that it happened last night, but they were just hearing about it.

While they were walking, Gug said, "Damn, that's fucked up."

All of them had stale faces.

One of them said, "We gotta smash on some shit. If not, we gone be on some dick shit, and them pussy-ass niggas gone keep mercing us out here!"

Dump agreed, "Real nigga shit."

Lung said, "It's crazy. How come we always believe a story we hear the streets say?"

Dump replied, "What are we supposed to believe nothing if we hear nothing, or something if we hear something?"

Shit-O said, "Sometimes when we listen to somebody in the streets that knows nothing about the streets, and they don't have the inside scoop, shit, nigga, it's like we out here with the blind leading the blind."

Then Lung said, "But Ma is heavy in the streets outchea for real. She knows what she talking 'bout."

Gug stopped and said, "Look, my nigga, either we gone ride together or die separately. It's our choice."

He was looking at Pook. Pook was looking at Shit-O. Shit-O was looking at O-Head. O-Head was looking at Slob. Slob was looking at Donkey, and Donkey was looking at Dump, and Dump was looking at them all.

Dump told them, "Something doesn't feel right. Let's keep it moving."

Once they reached the school, they walked through the gate thirteen deep, rocking their Bally Animals. It was the first time that environment saw anything from a group on that level. When they walked through, every group of people they walked by was looking at their feet. Some people made eye contact with the most popular boys in the gang. Some tapped their friends, pointing at their shoes while they started to whisper. Dump was feeling like a king on some boss shit. He was grinning, showing his two gold teeth on the side of his two front teeth. All of a sudden, out the blue, a chick walked past him and bumped him, walking up to Slob.

She leaned over and whispered in his ear.

He busted out laughing then said, "Bet! I got you!"

After breakfast, they got up from their table and dipped to class.

Slob told 'em, "Boy, after school, I got something for y'all ass."

O-Head said, "Oh yeee?"

Dump was like, "Double up!"

They all split up. Dump made it to his first class. His teacher was a female named Ms. Johnson. When he first saw her, the first thing that crossed his mind was, "Damn, she thicker than a Snicker." He never took his eyes off her, noticing her breasts were plump, her waist was slim, her ass was round, and her hips were wide, and her thighs were thick as fuck. Her hair was short, blonde, and cut perfect.

With a sweet, soft, confident tone, she said, "Good morning. Welcome to my world."

Ms. Johnson was the finest teacher Dump ever saw. She could tell by the look in his eyes, he was turned on like a light switch.

She walked behind her desk, looking down in her phone briefly and said, "Everyone is late but you. What's your name?"

Dump didn't answer her because he was zoned out, looking directly in her eyes, trying to read her mind, thinking to himself, "I would fuck you like a dog on some one-night-only shit."

Ms. Johnson saw the look in his eyes and read his mind.

She said, "Remember, in this class, opportunities somehow always present themselves. What's your name?"

Dump responded, "Cage Coleman."

She replied, "It's good to meet you, Cage. Stay focused," as she grinned.

Other students started walking in, groups by groups—two here, three there, and four or five at a time until the class was full.

Ms. Johnson stood up behind her desk, looked at the class, and said, "Good morning," as she wrote, "Never Fail to Plan" on the chalkboard.

She turned around to the class and stated, "From the first person to the last person who entered this classroom, by the way you entered, I can tell that many are alike, a few are odd, but two of us are very different."

She blinked her beautiful eyes once then made eye contact with Dump. She was swift and brief. To others it wasn't noticed, but Dump caught it clearly. He wanted to smile, but on some chess-game shit, he made no facial expression. Dump patiently waited for her to look at him so he could respond by blinking his eyes once. Ms. Johnson never made eye contact with him until the class bell rang for the next class. When it sounded, she raised her head and looked back at Dump. He blinked his eyes once, got up, and walked out.

Dump was walking through the hall on his way to his second period class, when he saw the dark chocolate thick chic that was with her friends earlier pointing at his feet and whispering. Dump jammed her up quick while she was bent over poking her ass out drinking from the water fountain. When he got close, he slowly walked up behind her, brushing himself lightly against her super thick ass. She pretended that she didn't feel it. So he did it again.

That's when she pushed her ass back on him and said, "Boy, what do you think you're doing?"

Dump looked at her slick and said, "All that pointing and whispering shit gone get your ass *fucked* up, yeah!"

She responded, "Oh, you got jokes, huh? You never know. I might want that."

As she was saying that, Dump was walking off and said, "Don't trip. I got chu."

He was still on his way to class when the tardy bell rung.

As soon as Dump made it to class, he walked in a saw four of the Desire Back Boys sitting together in the back of the class. That feeling came back from this morning. It changed the whole vibe. Them boys started smirking and talking under their breaths. All Dump could see when he looked at them were flashbacks of him and Snoopy at the trap house that day with him and Blow. He mentally flashed out, looked at them, booted the fuck up, and sat down behind them. Everything from that moment when Ma walked up on them this morning rewound in his head.

Then he heard Gug say, "Look, my nigga, either we gone ride together or die separately."

The teacher was talking, but Dump didn't hear a word. All he heard was Gug's voice on repeat. The teacher couldn't tell what was going on because he was doing his class work on auto pilot. Class was over quick the rest of the day was interesting.

Third period came and went. Then it was lunch time. The whole gang met up on the first floor in their well-known spot. It was different. Females were hanging close to their left, in range to their right, and ten feet away right in front their faces laughing and kee-keeing, letting it be known they was checking them out on the call.

Dump started telling the homies about the vibe in his class with the Back Boys. He broke it down to them how the play went.

He stopped in the middle and said, "Ma had to be telling the truth 'cause these clowns found something funny when I walked in the classroom."

Louie said, "Oh yeee?"

Dump was like, "Real shit."

When they started walking to the cafeteria all the girls broke out and went separate ways in their groups. The Up Front Boys were looking, paying close attention to Dump and his team.

One of The Up Front Boys said, "Man, them niggas doing too much."

He said it loud so everybody could hear it. Shit-O looked back, booted up, but kept walking. When they walked in the door, everybody started to look at them.

One of the Desire Back Girls screamed, "Park Boys deep in this bitch!"

That's when Dump hollered, "Park Life! Tell them bitch niggas get right!"

Girls from the Florida Project started laughing. One of them leaned over and started whispering in her friend's ear, then they all looked at the Back Girls. Dump was paying attention.

Big Donkey said, "Damn! Y'all got these hoes jock'n."

Dump said, "Yeah! But these hoes being messy."

And the whole gang started laughing. They found it funny, but Dump didn't because he knew some dumb shit was in the mix. All the other students from ever other hood sat together at every table, but the Park Boys table. It was a table with fifty seats, but the max seating at their table everyday was twelve, no more, no less. The way they operated made the Park Boys a hot topic. They sat at the table, ate, joked out, ribbing the fuck out of each other, and chilling until the bell rang.

When it rung, they cut the next class.

Louie said, "Let's go by the gym."

So they walked to it and went behind it. They rolled up a couple of blunts while they talked about their next move. Dump started talking to Shit-O while Louie sparked up the first gar. Pook heard a sound coming from around the building. Then saw Coach Rese turn the corner.

When Coach Rese looked up and saw them, he screamed in a raspy voice, "All y'all come here!"

Pook said, "Oh, shit. We out!"

They all busted out laughing while running off to another ducked off spot. When they got there, Dump said, "I'm going home. I'm gone fuck with y'all later. I got some business to get into."

Dump gave 'em all dap and pilled straight to the block.

When Dump made it to the block he met with the plug and gave him the money he owed. Big Homie dug in his pocket and gave him another pack, but this time it was doubled up in size. Dump looked at it and knew he was digging deeper in the game. The field got colder, and the risk grew larger. Dump shot out straight to the house, went in his closet, chopped down, bagged up, and headed straight for the block, but before he made it to the dope spot, he saw half of the click in front Slob's house. He dipped over there to see what was going on.

When he walked up, he saw O'Neal smiling.

O'Neal said, "Boy, you late. It's going down in this bitch."

Dump was like, "Oh yeah? What's good?"

O'Neal said, "Ya girl Big Kendra upstairs. Gug, Slob, Louie, and I already hit that. Big Donkey bending that hoe up right nah."

When he said that, a loud sound started banging in the room.

"Damn, Big Donkey going donkey in that hoe, huh?" said Dump.

Then he busted out laughing. He knocked on the door, so Slob let him in and said, "What's up, shaggy?"

Dump gave Slob dap and shot upstairs. When he got up there, four of the homies were already at the door.

Lung had his hands in his pants, Snook had his ear to the door, Pickle had his back on the wall, and Da-Da was looking at Dump, smiling ear to ear, saying, "Boy, fall back! I'm next!"

At that moment Big Donkey walked out, sweating bricks. Dump looked in the room and saw four more homies in there with Big Kendra half naked, standing there like they were waiting in line. Big Kendra looked Dump in his eyes smiling at him while she lay there naked. One of the homies closed the door. The way she looked at Dump actually turned him on. He ain't never met a freak like her before.

As Dump was fucking Big Kendra, she was fucking him back and from that point, he always wanted her type while the rest of that week blew by. All he did was think about how Big Kendra threw that ass back. From the hoes to the dope, that whole week was popping heavy. It was already Thursday, but it felt like Monday was just yesterday.

Chapter Seven

The week was ill. Dump woke up late for school on Friday in a cold sweat from a dream he had where two dudes wearing ski mask were chasing him down, shooting at him, but was missing every shot. Dump didn't understand his dream at all. He got dressed and rushed out the door. The closer he got to the school the less people he saw. It was to the point where he saw no one, but he could feel somebody was watching him. He picked up the pace. Once Dump made it to school, he felt more comfortable, but something still felt out of place. As he was walking through the halls, everyone was in class. It was so quiet, he could hear his own heart beating slow as he was breathing deeply. Even though Dump was alone, he still felt a presence tailing him. He walked into the office and asked the lady for a tardy slip, then went to class.

After third period, the click met up as usual at the spot for lunch. Louie went dumb like, "What's up with that back-to-school dance tonight? We in that or what?"

Pook turned up like, "Man you know we in there!"

Shit-O said, "Bet!"

The Back Boys walked by looking at them on some gutter shit, but none of them paid attention to it except for Dump.

Later that night they all get ready for the dance then met by Slob house. A few of the homies that went to other schools decided to go to the dance with them. Bo, Flee, and Frank popped up ready to dip with the click. They were different from the rest of the gang. They were good boys, but they wanted to be down because they wanted to be noticed with the most popular gang in the school. The homies weren't tripping. At an event like this, the deeper they were, the better. With Bo, Flee, and Frank, they were twenty deep.

Gug looked at Slow and said, "Come on. Let's rock."

They walked out the door, and Slob locked up. They took the short cut to the gym, walking the back way through the elementary school gates, cracking jokes. There wasn't a cloud in the sky. The moon and the stars were shining bright down on them as they walked behind the school with no lights. They were zoning out, ready to go dumb in the gym. The closer they got to the dance the music got louder, and they began to talk less. It reached a point where they all were quiet. Truth be told they were nervous.

Twenty feet away from the entrance as they were approaching, nothing changed. Everybody started looking at them making eye contact, talking low, almost whispering. That impressed most of the gang because they loved being relevant, but on the other hand, it made Dump uncomfortable because he had no idea what was being said about them. So he gave a slick mug to dudes but a stale face to the chicks. To him it was pros and cons. Either they were digging, or they were hating.

The gang blew right pass onlookers and walked through the doors of the gym. The gym was packed wall to wall; it was obvious that they were the hottest topic in the building. The first thing they did was shoot straight upstairs to the picture booth. They were too deep. Some had to sit on the floor, others had to squat down, and the rest bunched up behind them. Some threw up the 9th Ward sign, others held up cash.

The dope boys showed off their chains, holding them in their hands, while they smiled, showing their gold grills. The picture was a classic. All the Park Boys were there—from Head Busser Big Moe to Young C-Note, from Slow to Da-da, Louie, to Pickle, O'Neal to Rasco, and others along with Dump. After the flick was taken, they slid downstairs and turned the fuck up. The gym was dark and crowded, and the music was going live. As the gang was walking through, the crowd started splitting itself until it reached a certain point.

At that section, the Desire Project Back Boys had no thoughts of moving out the way. The DJ thought it would be very entertaining to play a hit single from the Back Boys' well-known rap group The YG's. As soon as the beat dropped, the Back Boys started bucking wild, throwing elbows from side to side, jumping up and down at the same time. The Park Boys stood still with a raw look in their eyes mugging. That made the Back Boys buck harder. They started coming toward them, but the Park Boys ain't move.

Everybody knew it was about to go down. As they were bucking while the song was playing, everybody from their project was screaming, "Desire! Desire!"

They were too young to understand that the DJ was being messy like a hoe. Soon as The YG's song went off, Fila Phil's hit single "Where My Hustlers At" came on. In a millisecond, Dump and his crew went dumb in their own zone, bucking face-to-face, body to body with them boys. Their movements were full of drama. The Back Boys' eyes were full of jealousy because the whole gym, except the Desire was singing that song. The Park Boys stopped bucking, folded their arms, then started bobbing their heads and sang it with 'em. "Rat ta tat, ratta tat tat trigga. Pass the AK to 'ah Press Park nigga!"

Then the song went off. Everybody went their separate ways. They felt like they made a statement, so the whole click was like fuck 'em.

Thirty minutes passed, and the homie Bo came back to the gang on some shook shit.

He told them, "Man, them niggas we bucked on ran up on me in the cut when I was by myself. It was too many of them. I didn't know what to do so, I dipped out."

Dump thought to himself, "They picked Bo out because they weren't used to him, plus he was alone." Being that he had no reputation, they tested him. As the dance went on, the vibe was sick in it. The Park Boys and Back Boys left it no secret, they were rivals. When Gug and them were leaving the dance, they noticed that their big homie Baldy from the hood was pulling through the front gate. They could tell something was about to happen, but they didn't know what it was. They knew Baldy was always strapped.

He pulled up and told 'em, "Get in!"

They asked no questions and hopped on the back of the 1500 Chevy. It was so tight. Twenty deep, they were shoulder to shoulder.

As they were exiting the front gate slowly, they noticed the crowd was trying to block the truck, but Big homie kept it moving through them. The closer the truck got to them, they moved out the way, but there was a group of knuckle heads from the Desire that refused to move. When Baldy started paying more attention, he realized that 95 percent of the faces he saw was from the Desire to the Up Front section, Benefit section, down to the Back Boys and Girls were all there talking major shit. It was over two hundred people there, and they were chaotic. The Park Boys were shook, but Baldy was calm as fuck.

The crowd got quiet then they heard a girl screaming *loud as fuck*, "Y'all niggas talk all that shit. Get off the back of that truck!"

Then a nigga said, "Yeah, get off the back of that truck!"

There was a brief moment of silence. They all looked at one another to see if any of themselves would get off the truck. None of them moved.

That's when Rosco said, "Fuck all that!" while climbing down off the truck walking with a limp like a gangster and his fist balled up saying, "Y'all niggas ain't fucking with none of my homies. What's up?"

It shocked Dump, because Rosco was one of the coolest laid-back homies, but at that moment, it was obvious he was fearless and ready to ride or get rode on for any of the homies.

None of the Desire Boys moved on him. Rosco left everybody mind boggled as he got back on the truck. After that, Baldy pulled off.

Chapter Eight

When they made it to the hood it was 11:30 p.m. They all chilled on the corner under the street lights. Half of them sat on the curb of one corner while the others were sitting on the curb across from them. It was so quiet they could hear a pin drop. Dump was paying close attention to each one of them. He was thinking about how gangster each of them appeared to be, but Rosco was the only one who hopped off the truck when real shit hit the fan. Then he thought it was a smart move for them not to. Then he said to himself under his breath, "Gangster shit ain't always smart," as he was looking at Shit-O.

Shit-O was looking at the sky while the white clouds were blowing by. He could tell that an embarrassing feeling was sitting on him.

One of them busted out, saying, "Them bitch niggas had us down bad tonight."

Dump said, "Yeah, they did, but what the fuck we gone do?"

Louie replied, "Man, look, all them people that was out there tonight ain't gone be there with them at school Monday. Fuck it! We up and at 'em! Bo, make sure you're there."

Slow said, "Dig!"

And Dump said, "Bet!"

They all shot out.

The next morning Ann woke up, getting ready for work. It crossed her mind that she hadn't seen Dump that much last week. She walked to his room, cracked the door, and saw him sleeping peacefully, so Ann didn't bother him. She left him and walked down the stairs, went into her purse, took out ten dollars, and put it in an oven mitt that was hanging on the wall for decoration, then she left.

It was about 12:00 p.m., and Dump was deep in his sleep, having a dream that a dog was running behind him, barking. The dog was close to catching him, but it wasn't fast enough. He hopped a fence and took away the opportunity from the dog. The dog started to bark in rage, then Dump woke up to the sound of the neighbor's dog barking. It took Dump a second to realize that the sound of the neighbor's dog barking was the dog in his dream. He thought to himself that sometimes dreams become reality. He dipped in the bathroom, washed his face, and brushed his teeth.

He looked in the mirror at himself, then said out loud, "It's a cold world you live in. Stay focused young."

Dump started getting dressed while he was listening to the news on the TV.

The reporter said, "In the lower 9th Ward across the canal, there were three bodies found execution style with their hands tied behind their backs, their feet duct-taped together, and one had a shot between the eyes. It has the neighborhood in disarray. Nobody feels safe. If you have any information, please call Crime Stoppers at 522-2222. Also, in the Desire Project, a man was found in a dumpster; his body was beheaded. He has not been identified. If you have any information, please call Crime Stoppers at 522-2222. There is a $2,500 reward. Your name will be confidential."

In Dump's mind, every day in the hood blood spilled. It was a bloodbath. The truth was, in the summer of 1996 in downtown New Orleans, the 9th Ward was the valley of death where it was ride or die and the blind was officially leading the blind. The youth grew up with a point to prove seeking to make a name for themselves. They were overlooking the probability of them possibly being murdered for being involved in certain situations. That thought never crossed their minds. The only thing that was on Dump's mind was hustling for the weekend, but the police were hot as fuck on the block, so he stopped by Lung to get a gar of piff. So they both rolled up and smoked.

"Man, we gone fuck them niggas up Monday, ya heard me! They gone regret pulling that shit off. Believe that!"

While they were talking, Lung's little niece Hazel came busting in the room. That's Dump's first time seeing her again in five years. She looked totally different. She used to be a lil girl, but now she had the body of a grown woman, 38-24-36. She was shaped like a Coke bottle, high yellow, looking Creole as fuck.

Before she started talking, she looked and made eye contact with Dump and said, "Why you biting your lip?"

Lung looked at him with a confused look.

Dump was like, "Girl, you tripping? Ain't nobody biting their lip."

She nodded and smiled, turned to Lung, and said, "We heard about what happened last night. Y'all bet not let that shit slide!"

She looked back at Dump and gave him a seductive grin then closed the door. Dump gave Lung a dap and went hit the block. While he was hustling on the block, all he could think about was how good Hazel's pussy would taste. Not only that, but how tight it could be. He wanted to fuck her bad, but he didn't want to go at her because she was his homie's niece. Just because it was Lung's niece, it didn't stop him from fantasizing about fucking her that whole day and the day after that.

Dump's dope went dumb for the weekend, but that blew by. It was early Monday morning, the whole gang met up by Slob's house. The two homies from other schools put on uniforms to match theirs, then they rolled out.

Once they made it to the front gates and walked up to the doors to the hallway, someone said, "If y'all looking for the Desire Boys, they're upstairs."

Shit-O broke out upstairs. He was the first one to make it up there. When he walked through the doors, he saw their best fighter and ran up on him. Dump was last up the stairs.

When he made it, he saw Nut and Shit-O fighting one on one, while both groups watched Shit-O beat the breaks off Nut. O'Neal was waiting for one of the Back Boys to say something, but none of them did. He was amped as fuck up.

He spazzed out and said, "Fuck that!" as he balled his fist up, making his way through the crowd and ran up on the first Back Boy he saw. Everyone was fighting one on one, but Nut who was standing in the doorway of the nurse's office with his nose leaking, he looked shook.

Dump ran up on him and snuck the fuck out him, punching him in his nose trying to Z him the fuck out. Nut dropped his head and grabbed his nose holding his face in pain. Dump dipped off to the next Back Boy fighting one of his homies. He ran on him from behind and banged him four times, and he fell.

Dump saw his short homie Lil Wayne fighting tall Bahdee. Wayne had his back to the wall, slinging jab after jab. He was holding his own, but he didn't have much room to maneuver. Dump caught Bahdee from behind hitting him with four blows and laid him down. Dump kept doing this with every homie he saw fighting.

Everybody he touched, they touched the floor. After the fight was over, the teachers and security stormed the hallway, blocking it off. The gang ran to the end of the hall to go down the back stairs, but the doors were chained. They were trapped with no place to run. They turned toward the teachers doing fake shake moves as if they were running and playing a legendary neighborhood game called humpty heads. The security guards could not grab ahold of them. Dump and the crew left school walking home smiling, feeling good that they got away from the teachers. Not only that, but the fact that they beat the fuck out them boys.

Chapter Nine

Two days passed, and Dump and his boys thought they got away scott-free, but to their surprise, they would all be suspended. They had no idea how the principle found out who all was in the fight. Dr. Moore came over the intercom with a loud statement.

"Attention, Back Boys and Press Park Boys, we are no longer going to tolerate any of your foolishness! All Press Park Boys report to my office now!"

They all went to the office and were suspended for three days. Some of them were worried because they knew they were going to get in trouble with their parents, but Dump ain't pay it no mind. He had no problem staying home alone every day blowing gar after gar.

On Monday, the school had required a meeting with all the boys' parents because of the fight. When Ann and Dump walked into the library, they saw ten long tables connected together shaped in the letter U. All the Park Boys were sitting at the tables, looking at one another, wondering what was about to happen. They all knew the meeting was for a reason. It was strange that even though they were all together as a group, none of their mothers interacted with one another. They all simply paid attention to each other seeing how they carried themselves in a critical situation involving their children.

Dump looked at Ann with big bubbled eyes and said, "I'm sorry that you have to come out to deal with this, making it seem as if you're not doing a good job."

She looked at him with a stone face as if she wanted to beat his ass like he stole something. As Ann started to say something sarcastic, a loud group of students opened the doors. Once they saw who was in the library, they shut up. The Back Boys and their parents walked in right behind them and sat on the left-hand side of the table. The Park Boys and their mothers were shocked because every Back Boy walked in with bandages on their noses. It wasn't a question about who won the fight. The question was, "What are the consequences the winners have to face?"

The assistant principle walked in the library and made it quick. She started to speak as the Desire Boys held their heads down. "Louie Johnson and Co Booth are expelled. The Rest of the gang will have to obey the rules and regulations, or you will be expelled as well. As for the Desire Boys, you all are on probation as well. If you're suspended two more times, you will be expelled. To all the parents, thank you for attending this meeting. Are there any questions?"

One of the mothers said, "How is it possible that you expelled two of our children and none of theirs?"

Mrs. Parker replied, "Ms. Pat, your boys are the gang that started the fight."

Ms. Pat said, "Okay, Mrs. Parker, obviously you don't know the whole story."

"Hold up! What do you mean?" said Mrs. Parker.

That was when Louie's mom stood up and said, "Excuse me! The truth is, those boys attacked our children at the dance, and our boys were outnumbered. Is there anything you're going to do about that?"

Mrs. Parker replied, "Yes, Mrs. Johnson. That's why they're on probation."

Chapter Ten

When the meeting ended, Ann and Dump started to walk home. When they made it, they saw Bubbles walking in the door, just making it home from work.

She asked, "Mom, what did they say?"

Ann mumbled, "If his ass gets into any more trouble, he's gone get put out Carver. I'm so sick of this shit."

As Bubbles sat down on the couch, she said, "When you have a minute, we need to talk."

Ann looked at her, "Let's talk now. What's going on?"

Bubbles said, "I'm pregnant."

Ann closed her eyes and put her head down.

"I'm sorry, Ma!" Bubbles said as she walked away to her room.

It seemed that everything started moving slow that week. All Dump did was hang on the block, smoke weed, and write raps.

On Monday, he hooked up with the gang and went to school. Everybody started doing their own thing, but he and Lung started to hang more. It was strange; the more they hung together, the more they realized they looked like brothers.

One day after school, Dump stopped by Lung's house, and one of the Desire Back Boys' girlfriend was there with him. It really caught Dump off guard, but it didn't shock him too much.

Dump gave him dap and screamed, "Park Life! It's going down in this bitch. Do ya thing. Imma fuck with you later," as he walked out the door, smiling.

When he was walking through the hood, he saw her boyfriend riding a bike up the block and could tell he was looking for her. He pulled up by Dump and slowed down on him, asking him, "Did you see Kayonna?"

Dump told him, "No."

He could tell that Kerie had a fucked-up attitude by the way he pedaled off in rage.

Later that night about 7:00 p.m., Dump was inside, sitting on the couch, writing a rap. Pook walked up and knocked on the window while screaming his name.

Dump got up and opened the door like, "What's up?"

Pook said, "Man, picture this fuck-ass nigga Kerie back here looking for you!"

"Stop playing," Dump said.

Pook said, "No bullshit. Come see."

Dump walked out the door and closed it behind himself. Dump and Pook walked four houses down, then he followed Pook into the court way with townhomes on each side. There he saw his homeboys standing there with Kerie and Boss sitting on their bikes, booting up. Boss was one of the Back Boys' most infamous assholes. Dump could tell the gang wanted to bush 'em. All he had to do was kick the shit off, but he really wanted to beat the fuck out of Kerie alone.

He asked Keire, "What's up?"

Kerie said, "Nigga, you know what's up. I asked you about my bitch earlier, and you lied. Did you fuck the bitch or not?"

Dump told him, "Look, that's on you and that hoe. Take it up with her!"

Kerie said, "Yeah, all right."

Louie was pissed because Dump didn't start the fight.

He told 'em, "Man, fuck all that! Y'all niggas get the fuck from back here before we beat the fuck out y'all!"

Pook said, "Straight up!"

Boss saw they were outnumbered, so they were quick to peel out. Shit-O, Louie, Slow, Pook, Pickle, O'Neal, and Lung were pissed because they didn't get the chance to jump them. Dump refused to start the fight because he felt like his own homies wouldn't let him win the fight alone. He wanted a one on one simple because on both sides, he had a point to prove.

When Dump walked off, none of them walked off with him. He didn't give a fuck because he knew on the low they hated him. The next morning when he got up, him and Big Donkey stopped by the lil homie Big Lip Terry's house and smoked a gar before school. He told Donkey about last night and how he was gone see Kerie and fuck him up.

Big Donkey told him, "When you sneak him, keep punching him until he drops. I'm telling you, Dump, don't stop jabbing the fuck out him."

Dump smiled and said, "Donkey, chill out. I got this shit over here."

Donkey gave Terry dap and said, "We gone fuck with you later, my nigga. We out."

Terry's house was a block away from school. As they started to walk, they stopped talking. Just like before with the Back Boys, it seemed like everybody at the school knew what was going on. When they walked up to the school, somebody told Dump, "If you're looking for Kerie, he's upstairs on the second floor."

Dump told Donkey, "Hold this book sack. I'm going up the back stairs."

When he walked off, Donkey said, "Remember what I told you."

When Dump got on the second floor, he walked through the double doors into the main hallway. That's where he saw Kerie talking to a female that borrowed Dump's jacket two days ago. When Kerie saw Dump walking up, he had to do a double-take and made full eye contact. Dump was walking cool as fuck with a limp. Kerie was mugging hard as the fuck, booting up like a nigga with thirty-two golds. Dump was ten feet away.

The girl told Dump, "I have your jacket. Do you want me to get it?"

Dump kept walking in their direction, nodding, and said, "Yeah."

Kerie folded his arms and started booting up harder. Dump took two more steps closer, and the chick walked off. Dump threw a quick, strong jab, followed by a bolo that stumbled the fuck out of Kerie, almost knocking him out. As he was going down, he held his arm out like a kickstand, in an attempt to stop himself from falling.

Dump jumped back, threw his set up, and said, "Let's get it!"

Kerie stood up as the class bell was ringing. He rushed Dump, hitting him with two jabs in the left eye before Dump started swinging. The class doors started opening while Dump started pounding the fuck out Kerie's face. It seemed like every time Dump jabbed Kerie, his knees buckled. It was so bad he tried to hold on to Dump to keep from going down by poking Dump in the left eye with his fingers.

Dump realized the hall was packed while Big Donkey was carrying him off.

He went to screaming, "Park Life Nigga! Press Park in this bitch!"

Donkey and Dump left school taking the back way. Dump's eye started to swell up. Before they made it to the hood, his eye swelled shut.

Big Donkey said, "Didn't I tell you not to stop punching him?"

Dump looked at him and said, "Yeah, you did."

Then he started smiling and said, "But I still beat the fuck out him, though."

Donkey said, "Yeah, you did that," as he busted out laughing.

The next morning when Dump woke up, he heard his mother and Bubbles fussing. He walked into the bathroom and washed his face. After he finished, he looked in the mirror. His eye was shut and black, looking like a pirate's patch.

He thought to himself, "Damn, I should've listened to Donkey."

He brushed his teeth then went downstairs.

He heard Ann tell Bubbles, "Yeah, you're a young woman. You can get your shit and move out. Just make sure you take care of that baby like I took care of your ass!"

Bubbles said, "Fine! I'm gone."

"Okay, bye," said Ann.

Ann then looked over at Dump and told him to put some witch hazel on his eye. Normally, days would blow by, but this day was like an hourglass moving in slow motion. Every thirty minutes, he walked up to the mirror, checking to see if the witch hazel was helping. The swelling was down, and the eye was open, but it had turned purple.

Chapter Eleven

Two days had passed, and Dump thought he should walk to school. It was 2:30 p.m., almost the end of the day at school. Dump was interested in showing his face in a place where it was known that he punched a nigga the fuck down. It didn't matter how his eye looked. He was in there, purple eye and all.

On his way to school, something in his head said, "You should pick up a big stick."

So he did. Once he made it to school, nothing happened, so he threw the stick down.

Chilling under the breezeway in the usual Park Boys spot. Dump and the gang were joked out.

Slow said, "Boy, everybody saying you bashed his ass!"

Dump gave him a grin, then Slow said, "But you looking like he whipped your ass! Bitch, that eye on Mardi Gras Mambo."

Everybody in the gang started laughing their asses off, including Dump. If he didn't win the fight, he probably wouldn't be laughing at all. The vibe at school felt different to Dump. It was obvious that he proved his point.

When school started letting out Dump and his crew left taking their usual back route through the elementary school. The gang didn't walk all together, but still together in separate groups. Three here, four there, and so forth they walked. They exited the elementary school and hit the main street as they continued to crack jokes.

Out of nowhere they heard a female's voice say, "Here they come!"

The gang looked around and saw nobody so, they kept walking.

Dump said, "What the fuck she talking about? Who coming? I don't see nobody."

As soon as he said that, he saw Kerie walking up the side street that met with the street they were on as a fork in the road. The click wasn't tripping because Keri appeared to be walking alone, but the houses was blocking the view of the people walking behind him. The closer they got they noticed he had a Desire mob with him, packing the street from curb to curb for a block long. The mob was carrying sticks, bottles, hammers, one of them even had a bike handle bar in his hand.

Rosco and Dump broke out running to the hood, but Dump saw a big stick, picked it up, and went back with a few homies.

When they made it back to the mob, Big Donkey said, "No jumping!"

It was odd. The whole crowd started dropping their weapons. Keri and Dump went in a quick blend. While they were fighting, a police car turned the block, so everybody broke out running. The most interesting thing was Dump never seen that many people come out for one person before. Ironically, after some time blew by, Dump and Kerie became friends.

It was the end of the school year, and Fat and Bubbles had moved out of the house. Ann was still working hard and praying harder. It seemed as if Dump was going out of control. Ann felt like there wasn't anything she could do about it, so she put it in God's hands. Every day and night Ann prayed for her son. Dump didn't know it, but she saw him taking a short cut to a dead end that she couldn't describe.

Chapter Twelve

It was the last two weeks before the school year ended. Dump started to have problems there with the assistant principle. He was caught cutting class and got suspended. One of the days he was suspended he rode his bike to school. When he made it there, he tied a black-and-white bandana around his face, stopped by the assistant principal's truck, pulled out a knife and slit all four tires, then shot back home. The next week he was expelled. Ann looked into alternative schools Dump could go to next year once summer was over.

Time blew by and the summer was over, and it was the '97-'98 school year. Louie was a senior, Dump was a junior, and Co was a sophomore all attending McDonough Senior High School. It was only three of them there, but somehow, they had become one of the most popular groups at the school. Dump and Loui started a rap group writing music together. Their music was good. It made them take their careers very serious.

At lunch it was impossible for Dump to walk through the halls without hugging girl after girl and dapping the dudes he knew. Everybody knew who he was, but he didn't understand why he was popular. The school had a talent show coming up so, him and Louie thought that they would perform. They took a week to write the song. It turned out to be a downtown anthem. When they started cutting up on the stage, the crowd started bouncing off the walls. That changed Dump's mind about music. He was addicted to rocking the crowd. That year came and went. Dump's life started to take a graphic twist. Within a blink of an eye four years blew by.

Dump was now grown. He had a baby boy with one of the girls he graduated with in high school. Dump's son was his twin, just like Dump was to Beaver. And just like Beaver and Ann, Dump and his baby's mother split a few years after they were together.

It was now 2003, and Dump was in the streets heavy. He was back to hustling in the hood. He switched from pushing crack to selling weed. On his first day hustling with it, he took his profits and went and bought a pit-bull puppy. He named him Hustler. Hustler was a zeebo and bullison bloodline. His color was all black with a white chest, four white feet and a white tip on his tail. Dump fell in love with Hustler. It was like him and DoDo all over again.

All day long, it was Hustler and Dump hustling on the block. Dump trained him every day, walking him while he dragged a five-pound weight on his chain behind him. As time passed, Hustler grew fast. He became a muscle-cut, blood-craving trained monster.

One morning on December 23, 2003, Dump woke up, got dressed, put on his jacket, grabbed his package, tucked it under his underwear, grabbed Hustler, and hit the block. While he was walking up the street, he saw a police car approaching slowly with the back door cracked open. It crossed his mind to run, but he knew that he couldn't get away with Hustler running behind him. The police pulled up three deep. Two of them jumped out of the back of the car and drew their guns.

One had his gun pointed at Dump, and the other raised his gun to Hustler, and said, "If that motherfucker move my way, I'm ah put a hot shot in his ass!"

Dump put his hands up. Hustler was so trained he just kept looking back and forth from Dump to them, simply waiting for Dump to say get 'em, but he never did. It was obvious to Dump that someone had ratted on him.

As he thought to himself, "These bitches spent on me early."

The cops were checking him for drugs, but it seemed they couldn't find them, but they knew it was there, so they kept checking his pockets. One cop decided to check Dump's waist for a gun.

He looked at his partners and said, "Bingo! We got him!"

The other police officer said, "Merry Christmas, you young slick motherfucker."

Dump held his head down. When he looked up, he saw Ann walking up. The cops were telling her what was going on while they were ducking his head down, placing him in the back of the police car. Ann looked at Dump with a tear in her eyes as she took Hustler and went home.

The next day on Christmas Eve, Dump's bond was paid, and he went home and went back to the same shit. Nothing changed. It was like nothing ever happened. Dump and Ann never talked about it, and he never brought it up again because he knew he really hurt his mother. Ann didn't bring it up because she was hoping that he learned a lesson. Dump didn't learn shit.

Chapter Thirteen

One night Dump was chilling by his homeboy Choppa's house.

Choppa said, "Man, I got these new pills. I want you to try one."

Dump told him, "No. I ain't gone fuck with it."

Choppa said, "Come on, man. You know these go for twenty. I'll give you this one for two."

Dump looked at him and said, "Okay. I pop one, you pop one."

Choppa replied, "Cool."

They walked to the car and shot to the gas station and picked up a couple of Heinekens, Keep Moving cigars, orange juices, and a pack of gum. After they got what they needed, they dipped back to the crib.

When they got there, they went into the back room, turned on the television, opened the beers, and then popped the pills.

Dump said, "That was the smallest pill I ever seen in my life."

Choppa was like, "Shit, that bitch gone get you right."

About an hour passed, and Dump didn't feel anything but the beer. They started to roll the gars up while they were watching TV. Dump started to feel his guts bubbling.

When Choppa saw the look on Dump's face, he said, "You feel that pill busting, huh?"

Dump didn't respond. Choppa lit the gar and passed Dump a gum. When he took it, his vision started to trip.

He said, "Man, what the fuck y'all gave me? This shit too strong!"

Choppa and EZ busted out laughing at him. He was seriously hallucinating. The television was getting bigger and bigger, then it got small. Dump held his hand out in front of his face and waved it from side to side.

When he did that, he saw an illusion. All together he saw five hands, one following the others. It had to be a drop of acid on the pill, because normally an ecstasy pill wouldn't have that effect on people. That phase spooked him out, but after that phase finished, he felt real good.

The first thing he asked them was, "Man, where them hoes at?"

His homies laughed at him because he always made fun of them for popping pills and swore he would never do it.

His eyes had started rolling in the back of his head while he said, "Fuck what they be talking 'bout. After tonight, every day I'm getting high off my own supply."

Dump was high, but he was serious as fuck, because for thirty-two days straight, Dump popped one or two, three, or four, possibly five pills a day. He stayed up every night. Sleep was nowhere on his mind. Dump was out of his body.

On the thirty-second day, Dump was chilling under the breezeway on autopilot, but his body couldn't take any more. It automatically shut down. Dump dozed off without even knowing it. Choppa woke him up and dropped him off at home. He went inside and went to sleep. When he woke up, he felt like a brand-new person in a brand-new world, with the same old people. Dump was looking for different results. The only thing that changed was his drug addiction and his product.

Dump was in love with the feeling of getting high off the pills. One day he was leaving the studio and saw a woman walking up the street, so he stopped and spoke with her.

He asked, "What's your name?"

She smiled and said, "Tori. What's yours?"

"They call me Dump. Where you from?"

Tori folded her arms and put her thick legs into a bowleg stance and said, "I'm from the 7th Ward right up the block. What about you?"

He grinned, showing his four golds because he liked the way she was standing. He also could tell she knew how to turn him on. Dump told her, "I'm from Press Park." Tori replied, "Hold up. My baby daddy from Press Park." "What's his name? Matter of fact, I don't even wanna know."

He saw how fine and cute she was and didn't give a fuck if her baby daddy was his homeboy; he wanted to fuck, and she knew it. Tori just smiled it off and gave him her number.

Dump went by Tori's house in New Orleans East one night. When he got there, he walked across the street to the gas station and brought a bottle of vodka and some orange juice. He had plans on slipping a pill in her drink to freak her ass out. When Dump made it back to the house, he heard music playing on the radio. He knocked on the door, Tori opened it and walked off with it cracked open.

When he walked in, he saw her walking to her room in some black laced boy shorts with her ass jiggling. He looked around the house and saw it was nice then proceeded to her room. Tori was in the bathroom with the door closed as her bath water was running. He sat the bag on the night stand then went to the kitchen, grabbed two glasses, put ice in them, and dipped back to the room.

Dump yelled to Tori, "You good in there, huh?" just to make sure she was in the tub.

"Yeah! I'll be out in a minute. Make yourself comfortable."

He put his hand in his pockets and pulled out the pills. Then took two out and crushed one. He dumped the powder in the glass then fixed her drink, hoping she couldn't tell the difference. He took off his pants and shirt while he laid in the bed in his underwear and wife beater, sipping on some shit.

Dump started to hear the water draining out of the tub, so he popped his pill and stirred her drink up. Tori opened the door and walked in the room wearing matching red lace bra and thong smelling like a dozen of roses with her hair in a ponytail. Dump was far past tender dick, just from the sight of her, he fell in love.

She walked around the bed to her side and climbed in.

She looked at Dump and asked, "Why is the cover sticking up like that?"

Dump replied, "Shit, you know what it's hitting for."

Tori grabbed her drink off the stand, took a sip, and said, "Damn this taste good. You mixed it just right."

He looked at her and thought to himself, "If only you knew."

Dump was ready to fuck Tori, but he wanted to wait until their pills kicked in. Because hers was crushed down, it hit her faster. Tori was sipping her drink and talking out the side of her neck. After every sentence she started a new one. The pill had her rolling so hard that she couldn't stop. He felt the pill bust inside his belly, and his stomach started bubbling. Dump slid over to her and put his hand on her thigh, but she paid it no mind.

He started moving his hand up her thigh closer to her pussy. Her actions didn't change. It was as if she didn't feel a thing; she just kept talking while his hand rubbed her pussy. His dick was thumping because his fingers felt her pussy soaking wet. He climbed on top of her while she spread her legs.

Tori was tongue-kissing Dump then bit him on his bottom lip and said, "Stick it in."

He took his hand and grabbed his dick and rubbed the head of it up against her clit.

Tori wrapped her legs around him and said, "Give me that dick."

Dump stuck his tongue down her throat while he dug his dick up in her pussy, grabbing her ass and looking her in her eyes. Dump knew she was loving the way she felt. Because of the pill, Tori's eyes were rolling in her head. Dump put his hands behind her knees and pinned her down, locking her legs in the air while he pounded her pussy. Her panties were dripping wet because he didn't take them off her. Tori pushed Dump off her and laid him on his back, licking him on his chest with his rocked up dick in her hand stroking it up and down. She came up and tongue kissed him then brought her head down to his stomach and started licking it while she continue to beat his dick.

Dump grabbed her head by the ponytail with both hands pushing her down further. Tori looked up at him with a seductive look as she was going down with ease. She opened her mouth took her tongue and circled it around the head of his dick, then deep-throated it making his toes curl. While her mouth went up and down her hand moved with it. She took her other hand, grabbed his balls, and started jiggling them. That made him bust in her mouth.

Tori didn't stop; she started to swallow. Dump started moaning, making noise, and couldn't stop, even if he wanted to. Tori drained him dry. He rolled over on top of her and went down. He licked on her pearl tongue, slurped, then spit on it. Tori's body jumped. She busted her legs wide open in the air holding his head. That turned him on even more. Dump licked both pussy lips then spread the lips and stuck his tongue in her pussy hole twice then sucked on her pearl tongue while he licked it. She started trembling, then her pussy started squirting in his mouth. Dump rolled over and they both dozed off. The next morning when he woke up, he kissed her on her forehead and dipped out.

Chapter Fourteen

Dump was chilling on the block with Choppa talking business. When Tori woke up, Dump was the only thing on her mind. What he did to her had her on a level that she never experienced before. She wanted to upgrade their friendship to a relationship, but she needed to talk to Dump first about who her baby's father was, so she gave him a call.

When he answered the phone, she said, "Did you enjoy last night?"

He looked at Choppa and smiled then said, "It was all right."

She said, "Oh yeah?"

He was like, "Nah, I'm just fucking with you. You're a fool with it, baby."

She started laughing, "I try."

Dump questioned, "How did you sleep?"

"I slept great," she replied. "But it's been on my mind that I wanted to tell you. Pepper is my children's father."

Dump felt relieved. "That's cool because me, and Pepper never been friends. On the other hand, I do know him."

Tori told him, "I just wanted to let you know. I'll give you a call later."

Dump responded, "Bet. Fuck with me."

Then Dump hung up the phone.

Choppa tapped him on the leg and said, "Don't get pussy whipped! Whip that pussy! Bang! Bang! Bang! Bang!"

They pulled up to Dump's house. Dump gave Choppa some dap and shot inside. He sat on the couch and fell asleep.

Dump started dreaming. In his dream he was looking up at the clouds on the back street. He was counting the stars and started hearing thunder. In his mind it was as if it was the voice of God talking to him. He began to be able to translate what was being said.

As the lighting struck he heard the thunder say, "Why are you being so foolish, child?"

As a car pulled up with no lights on, the wind started blowing. He saw two guys with guns hop out, running toward him, so he broke out running into the bushes as they opened fire, hitting him in his back. Dump just laid there as if he was dying thinking the dudes were going to walk up on him to finish him off, but they never showed up. His breaths got shorter, but before they stopped he woke up in a cold sweat.

He thought about what God told him in the dream, then he remembered his mother telling him about acting foolish. He started to question his actions wondering if his choices are foolish. It crossed his mind what Tori told him about Pepper when she called. Pepper was Aggie's brother, and Aggie was a wild bull in the streets. He had a graveyard under his belt. The dream Dump just had, got him to thinking that maybe he was making moves that was putting his life in jeopardy and the dream was a message that he needed to hear. Dump called Tori and told her that he was coming over tonight if she was free.

She said, "For you, I'm always free. Call when you're on your way."

He agreed, "Cool."

About 9:00 p.m., Dump hit Tori up. When she answered the phone, he told her that he was on his way. When he made it to her house, they had a conversation about upgrading their status. Dump decided to move in with her and change his lifestyle. He gave up the dope game and found a job. Some time went by, and he fell deeper in love with Tori. He loved her more than she loved him. Dump knew something about their relationship wasn't right, but he paid no mind.

Tori was cheating. In her mind their relationship was over, and she had intentions on ending it fast.

One day she went out to find a job, but the way she dressed made Dump think that she was doing something different. She left out the house. At that point he felt like she was going on a date. The feeling in his gut didn't sit too well.

When Tori returned home, she went straight to the bathroom, ran some water, and hopped in the tub. That was a dead giveaway that she fucked someone. It put him in his feelings. He truly loved her. As she was taking her bath, he sat on the edge of the bed, thinking to himself that maybe he was wrong. He got up and turned the TV on then turned around to sit back down. That's when he noticed Tori's purse was on the bed. Something told him to look through it, but he was nervous that he would find something that would make him regret the choices he made.

With no regards to his feelings Dump picked up the purse and unzipped it. As he started thumbing through it, he saw a number on a piece of paper with no mane on it. He grabbed his phone and dialed the number.

A man answered the phone, and immediately Dump went into a rage as he hung up the phone in the man's face.

"Bitch, come out that fucking bathroom!"

Tori answered, "Dump, what are you talking about?"

"Who fucking number this is in your purse? You out here playing games, huh?"

Dump pulled on the door, but it was locked. His blood was boiling. Tori could tell that he was out of his body. Taking her time to get out the tub, Tori thought it would give Dump a minute to calm down. After she put her clothes on, she came out.

Dump walked up to her with the number in his hand and said, "Who the fuck is this?"

She poked her lips out and said, "Boy, that's my cousin. What are you doing digging in my purse anyway?"

He cocked back and bat the piss out of her.

He grabbed her around the neck as she grabbed her face screaming, "Give me that ring off your finger, you lying hoe!"

As she grabbed her hand, she balled her fist up. He pulled her hand up to his mouth and bit down on her finger, bending the ring on it. It hurt her finger so much till she allowed him to take it off. Tori's feelings were hurt, but not as much as his. He was crushed.

Tori was lying in bed under the covers, watching TV as Dump got dressed for work. They never made eye contact or said a word to each other before he left. Everything had changed. They were never on this level. While Dump was at work washing dishes in the gallery, all night he kept thinking about his next move. When he got off, he and a coworker went on Bourbon Street and hung out, having drinks until five o'clock in the morning.

Dump hopped in a cab and caught a ride home. He got out the cab, stumbling full of alcohol. He walked up to the door, pulling his key out his pocket. When he stuck his key in, he twisted it, but it wouldn't turn. He pulled it out and looked at it, checking to see if it was the right key. It was, so he stuck it back in, shook it up and down, then tried it twist it again, but it still didn't turn. It became obvious that Tori changed the locks on the door. He knocked on the door, but she didn't answer, so he went around to the back and knocked still she didn't answer.

It made him furious. Dump thought to himself, "I helped her keep this place. I pay the bills. I changed my life for her, and this is how she fuck over me!"

Dump went stupid and kicked in the door, not giving a fuck about how Tori felt. He walked through the house looking for her, but she and the children were gone. He started packing his bags, knowing that it was time for him to move around. Not only did she cheat on him. She decided to end the relationship without discussing it.

After Dump finished packing his bags, he started to walk out the room. It felt strange that he was walking up the block early in the morning with a big garbage bag on his way to the Broad bus stop. He waited for the bus four blocks away from the home. As he looked up to the sky, he saw a big black cloud of smoke rising from the house. At that very moment, he regretted doing it, but it was done. He couldn't change a thing.

The bus was approaching, and he was anxious to hop on it. Dump picked up his bag and walked to the curb. The bus pulled up and opened the door. He walked straight to the back and took a seat. The bus was packed as usual. He looked at everyone hoping to see nobody he knew. Dump transferred from that but to another then reached the Park. He made sure he took the back route not walking up the main streets to the house.

When he made it, he knocked on the door. Ann opened it. She saw the bag in his hand but asked no questions.

Dump looked at Ann and said, "Good morning," and walked upstairs, put his bag in the closet, then lay down in his bed on his side, looking at the wall thinking, *I got away.*

About an hour passed. Dump woke up to Ann calling his name loud. He got up and walked down the stairs. When he made it, he saw a police officer standing in the doorway.

He wiped his eyes and said, "Yes, sir?"

The officer said, "Are you Cage Coleman?"

Dump replied, "Yes, sir."

"Would you come out, Mr. Coleman, and put your hands behind your back please?" said the officer.

Dump asked, "Why?"

He told Dump, "You're wanted on an arson charge."

Dump walked outside and put his hands behind his back, turning his back to the police. The officer walked to him and cuffed him, then walked Dump to the car and placed him in it. Dump felt foolish sitting in the back of the police car as the fire marshal pulled up to have him a gas test on his hands for anything chemical that is flammable.

Dump asked, "What is all this for?"

The marshal said, "If we find chemicals on your clothes or hands, you're going away for a very long time."

Dump smiled, saying to himself, "Shit, that hoe being hot in the ass is the only thing that set that house on fire."

He knew that he didn't use nothing but a lighter, so if that was the only way he could be convicted by this test, he thought he was scot-free.

When the officer took Dump down to jail, it took the jail three days to get him processed at Temperman on tier C3. Dump was now twenty-five, and his life was much more different from when he was fifteen.

When he walked in the tier, he could feel the cold blood running through there. It was as if he was in a different world. The truth about it, he was right. As he was doing a scan to count how many people was on the tier and separate the real from the fake, he noticed that his neighbor Big J, who grew up in a house across the street from him, was the tier rep on the flat. Big J was huge, standing six feet, two inches, weighing 295 lbs., with fist big and round like grapefruit.

Chapter Fifteen

Dump walked down on Big J while he was sitting down at the table playing dominos with three others and said, "What it do, homie?"

When Big J looked up and saw him, he jumped up with a big ole smile on his face, showing the one gold on his big front teeth. Big J gave Dump a dap, squeezing his hand, pulling him in to him, and gave him a hug. It was without a doubt that Big J was happy to see him. With the smile on Dump's face, it was obvious the feelings were mutual. Big J left the game and ran it with Dump for a minute, telling him about why he was in jail and how much longer he had before he would be released. After the conversation, Dump went and jumped in his rack to pay attention to other's actions plus think about his own. When he looked at his actions, he acknowledged the results and felt like shit.

One word was stuck on his brain, jamming it like a jackhammer. *Tori...* He thought one four-letter word produced a lot of pain. One thing about this situation would never change. He was thinking about some of the people, places, and things he loved was never worth loving. His heart became one of his biggest flaws.

Dump began to doze off in his feelings when he heard Big J say, "Any one of you niggas got a problem with me or how I'm running shit, come your pussy-ass out chea right now, and we can get it in!"

One of the inmates said, "Ain't nobody got a problem with you. You need to calm the fuck down."

Big J nodded up and down poking his lips out, looking at Dump. Dump shook his head from side to side with no words, saying "This stupid nigga" in body language. Big J waited for the perfect time to catch this dude off guard. About twenty minutes passed, and the opportunity presented itself. While he was walking up the lane to his bunk, dude was walking down it. When they got close, Big J snuck him and knocked him out then went laid in his rack like nothing happened. That was Dump's first time ever seeing J fight. On the streets, he saw Big J as a cool dude, but in jail, he saw he was a monster. After that Dump finally dozed off.

There were a group of dudes playing dominos, slamming them on the table right by Dump's bunk. When the noise woke him up, he came out of a dream and back to reality. He looked at the dudes with a stale face, pissed off because they were being disrespectful, but he was more pissed at himself for putting himself in the situation. Two trustees came to the door with three brown containers and a small plastic crate with two big spoons and one big scooper in it. Big J and two other inmates met them at the door. They grabbed the containers then walked to the table and sat them down.

Dump hopped in the back of the line. Big J and the other two inmates started serving the food. Everybody got one scoop and a slide. When Dump made it to the table, Big J overloaded his shit with two scoops of rice, three scoops of beans with sausage, a side of peas, and four slices of bread.

When Dump sat down at the table, he caught a few looking at him sideways, but he paid it no mind. By it being his first time in real jail, Dump didn't understand what was going on. Little did he know, he made a couple of jealous enemies, just because J flooded his tray.

A few weeks went by, and it was time for Big J to roll out.

At twelve midnight, the correctional officer got on the intercom and said, "Johnathan Allen ATW. Pack your shit. You're all the way out."

He went and tapped Dump's mat to wake him up like, "I'm out, my nigga. Hold ya head in this bitch."

Dump gave him dap and said, "Dig that. I'm gone fuck with you when I get out here."

"One hunnit," Big J said as he grabbed his mat with his bag and hit the door.

Dump woke up for roll call the next morning; he felt a void. Since Big J left, there was no more tier rep, and it was a whole different vibe. Two days past, Dump and an OG were playing dominos. Dump was busting his ass. The OG got in his feelings because Dump was shining on him, slamming the dominos while saying, "Bo Bo an' Blare! Ten here," pointing his finger, "And ten there!"

It was so quiet in there that his voice was echoing off the walls. Dump looked at his dominos and saw he could score fifteen. That was enough for him to win the game.

When he slammed the domino, he said, "Three switching bitches! Wash them fucking dishes!"

OG said, "Man, I don't wanna hear all that fuck shit."

Dump told him, "Get the fuck out cha feelings."

OG jumped up and rushed Dump while his legs were stuck under the table and gave him a quick blend. He was trying to come from under the table with his legs, but the way dude caught him, he was stuck. The correctional officer started walking toward the tier, so a few inmates blocked the view and another inmate broke them up. OG went and lay down in his bunk. Dump was pissed. He went by his rack put on his tennis and paced the floor back and forth waiting for OG to get out his bunk, but he never did. He saw that Dump was tweaking to fight. When he saw that OG wasn't moving, he figured he would lay down until OG got up.

Thirty minutes after he played sleep watching OG, he thought he was clear, so he got up and walked to the bathroom. Dump got out of his rack, silently ran up behind him, and snuck the fuck out of him with a serious blow.

When the lick touched him, his knees buckled, and OG's legs gave way. The whole tier went dumb screaming and hollering. OG was knocked out. Dump hopped in his bunk like nothing happened. OG was transferred to another tier.

The next morning the tier chose Dump to be the tier rep. Dump didn't want the job, but they wanted him to take Big J's place after they saw him Z OG the fuck out.

Six months passed, and Dump went to court. As he sat in the juror's case with the other inmates cuffed and shackled, he saw when

Tori walked in the court. She made sure she didn't look in his direction, but he never took his eyes off her. After she spoke with the clerk, she went to the back for a minute, then left.

Dump's lawyer walked over to him and said, "They couldn't find you guilty of the arson charge. They are offering you six months for domestic violence and giving you credit for time served. Do you want to take the deal? If so, you will be released tonight."

Dump nodded. The lawyer walked over to the prosecutor and arranged it. After court, Dump went back to jail. At twelve midnight on August 2, 2005, he was released to a world that he wasn't mentally ready for.

Chapter Sixteen

Dump went home with Ann. The hood remained the same. She was happy to have him home again and just to get out of that place. Dump was happy to be there. Ann spent a lot of time at work every day from nine in the morning to eleven at night. Therefore, he spent a lot of time alone in the house.

One day he decided to hit the block and chill under the breezeway. He was chilling by himself for a minute until a few homies walked up.

Lung said, "Welcome home, nigga."

Dump was like, "Bet! What's been going on out here?"

"Ain't a motherfucking thing changed, my nigga. Same shit, just a different day."

He tapped Slow and tipped his head back then tilted it in Dump's direction while he wasn't paying attention.

Slow came out and said, "You fucked around and burned that hoe shit down huh?"

Dump looked at them both and said, "You got jokes? That ain't my lick. My charge was domestic violence for smacking the bitch. I don't know how her shit went up in smoke."

Pook said, "Whatever, man. You're always doing some ill shit."

"Nah, my nigga, I do real shit."

Then Dump walked off. He could tell they came by him to talk about a situation that he was trying to forget about. He didn't feel bad for what he did, but it wasn't a charge he was willing to take. Pepper had a few problems with what Dump did, not because of Tori, but because it affected the kids. Pepper was waiting to cross Dump too.

Dump was ready, but it was some dumb shit he was defiantly trying to avoid. Tori never called Dump, and he never called her. To each other, it was like they both fell off the planet.

One day it was beautiful outside. The sun was shining bright, the sky was bright blue, and the breeze was cool. Dump was walking up the block on his way to the store. He saw Choppa pulling up, so he flagged him down and asked him for a ride.

When he opened the door and hopped in, Choppa said, "Did you hear about Pepper?"

"No," Dump said.

"He was in a bad accident. He lost control of his car, and it flipped over. He survived, but he a vegetable now," said Choppa.

Dump asked him, "What the fuck you mean he a vegetable?"

Choppa slowed down and stopped at the stop sign then looked at him and said, "He can't walk, talk, or move his body from the neck down. It would have been a blessing if he wouldn't have made it."

Then he pulled off and said, "You know the word on the block is he had plans on having you murdered out here behind that shit with that bitch."

Dump said, "Man, look, fuck the world and fuck the block. The block don't have no love for me out here. They always said when you dig a grave for someone else, make sure you dig one for yourself."

When they pulled up to the store, he hopped out and walked in. As he walked out, he saw a slim sexy dark-chocolate cougar. He could tell she was up in age, but her complexion and style tuned him on. He made eye contact with her, and she smiled.

Dump asked her, "What's up?"

She said, "Nothing much."

Then he asked," What's your name? I never seen you around here."

She laughed. "Why you all up in my business?"

Dump was like, "What's your number? I'll tell you when I call."

She said, "Cool," and put her number in his phone.

He got his phone, gave her a hug, then peeled out.

Choppa asked, "Who that was?"

Dump said, "I don't know, but I'm sure gone find out."

She saved her number without her name.

"One thing about her, she surely knows how to make things interesting."

Choppa said, "Yeah, I could tell she been out here."

Dump rubbed his hands together and said, "That bitch look like she knows how to treat a nigga."

Choppa busted out laughing and said, "Nigga, you're a freak. I know you gone eat that chocolate bitch."

Dump gave a slick smile, then said, "All red niggas dig that sexual chocolate shit. I'm gone crunch and munch on that bitch!"

"Shit, nigga, you better wrap your tongue up before you fuck around eat some alphabets."

"What fucking alphabets?" Dump asked.

Choppa looked at him, shook his head, and said, "ABCD-HIV for your dumb ass."

They busted out laughing when they pulled up to Dump's spot to drop him off.

Dump hopped out, and said, "I'm gone fuck with you, nigga."

Choppa gave Dump some dap and pulled off.

A couple days after he met chocolate, he gave her a call.

When she answered the phone, he said, "You ready to know why I'm in your business?"

She said, "First of all, my name is Trish, and yes. Why are you in my business?"

He told her, "Look, I'm gone cut the bullshit. You caught my attention. Your age and style turned me the fuck on. I want to get to know you. Maybe you can show me some tricks."

She started laughing.

He asked, "What's so funny?"

Trish responded, "Boy, you smooth with that mouth."

He replied, "Shit, only if you really knew."

She asked, "What do you mean if I really knew?"

He explained, "Baby, I been eating pussy before I started fucking. You do the math."

Trish said, "I don't know. Maybe you can come over tonight, and I can do the math while I add and subtract."

Dump told her, "Text me the time and place, and I'm in the building."

She said, "Okay. I'm ah do that. I'll talk to you later," then she hung up.

Trish text Dump the information and later that night Dump popped up at her spot.

He called her phone, "I'm outside."

Trish came and opened the door. When he walked in, it was dark with candles lit. Her spot was different with an odd energy. He didn't pay it any mind because he was still comfortable. He walked into the bedroom behind her and sat on the bed. She took a cigar off the dresser and busted it down.

She opened her draw and grabbed a bag of weed then rolled it up.

Dump said, "You have a gift? You know how to get a nigga in the mood."

As Trish lit the gar up, she said, "I'm just being myself."

Dump said to himself, "Shit, you're more than yourself right now, bitch. You're a blessing."

Trisha passed him the gar and got up and walked to the bathroom, shutting the door behind her. Dump hit the weed two more times then sat the gar in the ash tray. About ten minutes passed, and he wondered what she was doing because he didn't hear water running or the toilet flushing. He looked up when he heard the door opening and saw her walking out dressed in a purple lingerie teddy and stockings with the lace at the top to match.

Dump got hard immediately. She stopped at the foot of the bed and put her hands on her hips while Dump reached back over to the ash tray and sparked the weed back up. When they looked each other in the eyes, she bent over and started to crawl in the bed between his legs.

When her hands reached his waistline, she unbuckled his belt and pants then unzipped them. Trisha put her hands on the bed, then she used her mouth to find his dick and pulled it out of his boxers with no hands.

He said, "I guess this what I get for saying maybe you could show me some tricks?"

She deep-throated it and started to gag.

When she came up off it, she said, "You like that?"

He said, "What the fuck you think?"

She said, "I don't know. I can feel this dick thumping in my mouth. I want to feel it bust."

"What are you gone do when it bust?" he asked.

Trisha grabbed his dick and started beating it while she said, "You all up in my business again. You just lie back while I make your eyes roll."

Dump was over there to go hard, but the truth was she was in full control. He could tell she was having fun, but she didn't know she was the best he ever had. In her mind she just wanted to make a statement to his young ass for playing with her.

Trish did make a statement, but all that did was make him turn up.

She looked up at him and said, "I ain't thinking about pussy whipping you. This mouth gone whip this dick like a slave."

Dump grabbed her head and said, "Shut up!" while he pushed her back down on it.

She was turned on by that. She went to moaning while she was slurping on it. When he nutted, she swallowed it, crawled up, and laid on his chest.

He wrapped his arms around her and closed his eyes.

Trish said, "Can I ask you a question?"

"Yeah. What's up?" Dump asked.

She was like, "Do you believe in God?"

He answered, "Of course. What made you ask that?"

She said, "You just don't seem like the type."

Dump raised up and looked at her because her asking him that after what they just did hit him sideways.

He said, "It's funny that you asked me that. I grew up in a family that is close to God, but I don't have the relationship with Him like I'm s'posed to have."

Trish told him, "Maybe you should work on it. Tomorrow ain't promised. I chose to get to know you because the way you looked in my eyes gave me good vibes. Not many men that come on to me I get that feeling from."

Dump didn't know how to respond. He just heard a small vice in his head saying, "Everything happens for a reason."

Trisha said, "I see you're not responding. I guess I'm making you uncomfortable."

"No, baby," he said. "You just have me thinking, that's all."

They laid there for a minute until they dozed off. Dump woke up the next morning and heard Trish in the kitchen doing her thing. He grabbed the remote and turned on the TV to watch the news.

Trish walked in the room with a plate of fish and grits and said, "Good morning. How did you sleep?"

"I slept good. I see you're up early huh," said Dump.

"Yeah. You were talking in your sleep."

Dump said, "Hold up! What did I say?"

She replied, "I couldn't understand most of it, but I heard you say, 'Lord save me.'"

Dump suddenly heard the breaking news theme music, so he grabbed the remote and turned the TV up.

The reporter said, "This morning in Motel 6 two young ladies were murdered in cold blood. One was found in the bathtub, shot multiple times, and another was shot once in the head at the 9th Ward location. If you have any information, please call Crime Stoppers at 522-2222. Your identity will be kept confidential."

He said, "This city is fucked up."

Then he changed the channel and said, "Thanks for the breakfast. I'll be dipping in a minute."

Trish told him, "I told my daughter about you. She said to tell you you're lucky."

He asked, "How old is she?"

Trish smiled and answered, "She's fourteen and a handful."

Dump looked at her like really, "Tell her after last night I'm past lucky. I'm blessed."

Dump gave Trish a hug then walked to the bus stop of Chef Mature Highway where he caught one bus, transferred to another, then hit the hood.

As soon as Dump got home, he went to the kitchen and sat at the table then heard a knock at the door. He got up and walked out the living room then opened the door. He saw Big Donkey with a fucked-up look on his face.

He asked Donkey, "What's up?"

Donkey said, "Man, these bitch-ass niggas back here killed her!"

Dump asked, "Hold up. What the fuck you mean? Killed who?"

Donkey's eyes were bloodshot red. Tears started falling.

He said, "Marsha and Nelly! They're both dead! I know these fucking niggas killed them! I know they did it!"

Dump told him, "Donkey, you tripping. Why would the homies kill two homegirls from the hood? It had to be some other niggas."

Big Donkey said, "Fuck that! I feel it in my gut. When I find out which one of these bitch-ass niggas killed my girl, I'm gone kill 'em!"

As he was sobbing, he said, "That's my word."

Dump told Donkey, "Calm the fuck down, man. I'm ah find out what's up."

Two days passed, and Dump, Lung, and Choppa were out hanging on the block talking shit when they heard sirens screaming up the block. When they looked down the street, they saw five police cars blow by and stopped by Da-Da's house. They wondered what was going on.

T-Man rolled up on a bicycle and said, "Man, them dicks just hit Da-Da's house and took him for killing Nelly and Marsha."

Dump's face hit the ground. He couldn't believe it. He didn't understand why Da-Da spazzed the fuck out. It was no secret Marsha and Nelly were two of the coolest chicks in the hood.

Lung shook his head and said, "It gotta be more to this story."

Dump said, "This can't be life."

He felt fucked up because he told Big Donkey to chill out, but all the while he was right. Dump's head was fucked up. He didn't say nothing to nobody; instead, he just walked off headed to the crib.

Dump went to his room, lying down in the bed, pulled his phone out his pocket, and called Lil Wayne and asked him, "Damn, my nigga. What's going on in the hood? I heard you was in the spot last night."

Wayne said, "Fucking right. I was in the room last night. We all was chilling. Co and Da-Da ill ass was getting full of that pluck. Me and Slob was talking business. Head Busser, Big Moe, Lil C-Note, and Pickle slid through too. Everything was good. Nelly and Marsha were rolling on them tabs when Nelly went and hopped in the tub. Da-Da fucked around and snorted another line and ducked out unconscious for twenty minutes with forty dollars in his hand. One of them niggas took the money out his hand while he was ducking. When he woke up, everybody was gone but Pickle, Slob, Nelly, C-Note, Marsha, and me. He asked Marsha where his money was at. She said she didn't know. He told her to give him his money. She got jazzy and said, 'Nigga I don't have to take your money. I got my own money.' This nigga walked up to her and grabbed her by her ponytail, pulled out his gun, and blew her fucking brains out. Nelly went to screaming and hollering in the bathroom. Da ran to the bathroom door and went to kicking that bitch in. Man, she was screaming so loud I could tell she was terrified. When the door busted open, He ran in there and let off four shots in her."

Dump said, "Dog, you serious?"

"Fucking right I'm serious." Wayne confirmed then continued, "He came out the bathroom with the gun in his hand and asked us if we had a problem. I don't know what the fuck he was thinking. I should have never gave him that dope."

Dump said, "Look, let me take this other call. Imma hit you back."

When Dump hung up the phone, his whole life and mind frame changed. Dump trusted no one close to him. He laid there for a minute then dozed off into a deep sleep, wishing that everything that went down was a bad dream, but it was fucked up, he knew it wasn't.

He drifted off into a dream where he was walking into his neighborhood at night. He saw graffiti spray painted on the brick buildings as he walked through the cuts he felt evil energy. When he looked around, the graffiti started glowing and he began to see spirits floating not far from him. The spirits were all glowing the same color as the graffiti. He could tell they were demonic. Dump started to walk and pray as he moved forward. The deeper he got in the hood the spirits were more agitated because of his prayer they couldn't touch him or attack him. Dump was nervous and uncomfortable but still trusting God.

He saw that he was exiting the hood. Over the hood it was darkness, but at the exit he could see light everywhere. When he was a hundred yards from the exit, he felt a greater demonic force approaching him. He heard a noise as if something was hovering, so he looked up. When he did, he saw a huge oval shaped space ship with green lights glowing from the top to the bottom.

Then he saw green lights going clockwise in a circle around the black ship. His spirit told him it was the devil himself. The ship started to suck him up slowly off the ground as if it was abducting him.

Dump remembered hearing before that someone said that the devil will flee from the name of Jesus, so he began to say it, "Jesus! Jesus! Jesus! Jesus!"

The closer Dump and the ship got to each other, the louder he screamed, "Jesus!"

His head got so close to the ship that the fear forced Dump to wake up out of his dream. Dump didn't understand the dream and was upset that the name of Jesus didn't make the devil leave him alone.

Chapter Seventeen

Dump did a lot of thinking about the dream trying to understand it, but the only thing that he could think of is Trish asking him did he believe in God and telling him maybe he should work on his relationship with Him. He looked at his phone to check the time and saw it was 9:00 p.m., so he figured he should give her a call.

When he hit her line, she answered and said, "Hey, baby. I thought you forgot about me."

He said, "No. I just been trying to stay focused out here."

She asked, "What's going on?"

Dump told her, "Do you remember the shit we saw on the news about those two girls at Motel 6?"

Trish paused, then said, "Yeah. I remember. Why?"

He said, "That was two of my friends. I used to mess around with one of them."

"Hold up, Dump. What do you mean mess around? Was she your girlfriend or your ex?" Trish asked.

Dump was like, "It wasn't like that. We just had sex, but besides that, we all grew up together. What's really fucked up about it is, a nigga that grew up with us killed them."

She said, "When you need to talk about anything, I'm always here."

He said, "Fasho."

Trish told him, "I'm moving from New Orleans East to across the canal in lower 9th Ward next week. When I settle in, I want you to come to visit. Maybe you can help me break it in." And she laughed it off.

Dump had no problem with it. "Cool. Just let me know, baby. I'm in there."

She said, "Let me deal with this child. I'll call you later."

Then she hung up. That week blew by.

It was August 27, 2005. The weather was beautiful, and the city was going down. Dump and the gang was uptown by the Magnolia Project in the Third Ward at the park for Super Sunday. It was thousands of people out there. From the hot boys with the foreign cars to the hottest girls with the high shorts, thick thighs, and fat asses. From the hustlers to the head busters. The brass band and the Indians had it going dumb in the streets. Dump and Koonta were sitting on the truck of a black and gold old-school Chevy Caprice squatting on twenty-fours.

As he and Dump were talking about their next move after the second line, Louie walked over to them and said, "What's good?" And he gave them dap.

When Dump said, "We chilling," a whole lot of gunshots started ringing out.

The crowd broke out, running in one direction, away from the shooters. Dump, Louie, and Koonta hopped in the car and screeched off. At that point, Dump decided. He felt like he needed to buy a gun and stay strapped with it. They drove over the Almonaster bridge, made a right turn at the first street, drove down it slow, then made another right turn into the hood. It was 7:30 p.m., and all the homies met on the block.

O-Head said, "Man, it just went down uptown I heard."

Koonta said, "Ain't nothing new. That's everywhere we go."

Head Busser Big Moe were like, "Fuck all that! We going to club New Edition in the 7th Ward tonight. I'm about to go get ready. We rolling for ten."

Dump dipped out and went to the house. As soon as he was walking in the door, he felt his phone vibrating in his pocket. He looked at it and saw it was Trish calling.

He answered, "Wut up!"

She asked, "Did you hear about the hurricane headed this way?"

"No, I didn't. What is it looking like?" he asked.

She said, "Its name is Hurricane Katrina. It's a category three right now. That's pretty bad."

He said, "Damn. When will it hit land?"

"It's going to hit on the twenty-ninth. If you're not leaving, I think you should come over and stick it out with me," said Trish.

Dump replied, "Cool. That's what, two days from now? I'll be over there tomorrow night, love."

She said, "I'll be ready and waiting. Baby, be safe out there."

He said, "Okay. I'll talk to you later." Then he hung up.

Later that night, Dump and Koonta pulled up at the club. It was packed out in front. Koonta pulled up on the neutral ground in between the two streets and parked. When they hopped out, the homies were already posted. Half of them was in front the club's door, and the other half was in the spot. Koonta walked straight in the club, but Dump walked up to O-Head and Lox and gave them daps talking some hype shit.

Lox told him, "What's up, Nasty Man? I see you turned up and fresh as fuck!"

Dump said, "Tonight I'm fucking somebody's daughter. Fuck her being a dime, she gone be a quarter."

They kept talking for a minute then he walked in the club. It was a very small spot packed wall to wall. The crowd was straight hood. Everybody was gutter as fuck. Dump walked to the back of the club and saw the gang clicked up ten deep catching the small dance floor, while the pussy poppers were cutting up.

Dump saw Head Busser, Big Moe, and the rest of the homies sipping on drinks, so he ordered one, downed that, then got another one. He was feeling the vibe from the chicks, so he started fucking with a few of them. Before he knew it, he was drunk as fuck and feeling good. He walked outside and hooked up with Koonta.

They chilled for a minute, then Koonta said, "I'm surprised a nigga ain't let off fifty shots around this motherfucker."

Dump said, "Shit, don't speak too fast. It's still early."

Then Koonta went back in the spot. Dump and O-Head chilled in front talking for thirty minutes.

Koonta popped up out the blue, saying, "I'm gone fuck with you later, woah. I'm about to leave with this bitch."

Dump said, "Bet! Be easy, my nigga!"

All the homies started getting ghost, but a few of them hung around. Twenty minutes passed. O-Head and Dump were standing in front the door, but Dump walked in the door. As the door was closing behind him, he started hearing gunshots in front the club. He figured that somebody out there was shooting at somebody, and once they let off, a few shots they would stop, but they didn't. It went from five to seven, to twelve shots, and didn't stop. They kept ringing, getting closer to the door. *Pop, pop, pop, pop, pop, pop, pop!* Dump heard it before everybody in the club, so he quickly made his way to the bathroom in the back.

When he made it there, they still were plucking. *Pop, pop, pop, pop, pop, pop!* Nonstop. The bathroom was super small. As soon as Dump gets to the ladies' bathroom door, seven women and a man rushed in behind him. It was seven chicks and a man jammed in the bathroom stall with him. He was pressed against the toilet.

As he looked up he could see all their faces. They were terrified. Each one of them was crying on their phones, talking to the police. As he was watching them cry and listening to them talk, he still heard shots. *Pop! Pop! Pop! Pop! Pop! Pop! Pop!* People started banging on the door, trying to get in.

Dump said, "Don't open that fucking door!"

There was only one other man in the bathroom with them, and he was the one standing pressed up against the door as shots still rang out. Dump looked up at one of the girls, and tears were falling down her face. She looked as if she never been so afraid in her life before. Then they heard the door *Bam! Bam! Bam!* And a voice outside of the door said, "Open the door please!"

Dump warned, "Dog, don't open that door."

A female said, "Are you who they looking for?"

Dump said, "No."

Then gunshots went silent.

Then the dude in the bathroom said, "I'm about to go out there."

Dump said, "If you open that fucking door and a nigga starts busting in this bitch, I'm way in the back. That shit gone hit all y'all. I'm good!"

Then Dump thought to himself, *I hope these niggas don't come through.*

Then he heard a female voice say, "Oh my god! They coming through!"

Dump said out loud, "What you mean they coming through?"

Pop! Pop! Pop! It sounded as if the shooter was right in front of the bathroom door. They waited about ten minutes until they heard people talking, then they came out the door. Dump walked up to the front door. Between there and the bathroom, he saw a tall dark-skinned dude with long dreads lying on the floor bleeding. He walked right past him and went out the front door. He walked over to the netural ground where he saw Pickle and O-Head.

He told O-Head, "Dog, Koonta just said he was surprised a nigga ain't let off fifty shots out here."

O-Head said, "Man, I seen everything. A nigga came waling up the block popping at a nigga in front the club. One of the dude's homies was on the netural ground saw the shooter shooting at his homie, so he pulled out his pistol and started plucking at the shooter. The shooter dipped in between the parked cars then came back shooting at the dude's homie that was shooting at him. Dude's homie saw the shooter running back toward the club busting at him nonstop, so he ran in the club. Dude must have waited in the club beside the door because when the shooter walked in the door he got hit up."

Dump said, "I just saw that boy leaking on the floor. I'm ready to get the fuck outta here. Let's roll."

They pulled off as the ambulance pulled up with the cops right behind them. When Dump made it home, he went straight to sleep.

The next morning when Dump woke up, the sky was the most beautiful he had ever seen in his life. The clouds were puffy and snow white. The air was fresh, and the sky was baby blue. The birds were flying together in large groups in the same direction. The sun was shining hard, and the breeze was blowing perfect. Dump was sitting in his backyard rolling a gar.

Ann walked to the door and said, "Me and Albert are leaving the city for the storm today. Are you coming?"

He replied, "No, Ma, I'mma stay."

She said, "Okay. Be careful. I love you."

And she closed the door as the homie Author better known as Aw-Aw walked up.

Author said, "There you go putting that shit up in smoke, huh?"

Dump was like, "What's up? You already know."

Aw-Aw grabbed a chair and sat down. While they were smoking, they saw an SUV pull up. The passenger door opened, and Dump recognized the dude that hopped out. When the dude took two steps in their direction, a gunshot went off. The dude grabbed his leg and started hopping back to the SUV, and they peeled off. Then they noticed another car was following behind the SUV, but he couldn't see who was in it.

He told Aw-Aw, "This duck-ass nigga tried to jack something. He fucked around and shot himself."

Aw-Aw said, "Chedda Bob—ass nigga!"

Then they busted out laughing. Aw-Aw dipped out after the weed was gone. When Dump went inside, he saw Ann was gone. He went to his room and gave Trish a call. He told her that he would be over by eight o'clock.

Dump dozed off and ended up waking up almost five in the evening. He dipped by Choppa to get an ecstasy pill.

When he got the pill, he gave Steelo a call and asked, "What's up, fam? Can I get a ride across the canal in that nine?"

Stello said, "My nigga, what the fuck you going cross the canal for and you know a hurricane is coming in the am?"

Dump popped the blue dolphin pill, took a sip of water, and said, "I'm about to go lay up with this chocolate hoe. She asked me to ride it out with her."

Steelo laughed and said, "Boy, you're a real nigga. I'll be there to scoop you in a minute."

Dump said, "Cool." Then he hung up the phone.

He took a shower, packed a bag, and waited for Steelo to slide through to pick him up. About an hour and a half had passed when he heard Steelo blowing his horn. Dump grabbed his bag, shot out the door, and locked it behind him. He walked up to the white Cadillac, opened the door, then sat in. When he closed the door, he felt the pill busting in his stomach.

He told Steelo, "There go them butterflies."

Steelo looked at him and said, "Pop one, pop two! Nigga that ain't shit!"

Dump looked back at him and said, "Pop three, pop four! Nigga that ain't shit!"

Steelo said, "Oh no!" And he pulled off, smiling.

Steelo told Dump, "I been listening to your music. You're sleeping on yourself. I think you need to get in that lab and turn the fuck up. You too nice to not be recording homie."

Dump asked, "So you really like that CD?"

Steelo sucked his teeth and said, "Fucking right. I'm just telling you, man, wake the fuck up."

Dump looked at him and could tell he was serious as they pulled up to Trish's new spot.

Dump said, "I'm serious about this business. I just need the right connections."

Steelo said, "You know, this hurricane serious on this side. You sure you want to make this move?"

"We been through this shit in the city before," Dump said. "This ain't our first rodeo."

Steelo said, "Okay!" And he gave him dap, then he hopped out.

Trish's house was on the second floor of a two-story building with high ceilings built with bricks. As he walked up the stairs, he saw the door was cracked so he didn't knock on it; he just walked in. When he did, he saw Trish and her daughter, Trell, sitting on the sofa, watching the weather channel. Trish looked at him and smiled. She got up and gave him a hug.

Trell said, "I finally meet the lucky man!" as she laughed it off.

Dump just smiled and sat between them. He put his arm around Trish and looked at Trell, and said, "You're a cutie pie with a bad attitude, I heard."

She said, "Everything I got, I get it from my mamma."

Then she puckered her lips out, looking at Trish.

Trish said, "Girl, whatever. Go in your room."

Trell told Dump, "Nice to meet you," as she walked in the room.

Trish started rolling a blunt. She could tell that Dump was rolling off ecstasy hard as fuck by the way his eyes kept tilting to the back of his head.

She sat down next to him, lit the gar, then said, "Somebody looks like they feeling good."

He put his arm around her while his eyes rolled in his head, and said, "Baby, I'm feeling great."

She passed him the weed with intentions of letting him fuck the shit out of her once Trell went to sleep because she knew the pill would make him make her come back to back. Dump passed the piff to her. She hit it, straddled his lap, then put the gar backward in her mouth and blew him a gun while she looked him in his eyes.

It turned him on. She began to feel his dick rocking up, so she grabbed it, and asked, "You ready?"

He replied, "Always."

They chilled on the sofa for about an hour, talking, kissing, and touching.

When Dump and Trish were in the mood and she felt like Trell was sleeping, she grabbed Dump's hand and started walking to the bed.

Trell came busting out of her room, screaming, waving her hands wild in the air, saying, "I had a dream! We have to leave! We got to get out of here! Now! It's going to kill us! Ma, please! We got to go!"

Dump put his palms up toward her and said, "Baby, we been doing this for years. It's going to blow by. We gone be alright. Just calm down. We got this."

Trell went in her room, packed her bags, and called her aunt to come pick her up. When her aunt made it there, Trell gave Trish a hug and said, "I'm gone."

Trish told her, "Call me and let me know when you make it where you're going."

After Trish's daughter left her and Dump, they smoked a shit-load of weed. Trish was waiting on Dump to come down off his high from the ecstasy pill, but he was so lit he couldn't get right. They both just fell asleep laying up under each other.

Dump woke up the next morning to Trish fumbling around in the living room. He could tell that she was nervous. It was ten o'clock in the morning, and Hurricane Katrina was a couple of hours away from hitting land.

He said, "Good morning, bae. I'm sorry about last night."

She said, "That's okay."

Dump got out the bed and walked to the window because he heard the rain slapping against it from the wind blowing. When he looked out the window, there was two feet of water flooded on the street. It shocked him because the storm itself didn't hit. He asked Trish to turn on the news to catch the weather report. When she did, they found out that the hurricane went from a category three storm to a category five.

Dump grabbed the remote control, and as he started to turn up the volume, he heard the weather lady say, "The winds are one hundred and fifty miles per hour. Please pack and leave. Mayor Nagin said that evacuation is mandatory."

He thought to himself, "Damn, Trell's dream was reality."

He turned his head and looked at Trish. She was so terrified he could see her soul was troubled through her eyes. They both didn't know what to expect. It's been fifty years since the city was hit by a storm of this size and power.

Dump was real nervous, but from his attitude, Trish couldn't tell. At that moment in her mind, he was going to make sure she was alright. And in his mind, he was willing to do whatever it would take to survive. Trish went to lie down in the bed. Dump grabbed a fold-ing chair from the closet, unfolded it, then pulled it to the window to watch the conditions he had to prepare himself for.

As time went by, the water went from two feet to five feet of water moving up the street with a current the wind was whistling at the window seals. Trish saw how he planted himself at the window, so she went over to him and sat on his lap.

He put his arms around her and asked, "Did Trell ever call you?"

"Yes," she said. "She's in Houston, Texas, by her cousin."

Dump then said, "God sent us a message through her dream last night."

She turned and looked out the window and said, "I feel the same way. I prayed this morning and asked God to watch over us."

He said, "We good."

It was raining hard. They heard a loud pop sound, then the power went out. He asked her did she have a radio that took batteries.

She said, "I don't know. Let me check."

She went in the closet and started digging in it. It had been raining since early in the morning, but now everything changed. It was now noon, and *Karina* had reached land. It was pounding down on the city. He had never saw rain and wind together like that before. As Trish gave Dump the small radio, they could hear the wind blowing howling like a wolf. As he still sat by the window he could hear it rattling from the wind. He looked up to the sky, and the whole city was covered with one huge dark smoke gray cloud. Trish started to cry.

She asked, "What are we going to do, Dump?"

He said, "Swim?" He asked, "Do you know how?"

She looked out the window and said, "No!"

The flood was at ten feet and still rising constantly. He knew how to swim, but he wasn't sure if he could still do it with carrying her along. Not only that, the flow of the water was like a river rushing up the block. The thought crossed his mind that not even a Navy SEAL could swim through it.

He said, "Keep calm. I got you, baby."

Dump dug in his pocket and pulled out his phone to call Steelo, but he had no signal. He asked Trish for her phone, but when he got it, hers didn't have a signal either. That really put his thoughts in a jam. As he stood up looking out the window, Trish walked up behind him and wrapped her arms around his waist.

He looked at the corner and told her, "Look at this shit. You could only see the tip of the fucking stop signs."

She was so discombobulated she said nothing; she just squeezed him tighter, speaking to him with her body language, saying, "By God, I'm depending on you."

The wind started blowing and slamming against the big window making a loud thumping sound. The air was full of debris. The wind was so violent he could actually see it literally swirling before his eyes. It shook him. He grabbed Trish and stepped back from the window. All of a sudden the window busted, shattering glass in their faces. As the wind and glass hit them, it felt like someone threw it at them.

The sky grew darker, but suddenly, the storm calmed down, and the sun started to shine a little.

Trish asked, "Is it over?"

He replied, "No. This is the eye of the storm. There's more after this."

He didn't tell her, but he knew that the hurricane is always more rough after the eye of the storm passes. Trish's house was on the corner of Flood Street and Mirage Street, a half of a mile from the Coastal Water Canal and the main levy that protect the city. The canal that they were across from connected the Mississippi River, which was the location of the Port of New Orleans to Lake Pontchartrain, and that was connect to the Gulf of Mexico, where hurricane Katrina was coming from. About thirty minutes passed, and it started to drizzle a little. Dump took the batteries out of the TV remote. As he went to place them in the radio, they heard a loud explosion. It was the sound of the dynamite that the government used to blow up the levies to allow the poor urban area of the city to overflood in order to redirect the flooding water from the most known historical part of the city, which was the French Quarters and the Downtown New Orleans CBD area.

It was now 5:00 p.m., and the rain stopped. Now the water was still rising and flowing fast up the street. The water was now up to fifteen feet in front the door. He opened the door and looked down. There he noticed a light brown dog that was literally swimming up against the house. The dog was pedaling out of control with a look in its eyes as if it was afraid that it wouldn't make it. That really engraved itself in Dump's mind because logically dogs are known as the best swimmers in the world.

Then he looked across the street. There was a yellow-and-white one-story house that was halfway under water. He noticed that there were two crack heads, a man and a woman that were stranded on the roof. He could tell that the man was seriously panicking as the woman was crying. The woman stayed sitting at the tip top of the roof while the man kept walking up and down from the front to the back of the roof looking down at the rising quick flowing water. Before they knew it, water rose to the energy power lines. The radio was small enough for Dump to hold it in one hand. It had one speaker on it with a long antenna. It started too static.

As Dump pulled the antenna to make it longer so he could get more information about the storm, he heard the broadcaster say, "This storm is devastating. In the lower 9th Ward across the Canal we have twenty-one feet of water."

When Dump heard that he looked out the window and saw it. If he was anywhere else in the world, he would have thought that the informer was exaggerating, but he was looking at it with his own eyes feeling like they were in the middle of the ocean. He looked back at the houses across the street and saw a house floating up the street behind them.

He called Trish, and said, "Oh my god. Look at that!"

She was speechless. He looked back to the corner to the yellow-and-white house and saw the woman looking at them with her hands on her head pulling her hair, screaming at them continuously. "Save me! Please! Save me!"

Dump looked for the man that was with her, but he didn't see him anywhere. From the level of the water and how fast the current was moving, he knew that if the man tried to swim in the water, he wouldn't survive. Dump and Trish heard the neighbor next door, hollering, "Are y'all okay over there?"

Trish said, "Yes!" She said to Dump, "Do you want to go over there?"

He answered "I don't know him. That's up to you."

She said, "He's cool."

Dump said, "Dig."

So they walked on the porch, and the neighbor opened the door, and they walked in. When Dump walked in, he saw it was two dudes. They introduced themselves, then Dump looked around the house. He saw in the kitchen there was a stack of juice containers like the big ones they put juice in, in jail. It was something like an igloo. Dump asked the dude, "Do you have any duct tape?"

The dude opened the draw under the microwave and pulled it out then tossed it to him. He caught it then sat it on the table. As he heard the crack addict on the roof across the street still screaming. He grabbed five of the brown containers and locked their tops closed. After that, he started wrapping the duct tape around them all so they would not come apart.

When he finished, he laid it down like a surf board. He saw an extension cord, picked it up, and wrapped it around the handles so they had something they could all hold on to. Dump walked to the front door to check on the lady on the roof. He saw she was broken mentally. She had maybe five more feet left clear of her roof before the water would rise and sweep her away. Dump couldn't imagine seeing that. He felt sorry for her and walked away.

Dump was in a position he had never been in before. He was with four people, but he felt alone. It was two people he just met and a woman he barely knew. He was uncomfortable, but the fear of swimming in the storm made that feeling irrelevant. About forty-five minutes passed, and everything stopped. It was no longer raining, the water stopped rising, and the fear ceased to exist. Dump thought to himself that the Lord spared the woman on the roof.

When he looked, she maybe had three and a half feet of her roof still above the water. As the sun started to set, Trish and Dump told the neighbors that they were going back next door.

Once they made it inside, the sun had disappeared. He looked up to the sky, and there wasn't a cloud there. It was so quiet he could hear people talking from up the block. He was mentally and physically tired because of the circumstances throughout the day.

He said, "Trisha, I'm going to sleep. Wake me up if the water start rising again."

Trisha agreed with an, "Okay."

Dump dozed off quick, but in less than fifteen minutes, he heard Trish say, "Bae, get up! The water is rising again!"

Dump's heart dropped. The statement she just made drove him berserk. He had just watched the water rise nonstop for nine hours to twenty-one feet. It was dark. The only light they had was the moon and stars glistening off the water. It rose three more feet and stopped at the door seal. He didn't know it, but it affected him mentally. The word *deranged* defined his frame of mind. Trish looked Dump in his eyes and could tell he was thinking crazy.

As she stood at the door looking at the water Dump grabbed a big flashlight and turned it on as he walked to the door and stood behind her.

He flashed it up the block and said, "I never seen this much water on land before in my life."

Trish said, "I'm happy you are here with me."

He hugged her from behind and gave her a kiss on her cheek. Suddenly they saw a bright light shining coming up the side street. The closer it got, they started to hear the motor of a boat. When the boat reached the corner, he saw it was police in a marked boat. Dump pointed the flashlight at them and flashed the SOS code Flick. Flick. Flick. Flick. Flick. Flick. Flick. Flick.

The boat immediately turned up the street and pulled up to the porch. As Dump and Trish boarded the boat, the neighbors walked out their house and entered the boat too. While the boat floated away from the house, the police started asking questions. Dump paid them no mind. His eyes and mind were extremely focused on the devastation; all he saw and thought about was death and how many poor people the government just murdered intentionally to save the upper-scale part of the city. As the boat passed the houses, he saw people climbing out of holes in their roofs.

The boat reached the bridge at the levy that crossed over the canal and let them off on St. Claude Street. When the four of them walked down the bridge, the water was only to their ankles. They followed a crowd because they were told that people were all going to the elementary school across the street from Nichols Senior High School.

They walked four blocks and when they made it to the bottom of the stairs at the school Dump looked up the stairs and saw it was a crowd of people fighting one man. He saw a female pull out a knife and started stabbing him. The school was full of chaos. When they walked through the doors, it was dark in the halls. Parents and their children were sitting close to each other on the floor along the walls.

Each window along the wall was open. The only light in the school was from the moon and stars. Dump and Trish walked through, and he held her hand. From the way the people were carrying themselves, he knew it was an unsafe place. They looked back and saw that the two neighbor guys were still following them. He looked in a classroom and saw nobody was in it so; he stopped, and they all went in and took a seat. It was quiet for a few minutes.

Then Dump said, "Man, that shit was sick."

Chuck said, "I thought we were dead."

Trish said, "Thank God we made it."

Dump felt like he needed a moment to himself, so he said, "I'll be back."

While he walked out the door, closing it behind him, Trish got up, and she followed behind him.

He walked to the end of the hall then walked into the doors of the hall then walked into the doors of the staircase as Trish hollered, Dump, hold up!"

He stopped on the stairs and turned around, waiting for her.

When she walked through the door she said, "What is wrong with you?"

He walked up to her and pulled her to him. He put his hand around her neck, slightly choking her while he slid his tongue down her throat. It caught her off guard, but she needed that. As Trish kissed him back, she wrapped her arms around Dump tight. He unbuttons her pants then pulled them down halfway. Then Dump walked her up two steps to the flat point then spun her around, bending her over aggressively.

He unzipped his pants, pulled his dick out, then stuck it in her without a condom. When he pushed it in Trish, gasped for breath, then moaned when he dug deeper in her. She grabbed the rail while he grabbed her by the hips jerking her back quick on the dick. Because of the circumstances and the situation, it literally blew her mind. It made her throw that ass back like she never did before. Dump could feel her flexing her pussy muscles. When he pulled her to him, she made it tight. When she bounced away from him, she let her muscles relax. The more he felt his nut coming the harder his dick got, the louder she moaned and the harder she bounced her ass back. Right before he busted, he pulled it out beating it as it skeeted everywhere. Trish turned around and kissed him because her body fell in love with him.

Dump and Trish took a walk through the halls, holding hands, then returned to the classroom. When they made it back, Chuck and his homie was still sitting there. After they sat down and chilled with them for a minute, Trish announced, "I'm hungry."

Dump replied, "Maybe there is something to eat in the high school's cafeteria across the street."

Chapter Eighteen

Chuck pulled a flashlight out of his bag and said, "Come on, let's go see."

Dump went in Trish's bag to grab the flashlight, and they left.

When they walked down the stairs and stepped into the street to cross it, the water was up to their shins. When Dump stepped up on the neutral ground, he turned and looked back toward the school and saw Trish looking at him through the window from the classroom. He turned around and kept it moving. When they made it to the door they busted the window. Dump slid in first and Chuck followed him. They went into the cafeteria and found honeybuns, cookies, milks, and juice. They grabbed a plastic milk crate and loaded it up then shot back across the street.

After they made it back, Dump said, "I'm sure they have some more valuable stuff over there. I'm going back. What's up, Chuck, you coming or chilling?"

"No. I'm good" Dump dipped out.

When he made it to the school he saw the principal's office and went in. He opened the desk draw and found hundreds of regional transportation bus tokens. When he looked over o the counter he saw a line of walkie-talkie radios. He grabbed a big garbage bag and started loading everything worth money in it. Once the bag was full, he walked to the window and put the bag through it then he slid out. Dump stood up and noticed a pair of bright headlights approaching slowly from the left on the neutral ground. It was a U-Haul truck. He began to flag it down as it started pulling up to him. When it stopped in front of him, he walked up to the passenger side window.

Before he knew it, a police officer that was driving, drew a big black Desert Eagle and pointed it at point blank range in Dump's face, and said, "Back the fuck up!"

He raised his hands and said, "I was just looking for a ride," as he backed away while the officer pulled off. Dump felt like he just looked death in the eyes as he walked through the water crossing the street.

Dump walked in the classroom where Trish, Chuck and his homie was. He felt the whole vibe changed. It was obvious that a conversation about him took place while he was gone. Later on that night, he and Trish got into an argument. The next morning what Trish said to him in the argument was still on his mind. That made him feel like she was disrespectful, and he should leave her with Chuck since he dropped some shit in her ear. Dump walked up to Chuck and said, "I'm gone. That hoe good with y'all."

He then grabbed his bag full of shit and dipped out. He thought back throughout all the storms that hit New Orleans. On the corner his house was on, it never flooded. Two blocks away could have ten feet of water, but his corner was dry as an island. In his mind the flood on this side was nothing like the flood across the canal, so he had to make it home. He tossed his heavy bag over his shoulder and started hiking up St. Claude Street.

He walked seven blocks down and turned right on Louisa Street. As he walked down the street he noticed the water got deeper and darker.

At the first block the water was at his shins. On the fourth block the water was past his knees. By the sixth block, it was at his waist. He lifted his bag up and sat it on his shoulder as he looked around and saw oil patches all over the top of the water with debris floating through it. He started to grow nervous thinking about snakes and alligators could possibly be in the water. As Dump kept walking, he realized the way it was looking that the water was getting too deep for him to make it home. He was now ten blocks down deep with the garbage bag on his head and the water to his chest. He had made it to North Claiborne Street, where he looked to the left and saw the bridge. He figured it was his best option to go across it because he didn't like where he came from and he was not for turning around and going back.

Dump made it to the top of the bridge. When he looked down, he saw that it was dry land. It made him feel safe and gave him hope. As he began to walk down, he saw a few people busting the store windows and going in, while across the street more people were looting in and out of the Chevron gas station carrying bags. He paid it no mind. He simply continued his route. Once he reached the bottom of the bridge, he walked to the corner of Claiborne and Franklin Avenue then looked to the right and saw that the water flooded the whole neighborhood.

He couldn't tell how deep the water was further down, but from where he was standing, it was once again at his ankles.

Dump heard a voice say, "What's up!"

When he turned around and looked, he saw DJ Slick from the hood.

Dump dapped him then said, "My nigga, what up?"

Slick said, "We fucked out here."

Dump turned back to the right and pointed to the Almonaster Bridge and said, "You see all them motherfuckers on that bridge? The homies have to be up there. I'm trying to make it to the hood."

Slick said, "Me too."

Dump asked, "Do you know how to swim?"

"Fuck no," Slick answered.

Dump looked around and saw three car tires on factory rims on side of a Dumpster.

Dump said, "Man, we could grab those and float on 'em to the bridge."

Slick said, "Cool."

They went and grabbed 'em then shot out. He was calm, but as the water got deeper, Slick got fidgety. He started to bobble on the tire.

Slick told Dump, "Man, I can't do it. I'm going back."

He looked at Slick and understood, but it disappointed him.

Dump was dedicated to moving forward, so he told Slick, "Okay. I'mma fuck with you later."

Slick turned back. Dump took the bag and sat it on top of the tire pushing it as he walked through the water behind it. He was two blocks down, and the water was already up to his chest. It was eight more blocks before he could make it to the bridge. The thought crossed his mind that there was over a thousand people on the bridge, and he was in the water alone. Just as it was before, turning around and going back wasn't an option. As the water got deeper, he started to walk a straight line balancing himself on top of the gates as he pushed the tire along the block.

The sun was beaming, and the water was warm. It was beginning to take a toll on him.

Dump reached the corner of Almonaster and Galvez Streets. Galvez was a main street just like Almonaster, so the intersection was wide. Before he crossed that point, he decided to stand on the porch of the house that was on that corner just so he could catch his breath. Once he regained, Dump swam over to the gate and looked both ways seeing that it was clear. That was when he pushed the tire across the street then used the gate to push himself off with his feet to swim across the eight feet of water.

When Dump made it to the center of the intersection, his legs started to tighening up on him. As he started to sink, he began doggie peddling to stay afloat. There was a building with a porch nearby where he could stop and rest, but Dump couldn't see the porch on the side of the building because of the flood, but he knew it was there. He was halfway to it, but his arms were getting tired, so he started to panic. His arms wanted to give out, but he knew if he stopped he would drown, so he kept pushing until he made it to the porch.

When he did, he stood up stretching his legs out and massaging the muscles to help relax them. At that moment, Dump was stuck on the porch and couldn't move hoping nothing attacked him. Ten minutes passed, and Dump moved along. He found a way to cling himself to the side of houses with his hands and feet without sinking. He had no idea how he was able to do it, but it was getting done.

Before long, Dump was three blocks away from the bridge, but he was too tired. He couldn't go any further, so he pushed the tire to a house and stood on its porch. Then a small float boat with two men on it began to approach him slowly and they asked him did he want a ride to the bridge.

He said, "Yes."

Then grabbed his bag and got in the boat.

As the boat reached the foot of the bridge, Dump notice a young man was holding a case of bottled water while issuing it to the people. As soon as Dump set a foot on the bridge he saw a man come from the side and knocked out the man that was issuing out the waters. Then he took the case and walked off. It seemed as if every destination, Dump made it to was chaotic. He walked up the bridge and looked around to see if he saw one of the homies, but out of a thousand people, he saw not one. It really drove Dump even more crazy. He lived in that neighborhood for twenty years and didn't know a soul on the bridge.

It left him mind boggled. He thought to himself, "How could I not know once person on this bridge?"

At that moment a young boy walked up behind him and said, "What's up, big homie?"

Dump turned around and said, "What's good?"

Noticing he was someone who stayed across the street from Press Park, the lil homie said, "I'm just trying to survive out here big brother. If you want to, you can put your bag in the car."

Dump asked, "Which one?"

Little Dee pointed out, "The white one."

Dump walked over and placed the bag in it, then the lil homie locked the door. They gave each other daps and looked down on the other side of the bridge which was the side they lived on.

Dump asked, "Have you been down there?"

Little Dee said, "Yes! It's deep as fuck!"

Dump told him, "I know. All I could see was the tip of the roof of the houses. It has to be more than fifteen feet of water."

Two people was floating toward the bridge inside of a refrigerator as they peddled with boards one on each side. Right behind them was a person floating on an air mattress.

Dump said, "Damn, my nigga. I'm trying to get to the block, but I'm not going that way. I'm gone cut through the field."

He and Little Dee split up. Dee stayed on that side, while Dump went to the other side. When Dump reached the foot of the bridge, a huge fishing boat without a motor floated up with three guys paddling and one older guy with long black and gray dreadlocks hanging from his head standing at the nose of the boat with one leg cocked on the tip of it. Dump noticed he had a bloody T-shirt wrapped around his forearm.

The older guy looked Dump in his eyes as Dump asked, "Where y'all going?"

The man with the dreads said, "To help people out of their houses. Do you want to come?"

Dump hopped in the boat and one of the other dudes hopped off. As they peddled away, the boat moved forward, swaying from left to right. Because they were peddling a big boat without a motor it took them at least five minutes or longer to make it up every block.

Dump asked, "Say OG, why you wearing that shirt on your arm?"

The OG looked back at Dump and said, "When I was in the water, a baby shark bit me. I gutted it with this knife."

They paddled block after block and picked up a few people that were trapped in their homes. They took them to the bridge. Once they made it the people got off and others asked for a ride to Claiborne Street.

OG told them, "Okay."

So they hopped aboard. When they were four blocks from the bridge, they saw a young teenage girl's dead body floating beside the boat. Everybody got quiet. It went from everyone, but Dump talking to complete silence. As they floated up to the fork in the road where Almonaster met with Franklin Avenue, there was an old school station wagon parked on the sidewalk in front of a house on Franklin. The water covered the majority of the vehicle. All he could see was the flat top of the station wagon, where a dead body laid on its stomach as his face was literally lying flat as if his facial structure was crushed by something.

When they got right on the side of it, one of the dudes that was paddling said, "That look like my boss who owes me money."

The other dude paddling said, "Shit, look at that fat ass wallet in his back pocket."

Dump said, "We'll check it for money when we come back."

After they dropped the people off a block away, they turned around and floated back up to the body.

One dude jumped off the boat and splashed into the water. He walked over to the man and grabbed the wallet out of his pocket.

When he opened it, he looked at the ID and said, "This is my boss!"

As he checked it for money, he said, "Ain't no fucking money in here!"

Dump said," Damn!" as dude hopped back on the boat soaking wet.

It was late in the evening when they pulled back up to the bridge.

Little Dee saw Dump and asked, "You still trying to go home?"
Dump said, "Yeah."

Dee started taking off his life jacket and said, "Here, take this. You should be good."

He took the life jacket and put it on then looked up to the sky and saw the sun was getting ready to set, so he gave Dee dap and set out on his way. When he walked down to the foot of the bridge, his guts started to bubble. He was more nervous than before. When he made it to the gate around the big field, he slid his body through a hole in it. The water was five and a half feet, so he floated across the field.

He reached a deeper part where the field had very high grass and weeds in the water. It started to wrap around his legs pulling him down into the water. The life jacket barely kept him afloat. His eyes grew wide. His heart started to beat fast. As he took his hands and began to free his legs from the weeds, he thought to himself that crossing that field in a flood was one of the stupidest choices he ever made in his life.

When Dump freed himself, he moved quick because it was now dark. He slid out the gate a block away from his house. The water was five feet there. When he looked up the street, he saw that his corner was flooded. That was his first time swimming in the water at night. His heart was now racing. He was actually getting paranoid. At that moment, Dump noticed that he could see the roofs of the cars parked on that street.

He walked on top of the first one and down it. Then up the next one, then down it. He kept doing that until he reached the corner. When he made it there, it was at least eight feet of water. There he was in the middle of the street floating feeling stranded. Then he looked over to the backyard of the town house next to his house and saw the roof of a white van. He decided to swim up to his front door, but he couldn't open the bar door because the wooden frame was swollen around it from the water. It was jammed tight. Dump rushed over to the side of the building and sat on top of the van. As he sat there, his heart was beating hard. It was so quiet that all he could hear is the helicopters chopping in the air flying over the city shining their lights down on it.

He became paranoid. Nothing but chaotic thoughts crossed his mind. His first thought was, what if a gator started swimming up to him. He had nowhere to run, so he was dead. Next he thought, what if someone from other neighborhoods that he had beef with came by on a boat with a gun and killed him. Nobody would know what happened. He would just be another dead body floating in the water. Dump looked up at the sky.

The whole city was so dark he could see every star like it was literally a million of them shinning down on him. The moon was so bright it looked like he could reach up and touch it. He laid flat on his back and stretched his arms and legs out wide open. At that moment, he heard his own heart beating and felt more alone than ever.

He looked up to God and whispered, "God, I've been through too much in life. I don't deserve to die like this. Don't let me go like this."

Then he shut up for a short second as the pain and destruction hit him.

He screamed, "*Fuuuuuuuuuuuck!*"

Then he heard a lot of people screaming and hollering back at him out the second floor windows of their homes. That lifted a ton of weight off his shoulders just to know that he wasn't there alone. They began to ask Dump questions and he kept answering them as time went by.

Almost an hour passed, and Dump heard a noise like a big fan blowing. When he sat up and looked down the street, he saw a trail of air boats coming up the street shinning their lights looking for people to save.

Dump yelled, "We have a ride y'all. The boats are here."

Kerrie's mom looked down at him and said, "Thank you, God!"

When the boats made it, he was first on. Once everyone was loaded up, the airboats went back the way they came from and pulled out on Almonaster then floated up to Louisa Street. From there, they dropped everybody off on I-10 interstate at the Louisa street exit. It was hundreds of people lined up along the shoulders of the interstate. The vibe was rare. Dump looked over and saw a man take a seat on the side of the bridge rail. Dump blinked his eyes then saw the man jump into the water to commit suicide. Everyone ran to the edge of the bridge to look for him, but his body never surfaced again. And if it did, it was too dark under the interstate to see him.

Dump kicked it with a few of the homies he had been waiting to see since early that morning as they walked along the interstate. They stopped as two camouflaged hummers pulled up with a line of army trucks following behind them. When the trucks stopped, all the civilians were ordered to load up in the back of the trucks. So everyone loaded up. Once they did, the army trucks turned around and headed downtown to the CBD area and dropped everyone off at the National Convention Center. This place was dark, and the building was sitting at the end of the CBD are where the Mississippi River was right behind it. The building was two stories and three blocks long. As Dump walked into the spot he looked around and saw it was thousands of people there with no police or doctors present. He saw a young woman with a new born baby sitting in front of a very old man that was standing there alone. To be in a situation like that, in a place and time when New Orleans was literally considered the murder capital of the United States of America was something that Dump never would have imagine.

Dump walked through the building to see what was going on. He got to a section where it was so dark till he couldn't see the people's faces, but he could hear them talking. He saw the fire on a blunt blaze up as one of them puffed on it. The further he got in the building it became more hood, so he decided to walk outside to get some fresh air. When he made it out there he saw it was packed. As he looked around, he saw a dude talking loudly and pointing at another dude. When Dump looked to the left, he saw a dude walking toward him with a gray hoodie on. When the dude passed him, he walked up to the crowd, pulled out a gun and started shooting. It caught Dump off guard as he looked at the man finger squeezing the trigger while biting his bottom lip. Dump walked in the door to get away from the foolishness. When he made the move, the dude that was shooting, walked right in the door behind him tucking the gun under his sweater.

Under his breath Dump said, "Oh my fucking god!" thinking, *That somebody needs to come get dude ass before he starts shooting in here.*

Chapter Nineteen

Dump walked back to the front of the building and hooked up with Snick, Head Busser, and Big Moe and told them what just went down.

Big Moe said, "Man, it's so much noise in here we didn't even hear no shots."

Dump said, "Picture the hitter that was banging it out walked right in the door behind me. What the fuck was so crazy about it is, when I looked out the glass doors the army rushed the crowd and drew their assault rifles on them, forcing the young children and the old people on the fucking ground while that duck ass nigga walked right beside me."

Snick said, "What's more fucked up than that is a little girl and her mother were just raped in the restroom."

Dump turned and looked at all the people in the building and said, "You got to be kidding."

Big Moe put his head down as he shook it and said, "My nigga, this is hell on earth."

Turtle walked up and told them that the army just told them that martial law was now ordered.

"What in the hell is martial law?" asked Snick.

Big Moe explained, "If we disobey the police orders or the army, them bitches can shoot us dead on the spot and get away with it scot-free."

"Shit. Them motherfuckers going to have to catch me," Dump said as they laughed it off.

That's when the whole crowd broke out running in one direction toward them screaming, "The water is coming!"

They broke out, running with them. Dump was terrified because of the water he saw across the canal when he arrived he was mentally fucked up. He cut right and ran up the escalator behind a few other. When Dump made it to the top, he turned around and looked, waiting for the water to rush the building as he saw other people downstairs. Dump waited, waited, and waited, but no water came.

He walked down the escalator to the glass doors. When he walked out the doors, none of his homies were in sight. He looked down the street and squinted his eyes because it appeared as if it was flooded down there, but it wasn't. It was dry land. Because of all the water he saw flooding the city, every direction he looked in, it was if he saw water flooding the street in distance.

Dump had to pull himself together and try to shake out of it, but he couldn't. His character became the character of a person who was shell shocked. He was so focused on everybody else he would never realize his own actions, but in the future, he would have to deal with the consequences. He met back up with the homies, and they went to the section where the rest of the people from the hood were. There they all laid down and went to sleep while a couple stayed up to keep watch in case anything happened.

The next morning, Dump woke up to the sound of a baby crying. He could tell the baby was hungry, but the mother had nothing to give him. He looked and noticed the baby's Pampers was loaded with poo and piss. The look on the woman's face was as if it was the end of the world. Dump could feel her pain, but there was nothing he could do. Also he realized that the woman had nowhere to go or a way get what they needed, they were completely helpless, alone, and vulnerable.

Mayor Ray Nagin sent a message throughout the city on Wednesday afternoon. It informed the people that they were giving the right to go into stores and get whatever important items they needed such as food, medicine, and water. That made all the people go through the streets, urgently seeking what they needed.

Turtle pulled up on Dump in a four-wheel cart and told him, "Come on."

Dump hopped in and they drove through the street until they found a store in the Garden District. When he looked, he saw people swarming in and out the door, so he hopped off and went in. Once inside the store, he looked down and saw a young man lying on the floor in the middle of the doorway having a seizure as everyone walked over him, one after another. He couldn't understand why nobody stopped to help him. It was as if the man or his issue didn't exist. He had no idea how to help a person who was having a seizure. It bothered him how everybody was handling the situation, but he operated the same and looked down at the man foaming from the mouth as he stepped over him, entering the room. He grabbed everything he needed then exited the room, looking down on the man again.

He brought his stuff back to the center; he walked to their section and bent down and placed it in the corner. When he stood up and turned around, he saw a woman pushing a wheelchair with a dead body to the front of the center with a white sheet covering the body. Dump watched to see where she was going to put the body. The woman rolled to the front corner of the building where seven more bodies were there covered in sheets. Once again, he felt death in the place. Because there were no doctors in the center, the people were dying from high blood pressure, asthma, as well as minor heath issues.

A couple of the homies came to Dump and said "Say round. We about to go on Canal Street. I heard they're letting us take shit out any store we want."

Big Moe said, "Yeah, I just saw some people come back with a whole lot of fresh shit."

Dump said, "Dig."

So they shot out. When they walked up the block, they saw an out of state police office with a AR-15 assault rifle sitting on his shoulder as he looked at them coming toward him. When they walked by him, they all made eye contact with him, but no one said a word as the sounds of a helicopter flying low was chopping through the buildings echoing loud as fuck. The police watched them until they reached the corner of Canal Street then looked up at the jet black military chopper as it passed by with a .50-caliber machine gun hanging off the side. When they turned on to Canal Street, it was an epic moment. This area was historical in the city. It was the front door to the French Quarters. On each block there were four cops with big guns ready to kill anyone who caused an unwanted situation they didn't like. It was an organized riot, approved by the mayor and directed by cops.

Dump started to walk into one store with the fellas behind him.

An officer pointed his gun in their direction and said, "Don't go in that store. Go in the other one!"

So they went in the store next door. Dump and his homies grabbed some bags and stuffed it with Polo shirts and Levi jeans then walked out. When they came out the store, they looked over and some dudes exiting the other store with bags. The police ran up to them with their rifles pointed at them and ordered them to drop their bags. When the dudes dropped their bags, the officers took them. Dump and them were able to walk away with two bags in each hand. They went to the center, dropped their bags off, and shot right back around there.

When they made it halfway there, half of the gang said they didn't want to go because the police were doing too much to harmless people. The other half said that the police never harmed them. Dump already made up his mind, so he sat on the Harrahs Casino wall and lit a cigarette to smoke as the click bickered back and forth to make up their minds.

Dump looked to the left and saw five young women walking by going toward Canal Street as they laughed among each other, he said, "Man, check these hoes out. They fine asses going get it, and y'all bullshitting."

They looked at the chicks but paid them no mind.

Snick said, "I ain't fucking with it."

Flee said, "I'm fucking with that."

Willie said, "Either we all going or I ain't."

Dump sat back grinning at them as he lit up another joe.

After about five minutes passed Big Moe said, "Say y'all, check ya girls out."

When they all looked, they saw two of them crying while the other three looked pissed. One of the chick's hair was all over her head. When Dump looked down, he saw that they were all barefoot.

He asked, "Say shorty. What happened?"

She looked back at him and said, "Them pussy-ass police robbed us!"

Dump didn't say nothing, but he thought to himself, "The cops let the gang get away with the shit they took out the stores, but they jammed the girls up and fucked over them."

Most of the click went back to the center. Dump and a few went to Canal Street and went separate ways once they got there. Dump went in Foot Looker Shoe store and grabbed a few pair of sneakers, then he went in a jewelry store and grabbed the left over jewelry that the people that hit the spot before him left behind. When he made it to the center, he stashed the jewelry in a bag and stuffed it in a suitcase he got from one of the homies.

It was now the third day after the storm hit the city. Dump had been doing so much for the last three days. He was tired, so his body had to rest. He laid down for a minute and dozed off lying in the cut by his belongings.

The next morning Dump woke up, everything felt different. It was like the world wasn't the same. He overheard two females talking about some big buses are supposed to be arriving to pick up the people from the center and transport them to other cities. People were at their breaking point and the city was in an uproar. Dump watched sports on television, and he always heard the commentators say that the crowd was going into pandemonium, but he never experienced it until he walked out the glass doors.

Dump literally saw pandemonium with his own eyes. People were running around doing some of the wildest shit. Some were fussing, some were fighting, and everyone was making so much noise till he couldn't hear himself think. He looked up to the Mississippi River Bridge, which was called the Crest City Connection sitting up high over the convention center and saw a long line of buses sitting there.

Hours passed, and those buses never moved. He started to see cars drive by and pick people up.

He asked somebody next to him, "Where the hell all these cars coming from?"

The man replied, "You see that tall building right there?"

Dump looked at where the man was pointing and said, "Yeah."

The man then said, "That's a car garage." Dump walked off.

When he ran across people, he knew he asked did they have a flathead screwdriver. They all said no, but he never stopped looking for one until he met up with Fat's little brother from her daddy's side of the family and found one. At that moment there were a lot of things going on around him, but none of it mattered. He was determined to steal a car and leave the devastation behind.

Dump walked over to the parking garage and began to walk up the ramp. Once he made it to the second level, he started picking out the car he wanted. He walked over to a white Chevy Impala and busted the window. Once he opened the door and sat in it, he didn't know what to do because he never stole a car before. He leaned to the side and looked at the steering column for a place to stick the flat head to pry it open.

When he did find a spot and opened the column up, he didn't know what to do. Before he knew it, he was frustrated. He hopped out to try another car. As he was walking up the ramp to the next level, a Lexus passed him going down the ramps.

Then he saw a blue Corvette coming down the ramp toward him, so he flagged it down and asked, "How are Y'all getting these top-notch cars, big brother? They can't be easy to steal."

"The keys are in the cars. You have to check 'em," the guy told him.

After that he pulled off. Dump walked up to a black Cadillac and busted the window and searched for the keys, but found none. He went to the next car and did the same. He flipped down the sun visor and saw no key. He opened the arm rest compartment, and it was empty. When he opened the glove compartment, there he saw a brand-new Smith & Weston .22 cal.

Dump popped the clip out and saw it was loaded and said, "Bingo!"

He slid the clip back in and walked up the ramp some more and chose to check a white Lincoln Continental president edition for keys. When he pulled the visor down, the keys fell in his lap. Dump didn't waste any time after that. He cranked it up and burned out to the first level.

He made a left then made another left at the corner and pulled up in front of the convention center. He cut the car off and hopped out and walked in the building.

He went to their section and grabbed his suitcases as he said, "I have a ride out front. I'm about to get the fuck out! Who coming?"

Big Moe looked back at his family and said, "I'm chilling."

Dump dapped him and walked off out the glass doors. When he looked back, he saw Turtle and Willie following him. Dump popped the trunk and started loading up. It seemed as if a calm spirit came down on him. He looked around and saw people talking to each other, but he didn't hear a sound, he just saw their body language and their mouths moving. Willie and Turtle got in the car when he closed the trunk.

As Dump walked around to the driver side to hop in, he noticed a young white ma pushing an old white woman in a wheelchair up to the car flagging him down.

While he was closing the door, he said under his breath, "What the fuck he want?" while Willie and Turtle were looking at the man.

Dump rolled the window down and asked, "What's going on?"

The white man said, "Please, sir, my mother is sick. I think she is about to die. Can you please give my mom and my wife a ride to the hospital in Baton Rouge? Please," as he pointed to his mother with a desperate look in his eyes.

Dump looked over to her and saw death on her face. Dump then looked down at her body and saw she was skin and bones with her dark-green veins visible throughout her whole body. He thought about her age, knowing she grew up at a time when racism was evidently relevant and openly active with whites hating, depriving, and assaulting innocent black people because of their skin color.

Dump thought to himself, *I know she is a racist.* Even though his mind thought that and had him thinking he shouldn't do it, his heart made him say yes. He hopped out the car and helped the man put her in the back seat. After that, he popped the trunk and placed the wheelchair in it. Looking her son in his eyes as they pulled off, he could tell a heavy weight was lifted off his shoulders. Dump hit the interstate headed to Houston. He stopped in Baton Rouge and dropped the ladies off at the hospital. After that, he had to take the backroads as Interstate 10 was shut down.

Chapter Twenty

It was twelve midnight. Dump pulled up to a gas station and filed the tank up.

When he hopped back in the car, Willie said, "Let's stop at Grambling University and holler at Jermane and Scooby."

Dump said, "We don't have no more money for gas. Man, look, we gone drive until the gas get low. When it do, we gone stop and rob the first motherfucker we see, fill the tank up and keep moving."

Dump looked over at Willie then looked back at Turtle and saw they both had stale faces. Dump wasn't sure if they were afraid or it just caught them off guard. Either way, Dump was going with his move. They were both younger than him and didn't understand his mind frame because the statement he just made didn't match his old ways. His life was already going in a bad direction before the storm. Once the storm hit it literally took the icing off the cake.

It was about 10:00 a.m., and they were coasting up Highway 90 floating in a big body Lincoln, listening to Fifty Cent on the radio. The road was clear. Dump looked up into the rearview mirror and saw a cop car a mile away with the lights flashing.

He looked down at the dashboard and he was floating at 110 mph. "Man fuck! The laws behind us."

Dump thought to himself, *We're in a hot car with buku stolen shit and a gun*, and said, "Y'all don't say shit. Just agree to everything I say."

Then Dump pulled to the side and waited for the cop to roll up. When the cop car pulled behind them, he looked at the rearview mirror and saw the police were wearing a cowboy hat with a big shot-gun hanging on a rack in the back window.

"Fuck, this ah real red neck. We might be fucked, man."

They heard the officer say over the intercom, "Driver, cut the engine off now!"

Dump complied.

Then the officer instructed, "Put your hands out the window!"

Again, Dump complied. After that, the police exited his car and walked up to the window by Dump and asked, "Do you know how fast you were going, son?"

Dump answered, "No, sir."

The office said, "I clocked you in at 115. Let me see your license, registration, and insurance."

Dump replied, "I don't have my license. I—"

The cop cut him off, and said, "Step out of the car please."

When Dump got out the car, the cop asked, "Where are y'all coming from?"

That's when Dump let it all out. "We came from New Orleans. The hurricane devastated the city. The police are down there killing us. We don't know where our families are, and we're looking for them. My mother died, and the police robbed my friends!"

The officer said, "I'm sorry you had to deal with that, but we are nothing like them out here! Stand right here, and do not move!"

The officer walked back to his patrol car and sat in it, looked at Dump, then put his down, looking at something he grabbed. Dump looked through the window at the lil homies. Their eyes said they were nervous. Dump looked back to the cop car, and the police were getting out the car with a chart in his hand.

As he walked up to Dump, he said, "I'm supposed to take you to jail, but I'm going to let you go."

He handed Dump a ticket to sign and said, "Do y'all have money for gas to get where y'all going?"

"No, sir," Dump said.

The officer went in his pocket and gave him twenty dollars and said, "Y'all can follow me to get something to eat if you're hungry."

Dump shook his hand then said, "Thank you, but we are going to hit the road to find our families."

When they got into their cars, the cop pulled off first, and they pulled off behind him. The car was silent for a few miles, then Willie said, "I thought we were gone."

Dump said, "Me too."

Turtle asked, "Man, what the fuck you told him?"

Dump was like, "I hit him with a hot track. The police down there robbing and killing people. My mama died. Man, I fucked his head up so much, he wrote a ticket and gave me money."

They all busted out laughing.

Willie told him, "Boy, you a fool with it."

Dump turned the radio on and put the car on cruise control at sixty miles per hour. Willie picked up the car phone and called Jermane and told him that they will be there shortly.

When Dump and his passengers made it to the university, they found out that the homies were pushing weed. Turtle asked them who the connect was. Scooby avoided answering him because he knew that because of the circumstances, they wanted to rob the connect.

Jermane switched the subject and asked, "Where are y'all headed?"

Willie said, "Houston."

Dump said, "Our money low. I got some jewelry I can sell. We trying to move out in the AM."

Scooby brought a few watches for three hundred dollars and an ounce and a half of weed. That night they crashed on the couch.

In the morning they hit the highway. Although Dump had a few dollars, in his mind, he wasn't about to spend it on gas. He wanted to hold it until they made it to Houston. He didn't tell the lil homies, but he was still going to rob somebody when the gas got low. They rode down to Lake Charles, Louisiana and the gas tank was on E. Dump exited off I-10 and pulled up to the gas station. He reached down in the side of the door and grabbed the gun. When he hopped out and walked up toward a man, the man looked at the license plate while Dump was clutching on the gun with his hand in his pocket.

The man said, "Oh my god! Are y'all from New Orleans?"

It caught Dump off guard.

He said, "Yes."

The man pulled his wallet out of his back pocket and gave him twenty dollars and said, "I'm sorry for what happened. God bless you."

Dump grabbed it and said, "Thank you."

It fucked Dump up because the man had no idea that he was about to get robbed. Dump gassed up and hit the road on I-10 West. He was two hours away from Houston.

That night when they reached Houston they hooked up with O-Head and some more of the homies by his aunt's house. Ms. Hazel was there, and she was happy to see them. They slept outside in the car for a few nights until FEMA showed up and helped them to fill out their disaster application for assistance.

After that, they were able to get themselves hotel rooms. With the weed he had, Dump used the hotels to his advantage. Everybody from New Orleans had no transportation and were stressing, because they were basically stuck in their hotel rooms. So he sold nickel bags for ten dollars, dime bags for twenty, and twenty bags for forty. When he finished selling that ounce and a half, there he met found the connect and hit him with nine hundred dollars and got three pounds. It blew him away, because from working that small amount of weed put him in a position to score the largest amount of drugs he ever had.

Even though Dump was hustling, he still went to the pawn shops and got rid of the jewelry. With the money he got from that, he moved into his own apartment on the southeast side of Houston. It was very different from the southwest side of New Orleans where he was used to hanging and hustling. Dump met a beautiful female that was thick in all the right places with a lovely dark chocolate complexion.

One night she was over by his house lying under him on the couch.

Out of the blue, she asked, "What drugs you tried before?"

Dump asked, "What made you ask me that?"

She replied, "Because if you never tried something I like, I want you to try it with me."

He asked, "Try what?"

He got up grabbed her purse and sat back down beside him.

He looked down in it as she stuck her hand inside it and pulled a small bag with white powder in it and said, "This," showing her beautiful white teeth.

He thought about it then said, "I ain't fucking with that."

She sucked her teeth then said, "So you gone turn me down?"

He turned his head and said, "Man, I ain't fucking with that!"

She looked him in his eyes as she unzipped her pants and pulled out his dick.

As she went down on him, she looked up to him and said, "Please...for me," with his dick in her mouth.

He heard mumble with it while she was reaching him the bag in her hand. When he took the bag rom her, she made sure she was doing her best job to please him. He used his pinky fingernail to get a bump out the bag and watched her looking up at him as he snorted it. Immediately he got a rush that he never felt before. He liked the feeling.

She said, "Take another bump, daddy, so you can enjoy this nut."

When he did, he went from liking the feeling to loving it. When she made him cum, his body started trembling. At that moment, Tasha knew she had him right where she wanted him, so they could always be on the same page. Her only intention was to use him for money from day one. Dump was more about saving and stacking up.

One day Dump and Tasha were out riding through the city in her truck. He asked her to buy him a gun and put it in her name, because when he tried to buy one, they saw his record and wouldn't let him purchase one.

Tasha said, "Cool."

On their way to her house, they stopped at a pawnshop and looked around. Dump fell in love with a gray-and-black 9 mm Ruger P89 with a clip that held sixteen shots.

He told Tasha, "This the one."

So she filled out the paperwork and then left. Two days passed before they called Tasha back to tell her everything cleared and she could come pick up the gun. She text Dump that she was going to get the gun and bring it to him. He text back, "Okay."

Later that night they met up on the Southwest side. Dump jumped out his car and hopped in the truck with her.

When she handed him the gun he could tell that she had a bad attitude so Dump asked, "What's wrong?"

She said, "I have to go to court."

He asked, "For what?"

She answered, "Six months ago I was riding with this dude and the police pulled him over. They searched the car and found a kilo of cocaine."

Dump looked at her out the corner of his eye and asked, "Are you going as a defendant or a witness?"

She answered, "I'm going to clear myself." After that, Dump knew he couldn't trust Tasha, so he stopped fucking with her. Before she knew it, everything changed, and he was no longer around. When they were cool, he was hustling, but when they split, his cocaine addiction started to fuck all that up. His money started to slow up, and one day it disappeared. At that moment, Dump went back to the thought of robbing people. The lower his money got the more coke he snorted.

One night Dump was at home feeling down, starving and having no money. He kept looking at the Rugar sitting on the shelf in the living room. He got up and walked in his room.

Something told him, "Get the ski mask out the drawer. Grab the gun and go walk to the store."

So he did. He walked through the apartments wearing all black, but there was not a soul in sight. Dump walked out the gate and crossed the street, walking into the parking lot.

When he made it to the door, he pulled the mask over his face and ran in the store pointing his gun at the Indian man behind the counter and said, "Put them motherfuckers up!" and pointed his finger at the register.

"Give me everything out of there! If you do anything funny, I'mma smash your ass!"

The man started to open the register.

He said, "Hurry the fuck up!"

The man emptied the register and reached him the money. Dump snatched it and ran out the store. As he was running up the block to the corner, he heard the man's voice hollering, "Come back! I have more money!"

When he looked back, he saw the man standing in the door. Dump paid him no mind and kept on running until he made it home. He walked in the house trying to catch his breath. He tossed the cash on the table, sat down, and lit a cigarette. He counted up seventy-three dollars. That shit made him mad as fuck. He felt foolish taking a big risk for something so small.

The next night, Dump had a plan to sting something that would give him enough money to chill out and kick back for a minute. It was 8:32 p.m. He got dressed and put on an Oakland Raiders pull over Starter jacket, grabbed the Rugar, and walked out the door. Dump had no idea where he was going. He was just walking waiting to cross paths with his next victim.

When Dump walked out the gates of the apartments, he looked to the right and saw the store. Just the thought of last night ran his blood hot, so he walked to the left. When he made it to the corner, he turned right walking by a car lot that was next to a strip mall. Once he passed the lot he saw a black drop top 500 Mercedes Benz parked in front of a business door.

When he looked past the Benz, there he saw a woman with a big purse in her hand standing in front of a business door that was next door to the business where the 500 was parked. Dump zipped the jacket up over his face and walked up close to her, pulled out the nine, and said, "Give me the purse."

The lady said, "No."

He got mad and said, in an angry voice, "Give me the fucking purse before I shoot you!"

The woman clutched her purse under her arm and took a step back. Dump went into rage and grabbed the purse, trying to snatch it from her, but she refused to let it go and started screaming. Dump pointed the gun at her hand and popped her. She grabbed on to her purse tighter, so he aimed it at her leg and popped her again. As she was falling, she released the purse. He took it and ran off back the way he came.

When Dump made it to the spot, he counted up eighteen hundred and felt ten times better than he felt last night. He went out and got rid of the purse and jacket. After that, he went inside and laid down until he dozed off to sleep.

Dump started to have a dream where he was lying in a king-size bed in a room he was unfamiliar with. The bed was trembling while he heard rain falling on the window. When he looked over at the window, he heard snakes hissing. It spoked him out of the dream. He sat straight up on the sofa trying to understand the dream when he heard a knock on the door. "Who is it?" he asked.

"Chris!"

Dump walked over to the door and opened it and said, "What's up?"

As Chris walked in, he said, "Man, it's going down tonight at the New Orleans club they started downtown in the city."

Chris pulled out a bag of coke, made four flat lines on Dump's kitchen counter, and said, "We're in there!"

Then he snorted two of the lines and told Dump to get dressed. Dump walked up to the counter and snorted the lines. After that, he got dressed.

When they hopped in Chris's car, Dump put the nine on his lap.

Chris said, "I can't lie, my nigga. I like rolling with you. You make a nigga feel safe on that N.O. shit."

Dump looked at him and thought to himself, *This nigga on some bitch shit.*

It fucked his head up because he never heard another man say no shit like that. From that point, Dump never said anything. He just kept opening the bag and taking bumps until they reached the club. All the parking spots in front the door was full, so they had to pull all the way around to the parking lot on the side of the building.

When they pulled in the lot, it was packed, so they had to pull to the back of it and park. He slid his gun under the seat then hopped out checking himself out looking down at his black, red, and white Jordan's. Dump picked his feet up and dusted them off. Then he grabbed his black leather jacket with the gold hundred dollar bills stitched on it and opened it up looking down at his iced out cross and chain with white and cannery yellow diamonds shinning bright from the street lights.

Tonight, Dump was feeling himself. When they made it to the door they went through VIP. The DJ was going dumb and had the club live as fuck bouncing back and forth with some Doughboy to bounce music shit. Dump was posted at the bar and kept the drinks coming back to back.

One of Young Jezzy songs came on and Dump told Chris, "I'm 'bout to dip through this bitch."

When he walked off, Chris stayed by the bar. Because Chris was from Houston, he was new to the vibe in the club because it was full of New Orleans people that was totally different from how they rolled in Texas, but he was definitely feeling it. As Dump bounced through the crowd, the women were feeling him, but he didn't stop moving to holler at none. He had drunk a lot of drinks, so he stopped by the restroom.

When he walked in, he saw a short big head dude with curly hair selling some ecstasy pills.

After he pissed, he asked, "How much are they going for?"

"Ten dollars," the dude replied.

Dump said, "Give me two."

As he reached dude the money, the dude passed him the pills. Dump slid back through the crowd, swaging as the DJ was playing one of Juvenile's songs.

About ten minutes passed, and Dump bumped back into Chris. He put his hand on Dump's shoulder, leaned over to his ear, and said, "Man, these pussy-ass niggas tripping in here!"

Dump said, "Oh yeah! What niggas?"

Chris turned around looking through the club and pointed, "Them right there."

When Dump looked, he saw eight dudes and the same guy with the curly hair was with them.

"I just left out the restroom with dude. He wasn't tripping at all," Dump said.

That's when Chris said, "I'm telling you, they tripping!"

Dump said, "All right."

And he walked off. Chris followed behind him to the dance floor where Dump walked up and talked to one of the chicks. After that, Dump and Chris went to chill in the cut for a minute. Dump thought to himself that Chris didn't know how they got down in New Orleans. Killing one another inside the club was a regular, so he asked Chris what happened.

Chris said, "I don't know. They just started looking at me on some sideways shit."

Dump knew it had to be more to the story, but he was like fuck it, "It is what it is."

Dump went back to enjoying his night. That's when he dug in his pocket, grabbed the pill, put it in his mouth, chewed it up, then swallowed it.

Thirty minutes passed.

Chris walked up to Dump and said, "They still tripping!"

Dump looked at him and said, "Man, fuck them niggas. We can go get the strap out the car, wait for them asses outside, and smash 'em. Is that what you wanna do?"

Chis shook his head and said, "No."

Dump said, "Don't tell me nothing else about that shit then!"

And walked off through the crowd. Dump's pill started to kick in while he was standing in the crowd watching the women dance on the floor. The pill high mixed with the coke and alcohol made him feel like Superman. He looked to the right and saw the dudes that Chris had been talking about standing off in a distance. Dump noticed a dude with them dressed in all black was looking at him through some dark shades.

Dump thought maybe he was tripping, so Dump turned to see if the dude would stop looking, but when he turned back to see if dude was still looking, he saw him staring at him. Dump turned his head once more for a brief moment then turned back to check, and the dude never stopped beaming him down. Dump thought to himself that just as Chris put him on their click, his homies had to put the dude on him.

Dump instantly clicked out and walked over to the dude through the crowd. When the dude noticed Dump coming, he turned his head.

Dump walked up face-to-face to him and said, "What's good, homie? We got a problem or something? Because if we do, we can handle that now."

Dude looked at him and said, "Nah, homie. We ain't got no problems. It's all love."

Dump said, "Dig!" and walked off.

In his mind, he knew he just did something foolish, but as high as he was, he didn't give a fuck. He knew that it was possible that the gang probably had a gun in the club and could let it off if they wanted to. It was obvious that Chris fucked up the whole night.

It was 2:00 a.m., and the club was getting ready to shut down. Dump's mind clicked into the zone of what he learned from the OG's back in the city in the mid-'90s. He knew that nine times out of ten that the niggas would be waiting outside to kill them. His main concern was all he had to do is make it to the car to get the gun, so if he seen the dudes he could smash on 'em. Dump's next thought was to find a female he could put under his arm and walk with her through the parking lot to the car. He figured that nobody would open fire at him while he walked with someone that was innocent, but if they did, he would use her as a body shield and run off. Dump thought it was cold hearted, but to save his life, it was fair.

It was one way in the club and one way out, so he stood in the hallway everyone had to walk through to exit.

He started thinking, "Whichever one of these hoes that be on my dick is the one."

Standing there as the people were walking out, he made eye contact with every chick, but they all kept turning their heads. All of a sudden, he seen a sexy short dark-chocolate motherfucker walking through, smiling with a mouth full of golds and a rope chain with a medallion to match. When she got close to Dump, she locked eyes with him, smiled at him, then turned her head and walked by.

Dump never took his eyes off her as she walked down the hall thinking to himself, *If she looks back, I got her.*

As soon as he thought that, she turned and looked back.

Dump opened his arms and said, "What's up?"

She replied, "What's up with you?"

He cracked a smile and walked over to her. She introduced herself as Bird. As she bumped her waist up against him, so he threw his arm around her as his mind focused on the situation. Dump's body went on autopilot. Chris walked out the door before them. As she was talking, he was responding but wasn't paying no attention to her. She couldn't tell, but the only thing he was doing was scanning for the dudes and praying he'd make it to the gun before they run up on him.

Dump looked at the crowd and didn't see the dudes standing by any of the people parked in front. When they reached the bottom of the stairs, Dump saw Chris eyes get big as he looked at a dude standing in between two cars parked side by side, but he paid it no mind because it wasn't the guys they had beef with. Parked next to those two cars was a black and red Chevy Monte Carlo sitting on deep dish rims with butterfly doors on it. When Dump looked at it, he saw it was three dudes sitting in the back seat, while one of them turned around looking at him with a boot in his mouth.

At that moment, he heard Bird ask Chris, "What the hell you looking at?"

Dump said, "Hold up, baby. He with me."

"Oh, my bad, I didn't know," she explained to Dump.

Dump asked, "Why you stopped here?"

She replied, "This is my car."

They swapped numbers, then Dump and Chris peeled out.

When they made it to the car and hopped in, Chris said, "Man, you didn't see that nigga with that big ass gun pointed at me between them cars?"

Dump said, "No, but I did see your eyes get big as fuck."

"Man, I thought I was dead."

Dump started laughing as he pulled his phone out and called Bird. Dump and Bird talked until they pulled up in front Dump's door.

Bird asked, "Do you want to eat breakfast?"

He said, "Yeah, that's cool."

She replied, "Okay. Meet me at Denny's by Interstate 59."

"Okay, I'm on my way."

Dump hopped out the old-school Sedan De Ville Cadillac with Chris and jumped in his red-candy apple-red STS Cadillac, sitting on some twenty-two-inch buttons with tinted window and a big TV screen falling from the ceiling.

It took Dump an hour to make it from the Southeast side to the Southwest side, but when he pulled up, Bird was there waiting inside the place for him.

When he walked in the restaurant, she jumped up, smiling hard, and gave him a tight hug and said, "Hey, baby!"

Then they sat down across the table from each other. Their conversation went on for an hour about what attracted her to him, where they were from in New Orleans and everybody they knew. Bird was doing most of the talking, and she realized that they both knew a lot of the same people.

She was really digging that because she was gutter as fuck and if he knew the people she mentioned, he was a street nigga, Bird's favorite type.

Bird finished her food and said, "You look like someone I know."

He said, "I already know who you're talking about."

She sucked her teeth and said, "Who?"

Dump said, "E."

"Lord! Boy, how you know that?" she asked.

"That's my cousin. We're twins," once he said that, Bird was completely comfortable with him.

She said, "I'm about to go home. Are you coming?"

He said, "Yeah."

They shot out.

Dump followed her home. When they got there, they sat on the bed talking for a while.

The vibe was cool. A thought crossed his mind, he came out and told Bird, "I can't lie. Tonight was ill as fuck."

She asked, "What do you mean, baby?"

"Tonight it was about to go down. My lil homie got into it with some niggas in that bitch. It was fucked up, but to be sitting here with you, it turned out all right."

All of a sudden, a stale, shocked look came over her face.

She asked, "Hold up! What they looked like?"

Then he described them. She looked at Dump, pointing her finger at him, and said, "Oh my god, so you the red nigga?"

He said, "What are you talking about?"

Bird said, "Just hold up. Watch this."

She picked up her cell phone and made a call. As he looked at her, she said, "Hello. What's up? Where you at? Come over here?"

Dump didn't know whom she called, but he wasn't tripping. He grabbed his strap and thought to himself, "I will shoot my way out this bitch."

About ten minutes passed before Dump heard a knock at Bird's door. He got up, put the nine in his back pocket, then opened the door and saw it was Big Head Shorty with the curly hair from the club. Shorty's eyes grew wide because he was shocked to see Dump there.

When he walked in, she asked, "Boogie, do you know who this is?"

Boogie looked back at him and said, "No," trying to play it off.

Dump gave him a stupid look because he knew he was lying and said, "Come on, man."

Since Boogie knew Dump knew he was lying, he said, "Oh yeah, that's the dude from the club."

Dump said, "Dig. What was up with that shit? I don't know what happened."

Boogie said, "Your boy came, sat down next to SWERVE's girl-friend on the couch while he was in the restroom. Your boy was trying to holler at her, and she ignored him. When Swerv came back and asked for his seat, your boy went off talking crazy."

Dump said, "So this nigga about to get killed behind a chick? See, that's why I don't be fucking with niggas."

Boogie told him, "Shit crazy."

Boogie looked at Bird and said, "I'm gone. Be cool."

After Boogie left, Dump and Bird talked for a while until the sun came up.

She asked, "How old are you?"

He replied, "I'm twenty-five. What about you?"

"I'm forty-two," she said.

They laid up under each other until they fell asleep. A few hours passed, and Dump woke up, getting his dick sucked. After he nutted, he flipped her over then went down and started eating the piss out of her pussy while she busted her legs open grabbing his head. After she came in his mouth, Bird laid him down and sucked his dick until it rocked back up.

He climbed on top of her and started fucking her digging so deep he could feel the bottom. Her walls were tight as she worked her muscles. It made him think about Trish. Dump pulled out of the pussy and put Bird in the bed on her hands and knees. He spread her ass cheeks as he bent down and started licking her asshole sticking his tongue in and out of it. When Dump seen how much it turned her on, it made his dick harder. He stood up straight and went to pounding that pussy.

Before he nutted, he announced, "I'm 'bout to cum!"

Bird told him, "I can't get pregnant. Leave it in."

As he nutted, Dump felt Bird's pussy, constantly gripping his dick and letting it loose over and over again. He was pussy whipped from that moment and ain't even know it.

Bird went downstairs to fix him something to eat.

When she came back upstairs with it, she said, "I want you to meet my son and daughter. They were at the club with us last night."

He said, "Cool. I'm going to run home and freshen up. When I get back, you can hook it up."

After he ate, he left.

Once he made it to the apartment, he took a shower and chilled out for a minute. Bird hit his phone and asked what time he was coming back.

He said, "I'm on my way now."

When Dump pulled up to Bird's spot, she was walking down the stairs to her car. That's when he parked and hopped out. He heard her hit the alarm on her car to unlock the doors. When he looked over to her, he saw her lifting up the butterfly door in the air, so he did the same and they hopped in. He felt funny going to meet her son because they were about the same age.

Dump couldn't imagine being okay with Ann having sex with a young man his age. Bird was totally different from Ann. She looked younger, dressed younger, and definitely acted younger. When they pulled up to her son's Swerv's apartment, she blew her horn, and he walked out the door. Dump noticed that he was the guy from last night that was sitting in the back seat of her car, mugging him in front the club.

When Swerv walked down the stairs, he walked up to the car and said, "What's up?"

Bird said, "Dump that's Swerv. Swerv, that's Dump."

They gave each other dap.

Swerv said, "You dude from the club last night, huh?"

"Yeah, that's me," Dump answered. "Nigga told me about what happened with your girl. That nigga was on some fuck shit."

Swerv was like, "Yeah. That nigga was tripping."

Dump said, "I'm surprised nigga ain't try to bend his ass up in the club. It's a good thing they ain't have no guns in there."

Swerv said, "Shit, the nigga did come ask us for the strap, but we didn't give to them because we needed 'em."

Dump said, "Huh, brah?"

Swerv told him, "Nigga was waiting for y'all outside the club, but you walked outside hugged up with moms."

Dump said, "That shit crazy as fuck. Out of all the people in the spot, I walk out with her. God works in mysterious ways. I was looking for the dudes, but ain't see 'em."

"Them boys were sitting in a car parked across the street watching."

Bird said, "We are about to go grab something to eat. Tell Kash we gone pass by her later."

Then they pulled off.

As they rode up to the drive-through to get some chicken plates to eat. Dump could tell that Bird was serious about him.

After they got their food, they shot back to the apartment. They sat in the room and watched TV while they ate.

Dump asked, "Bird, what do you do?"

She took a paper towel and wiped her mouth and hands as she got up and looked at him as she walked out the room. Dump heard her open a closet door in the hallway then heard it close. When Bird walked back in the room, she had a white plastic bag in her hand and sat it on top of the dresser.

She said, "You want to know what I do?"

As she stuck her hand in the bag and pulled out a pound of weed compressed and tossed it on the bed, said, "This is what I do."

She dug in the bag and pulled out a big bag of ecstasy pills of all different colors. Dump never dealt with a female on this level before. She already whipped her pussy on him, and now her occupation piqued his interest. He looked at the plastic bag and seen it had more pounds in it.

Dump said, "So you're a hustler huh? That's what's up."

"Yeah. I'm that and then some," she said as she grabbed the weed and pills, putting it back in the bag.

Dump turned the TV to the news. Bird sat down on the end of the bed and started back eating her food as he sat up with his back to the backboard thinking about his next move.

The news showed the strip mall by his apartment while the reporter said, "On Thursday night at 18009 Fifty-Nine Freeway, a woman was robbed and shot by a man."

It blew Dump away because it was his work. After the reporter said that a sketch popped up. It really fucked him up then because it was a real good sketch looking like he sat in front when they sketched it. Bird stopped eating and looked at Dump.

She looked back at the TV then looked back at Dump, pointing her finger at him and said, "*Boy, that's you!*"

He shook his head, saying, "No…"

She said, "Whatever… That's you."

At that moment, Dump realized he fucked up. He didn't know what to do, so he figured he would sleep by Bird for a couple of nights.

Dump told her, "I need you to go to my house to pick up some clothes. I'm gone chill over here until I find out what the fuck is going on."

Bird said, "Okay, baby."

Later on that night, Bird took Dump around the corner by her daughter Kash's apartment.

When he saw her, she was a newer version of her mother. Tall, slim, gangster, beautiful, and super sexy at the age of twenty-five. When they looked at each other in the eyes, they didn't know it.

But they both thought to themselves, "Why the hell are you fucking with my mother? You supposed to be dealing with me."

They openly paid those thoughts no mind. Just like Bird, Kash was a hustler, but not with drugs. She was on a whole another level. Dump and Bird chilled over there for a minute while he just peeped out the scene. Dump noticed how the click was rocking.

Big Lips was a hit man. Roy was a laid-back shit talker. Swerv was a real hard hustler. J was a young wild killer down for whatever, and Bird was their shot caller. She operated as a big dog, saying slick shit to show off, because Dump was around. Dump didn't say a word. He had a lot on his mind just sitting there, soaking everything in. Everyone was paying attention to him, but by him chilling so hard, they didn't know what to make of it. When it got late, they left.

The next day about noon, Bird got the key from Dump and went to his apartment to pick up some things. It took her about three hours before she returned.

When she walked in the spot with the bag, she said, "You did right to send me."

Dump asked, "Why you say that?"

"Because when I pulled up and hopped out in front the door, I saw two white men in the parking lot pretending to be looking under the hood of a black truck, but every time I cut my eyes to look at them, they were watching me. I could tell the way their hair was cut they were cops," she said.

Dump said, "Damn, you gotta be kidding, love."

"I'm not kidding. Your spot is hot," Bird told him.

He was now in a jam. His crib was hot, his funds were low, and his face was being aired on TV.

Dump told Bird, "I need to go take care of some business. I'll be back."

And he peeled out on Interstate 45 and headed to the Southeast side to hook up with an associate known for hitting hustles. Dump had to get his money up.

When he made it by Dee, he said, "What's up?"

Dee said, "We're going to go hit a lick in the Fifth Ward, but we gone go pick up Man Man off the other side first."

Dee looked at him and said, "One of my hitters from uptown."

"Okay, cool."

So they rolled out, picked up Man Man and his two .40 calibers, and slid out.

When Dump looked at Man Man, he was tall, skinny, and dark skinned with long dreads hanging down, covering his face.

When Dump looked at him in the rearview mirror, Man Man made eye contact with him and said, "What's up?"

Dump said, "What's happening?"

Man Man replied, "Pull up by that white Acura."

When he did, Man Man hopped out and said, "Y'all follow me."

He pulled off, and they pulled off behind him. When they made it to the Fifth Ward, Dee hopped in the car with Man Man.

Dump and Tank followed them spot to spot, but none of the connects were around to hit. Dee got back in the car with Tank and Dump, and they were around looking for another lick while Man Man shot back to his spot.

Chapter Twenty-One

It was 10:15 p.m., and Dump was pulling in a parking lot of a club and saw a big dice game going down on the side.

He said, "We about to hit them."

Tank said, "Dig."

Dee said, "No. Let me play them to win."

They pulled up and parked. Dee and Tank got out and walked up to the game. Dump sat in the car watching and waiting to see what happens. About thirty minutes passed, and Dee wasn't winning.

Dump said to himself, "Fuck that."

He pulled the handle to pop the hood and hopped out. When one of the dudes seen him get out, he walked away from the game into the club. Dump raised up the hood and was pretending to check up under there, but he grabbed the Tech .22 rifle and unwrapped the white towel form around it, walked over to them, and said, "Don't nobody move! Come out y'all pockets!"

Tank pulled out his 9 mm and pointed at them.

Dee said, "The nigga with all the money just walked in. Hold these boys right here. Let me go get him."

And walked in the club.

Dump told the five dudes, "Sit the fuck down."

Tank didn't say a word. He was just ready to shoot for any reason.

Two minutes passed, and Dump saw a dripping wet pretty purple four door Cadillac pulling up on them slow. When it got close the driver hopped out looking at them and saw Dump walking with the rifle in his direction.

The driver immediately got back in the car as Dee walked out saying, "He don't wanna come out."

He was pulling off. Dump raised the rifle and started squeezing at the Cadillac as it burned out. Tank started busting at it shattering the back window. When the car made a right, the passenger window shattered. That was when Dump saw the passenger's face get hit with a bullet that opened his face up as if it was a rose blossoming. His whole body jumped then folded over as the tires screeched.

Dump said, "Come on!"

They got in the car and pulled off. When they exited the parking lot and turned right, they heard shots firing at them from the club.

Dee said, "Stop the car!"

Dump said, "Fuck that. Keep going!"

When they made it back to Dee's apartment, Dump was pissed with Dee because ain't shit pop in the Fifth Ward and being greedy, he fucked up the lick on the dice game. While Dee, his lil cousin, and Tank were talking he was quiet with a deranged look in his eyes. Dump felt like he wasted his time fucking with them. He lit a cigarette looking at two guys walking out an apartment next door.

Dee said, "Them niggas right there got that work."

Dump said, "Let's get them."

Dee said, "That's my neighbors. I can't fuck with that."

Dump looked at him, hit the cigarette, then blew the smoke in his face and walked downstairs. Dump saw the dudes walking to a black Benz parked between some other cars He gave them a second to get in, then he ran between the cars up on them from the driver side pointing the Rugar in the fat dude's face while the passenger looked at him spooked the fuck out.

Dump told them, "Put your fucking hands up!"

When they did, Dump then told then, "Lie down on the ground."

Fat boy got down on one knee then lay down.

Shorty didn't want to get down, so Dump said, "Don't make me pop your lil ass."

Shorty laid down on his stomach. "Come out your pockets with that money."

Shorty said, "I don't have any money."

Dump didn't believe him, so he bent over and checked his pockets. Dump felt a knot and pulled it out and saw all hundreds. It sent Dump into rage. He started to pistol whip Shorty over the head. The second time he hit him, the gun hit Shorty in the head and slipped out Dump's hand then slid under the car. Dump looked at the gun then looked back at them and saw they didn't move. He grabbed the gun then made them stand up and strip down to their underwear. After they did, Dump said, "Y'all get the fuck on."

The two guys broke out, running around the building, and Dump walked to his apartment. He did some coke and counted the money up. Then he called Tank and asked him to bring him his car so he could roll out. After that, Dump called Bird and said, "I'll be there in a lil bit."

"Okay. I'm here," she replied.

Tank walked up to Dump's door and knocked. When Dump opened it, tank walked in with his 9 mm and the Tech .22.

He sat the nine on the counter and laid the rifle up against the wall then sat on the sofa, and said, "Ya boy Dee on some other shit."

Dump said, "What you talking 'bout?"

Then they heard a knock at the door.

"Who is it?" Tank asked.

"This Dee!"

He looked at Dump and opened the door.

Dee walked in and said, "You got 'em, huh? Pop it off!"

Dump hit him with two hundred dollars.

Dee questioned, "Damn! This all I get?"

Dump said, "My nigga, did you hit the lick?"

Then he looked over at Tank. "Fuck, they ain't have much anyway."

Dee made a crazy face and said, "Bet."

He saw the rifle leaning on the wall. He picked it up and started to look at it as if he'd never seen it before. Dump caught the vibe, so he pulled out his pistol and said, "That bitch nice, huh?"

Dee looked at Dump and saw he was cocked and said, "Yeah," and laughed it off as he sat it back against the wall, "I'mma holler at y'all boys."

Then he walked out the door. Dump locked it behind him.

Tank said, "That's the shit I was talking about."

Dump nodded and said, "Don't trip young. I got it."

Tank gave him dap, and they left.

When Dump made it to Bird's spot, she was fresh out the tub, smelling good. He leaned over to her in the bed and gave her a kiss then went took a hot shower.

When he finished and hopped in the bed, she asked, "What's up?"

He said, "I just had to make a few runs. What's up with you?"

Bird scooted over to him and said, "Turn off the light, baby. Let's relax."

Dump reached up and pulled the light string hanging from the ceiling fan. Bird grabbed the remote control and turned the TV off. The room was dark, but they could see each other glowing from the moonlight through the window.

He started to kiss her, but she stopped him and said, "Just relax, baby."

As she leaned him back, Dump put his hands behind his head and laid there. Bird crawled on top of him and kissed him on the lips then stuck her sweet tasting tongue down his throat as she straddled him grinding on his hard dick. She reached her hand down and grabbed it then began rubbing it on her, soaking wet pussy.

She made it feel so good. Dump closed his eyes. That was when Bird came down on the dick and started riding it slowly. Dump grabbed her by the waist and flipped her on her back. Now he was on top. As he started kissing and deep stroking, he opened his eyes. At that moment, he saw snake scales all over her body. For some reason he didn't feel uncomfortable. Neither did he stop. He didn't understand what was happening. He just closed his eyes and kept fucking her as she tongue kissed him perfectly. When they finished, he never said what he saw and had too much going on in his life to think about it.

Bird said, "Are we in a relationship?"

He asked, "Is that what you want?"

"Boy, how you answer a question with a question?"

"You know what, Bird? Yeah, we are. Now what's next?" Dump asked.

"We learn each other."

After that, she laid on his chest and fell asleep. He just looked at the ceiling, thinking about his life until he dozed off.

Early in the morning Bird woke Dump up, sucking his dick like a pro.

"Damn, bitch. You got my toes curling."

She went down licking his balls while she beat the dick with both hands, one at the head, the other on the shaft, twisting the palm of her hand and fingers around on the head and the other hand up and down on the shaft. Then she took one hand and lifted his balls up. While she beat his meat with the other hand, she started to lick the bottom of his nuts between his legs.

No female ever licked that spot on him before. His eyes started rolling.

She asked, "You like that?"

"Yes," he told her.

After he answered, she went further down and licked his asshole. That made him feel played, but the truth was it felt so good he didn't stop her. When she seen he had no problem with it, she stopped beating his dick and used her hands to cock his legs in the air, eating his asshole like it was Thanksgiving, sticking her tongue in and out, swirling it round and round. She knew just what she was doing to freak him out. He couldn't tell it wasn't her first time. He was past pussy whipped; he was now addicted, and she knew it.

When she stopped eating his ass, he said, "Come up and sit that pussy in my face."

She rode his face until she came hard in his mouth. They laid back and chilled. All of a sudden they heard seventeen shots ring out from somewhere close by.

Ten minutes later Kash called Bird and said, "Big Lips just hit a duck up, but his homie got away."

"Okay. I'll be around there," Bird told her.

Dump came out and told her, "I need you to go pick up the rest of the clothes from my spot today?"

Bird said, "Okay. Let me go see what's up with this Lips shit first. I'll be back."

Later on that day, Dump and Bird had a conversation about everything that was going on in the streets with both of them. Bird told him how she took a few hits and sent a couple of hit out. She also told him that a dude named Boo front her all the work.

Dump gave Bird small pieces of information about his situation.

He said, "Right now, I'm hot. I have to lay low and stay off the radar."

She said, "Don't trip. I got you."

She asked him for the key to go get his clothes and left.

When she got back, she said, "I couldn't get in. The keys don't work. Oh yeah, those same two white boys were out there again."

Dump picked up his phone and called the office at his apartments. The manager answered the phone.

"Hello, Greenwood Apartments! How may I help you?"

"Yes. This is Cage Coleman from apartment 202. I tried to get in my apartment, but my keys didn't work."

She said, "Mr. Coleman, you have abandoned your apartment. You are never there. If you want to, you can come to the office and pick up your new key. We are here Monday through Friday from eight to four o'clock."

Dump said, "Okay." And he hung up the phone.

"Yeah. Them hoes trying to pop me. They want me to come to the office to get new keys. Like I'm stupid and don't know the police are waiting there for me."

Bird said, "Don't worry about them clothes. You're good. We gone hit the mall up."

Dump dipped out and hooked up with Swerv.

Dump and Swerv went by Kash's spot. It was Roy, Swerv, J, Big Lips, and him.

Dump asked Lips, "What happened earlier?"

Big Lips said, "Pussy-ass nigga was cracking jokes and called me a bitch-ass nigga. His homie was laughing, so I squeezed on his ass, and his boy ran. That bitch got hit nine times, but he survived."

Dump said, "Bitch, you're retarded out here!"

Roy got up and left. Big Lips had a gray .45-caliber Rugar, matching Dump's P89 with seventeen shots, but the .45 clip only held eight bullets. He figured since Lips had some shit popping off, he would let him use the P89 and he take the .45 for a minute. Dump called Tasha and told her to report the gun stolen ASAP.

She said, "Okay."

Then hung up. Dump sat his phone down on his lap and said, "Here, Lips. You have too much shit going on for eight shots. Give me that bitch. Whatever you do, don't toss this shit."

Lips said, "Okay."

Right after that, Bird came in the spot and said, "Big Lips, ya boy that got away is right around the corner. Dump stashed the .45 and then went got in the Monte Carlo with Bird. Lips and Swerv jumped in a blue Mustang. J followed behind them in a rust-color Durango.

When they pulled out the apartment gates, they saw a police SUV with a camera on top riding up the street. When it passed, they went in the opposite direction. Once they were nowhere to be found, they split up to cover more ground searching.

Five minutes passed, and Roy called Bird's phone and said, "Say, I got some niggas following me!"

Dump said, "Bring them niggas around here."

Roy, sounding nervous, said, "Where y'all at?"

Bird told him, "We on Eagle Street on side of Georgetown Apartments."

"Okay," Roy said.

Bird called Lips. Lips called J, and they all met on Eagle Street. The street had two curves in it like the letter S, so from the beginning, entering it, you couldn't see the end of the road. They met up at the end and blocked the road off with Dump and Bird parked in the middle and Swerv, Lips, and J parked on both sides. Two minutes passed. Then Roy came driving fast through the S curve, swerving.

The blue Eddie Bower Expedition pulled up, and he hopped out jumping up and down, excited, saying, "They coming! They coming!"

All of them pulled their guns out.

Big Lips asked Roy, "Are you sure that's some niggas?"

"Yes! I'm sure!"

Lips asked again, "Are you sure?"

Dump said, "He said he was sure."

After he said that, a sky-blue Dodge Intrepid started sending shot through the windshield cracking it up. It immediately stopped then went into reverse and started backing up. A marked police car swerved from behind returning fire with a male's hand out the windows shooting at Big Lips.

J dipped into the bushes then ran back out shooting at the cop car. Big Lips jumped the fence and tossed the gun as Swerv pulled off in the Mustang.

The police started shooting at J as he hopped in the Durango and screeched off. Everybody was gone, but Dump and Bird. The police pulled up on side of them and looked at Dump then over to Bird as they held their hands up.

The officer slowed down, stopped by them, turned his head, and went after J. It was obvious that the police didn't arrest them because they were not seen shooting. They got in the car and went in the same direction the cops went.

When they were exiting the neighborhood, they saw the police trying to apprehend J as he was fighting against them trying to get away from six cops crowding him. They drove by slow and made eye contact with him but couldn't stop.

Everybody met back up by Kash's spot.

Dump asked Big Lips, "Where that plucker at?"

Lips said, "I tossed that bitch!"

"My nigga, I told you not to toss it. And look, your duck ass got away," said Dump.

Big Lip said, "My bad."

Dump thought, *Man, I hope that hoe reported it stolen.*

Everyone got on Roy's ass thinking it was niggas and it turned out to be the police.

The next day they found out that the officer in the Intrepid was ATF and the driver was shot in the chest. The police also ran the number on the Rugar, and it was still registered to Tasha.

When they did the ballistics, it matched the bullet that hit the officer, so they called her.

"Hello, may I speak to Tasha Mills please?"

Tasha said, "Yes, this is her. Who is this?"

"I'm detective Shawn Smith. There was a situation where one of our officers was shot, and the gun that we have that was used to shoot him is registered to you."

She said, "I had nothing to do with that. Cage Coleman stole that gun from me."

The detective asked, "Excuse me, ma'am, what is the name again?"

"His name is Cage Coleman. He is tall, light-skinned, with a lot of tattoos," she said.

Detective Smith said, "Thank you. If we need any more information we will give you a call."

As the days were going by the police were getting hotter and hotter everyday looking for Dump. He stayed inside all day and barely moved at night. He let Bird do all the moving. They knew it was taking a bad turn, and it was time to get the fuck out that area.

One night, Swerv was on the phone talking to J. J told him that they keep asking him a lot of questions about Cage.

He said, "Tell Dump to lie low out there."

Six months passed by, and they rushed J to trail. When he lost, they gave him six years. That changed the whole game just like it did for Dump on the Southeast side. Bird's connect went dry, and it was time to move around. They all needed to hit a lick quick. If they didn't, they were fucked.

Chapter Twenty-Two

Bird told Dump she had a friend named Gonzo, who had a friend that needed some help to rob one of his connects. So they took a ride by Gonzo.

When they walked in Gonzo's house, Dump saw why they called him Gonzo. His nose was long and wide. As they stood in his bedroom door talking business, Dump looked at Gonzo's beautiful wife looking back at him lying under the comforter in a royal king-size bed. Because Gonzo and Bird were talking, they were not paying any attention. Dump could tell that Mona was rolling off ecstasy, and she liked what she saw. He looked on the floor and saw some six-inch yellow stilettos. He started to imagine her bending over with nothing on but the heels.

As he watched her bite her bottom lip, Gonzo asked, "Y'all ready?"

Dump and Bird hoped in the Benz minivan with Gonzo and went met up with his lil homie to talk.

When they pulled up to his apartment, he said, "Y'all come in."

They all hopped out and walked in.

Dump said, "What's up?"

Duck said, "These two boys are at Motel 6 off Freeway 610. They easy to hit."

Bird asked, "What do they have?"

Duck replied, "Thirty pounds, a quarter brick of coke, three thousand ex pills, twenty thousand dollars, some bars, a 223, and a Rugar with an extended clip."

Dump said, "So they stocked up, huh? How many in there?"

Duck told him, "It's normally two, but I can't tell until I get in the room."

Gonzo sat on a stool by the bar and said, "How you want to play Duck?"

Duck said, "I'm gone walk in there to score while y'all stand outside the door. When I get ready to walk out, I'm going to act like I'm calling my girl, but I'm gone call y'all phone. When I say I'm on my way home, that means I am about to walk out. When the door open, y'all can rush in."

Gonzo said, "Cool. We gone go and get ready and call you when we're on our way back."

They gave Duck dap and dipped out. Gonzo went home. Dump and Bird hopped in the Monte to go grab the gun and pick up Swerv.

When Swerv got into the car he didn't have a gun.

Dump said, "These niggas we going get at are strapped. When we hit the door busting in, we gone say HPD put your hands up. That will spook 'em out so they won't grab their guns."

Swerv said, "Okay. That's smart."

Bird was real quiet. It was reasons like this she liked street niggas. She loved to use them. They made it by Gonzo's, picked him up, and shot to Duck spot. Gonzo and Duck got in a white van. Bird followed behind them to the location.

When they got to the Motel 6, Duck got out and walked up the stairs. Gonzo hopped out and walked over to the Monte Carlo. Dump and Swerv got out. When they looked upstairs, they saw Duck knock on the door. The door opened, and Duck went in. Dump was the first one up the stairs. Next was Swerv with Gonzo following behind him.

They stayed in the stairway until Dump's phone rang.

He picked it up and heard Duck say, "Are the kids okay?"

"I'm on my way home."

In four seconds, Dump bust the door open and yelled, "HPD! Put your hands up!"

The two dealers in there with Duck had eyes that bucked out their sockets. They were spooked out, because Dump was pointing the four nickel in their faces. When they realized they weren't police, they felt stupid.

Dump and Swerv had the two dudes under control, but there was a female with a baby boy sitting on the sofa chair terrified, screaming and hollering. Dump saw their 9 mm sitting on the table. He picked it up and passed it to Swerv. Gonzo walked up to the female and talked to her to calm her down.

He said, "Baby, this has nothing to do with you. You're all right."

While she and Gonzo kept talking, Dump was asking the dudes, "Where is the money?"

As Swerv was duct taping their ankles. Dump smacked one of them with the pistol.

"The money is in my pocket."

Dump reached over and checked his pocket, but it was empty.

He yelled, "You lying! Ain't shit in your pocket."

Dump pistol whipped him as Swerv filled up the garbage bag with the weed and grabbed the 223 and put it in its case. After that, he walked out the door to go put it in the car. Dump started putting the pills and coke in a duffel bag when they heard a knock at the door. Dump looked through the peephole and saw a man with a badge on his chest.

Dump asked, "Who is it?"

"It's security. Can you please open the door?"

Dump said, "Okay, sir. Give me one minute."

Dump grabbed one of the dudes off the floor and dragged him to the restroom fast. Then he did the same with the other.

Dump told Duck to get in the restroom with the two men. Gonzo and the Latino woman were still standing face-to-face, talking it out. Dump walked up to the door and opened it, sweating from his fore head as he gripped the gun in his jacket pocket.

"Yes, sir, may I help you?"

The security officer looked him up and down then looked behind him and saw the chick and Gonzo talking and said, "We got a call saying that there was a disturbance going on in this room Is everything okay?"

Dump looked back at them and said, "Yes, sir. My homeboy and his girl were fussing, but they're okay now."

The security officer said, "Okay," with a funny look on his face.

Dump closed the door. He and Gonzo grabbed the two bags. Dump looked out the window to see if it was clear. It was, so they left out. When they made it downstairs, Bird and Swerv were gone.

They could hear police sirens screaming from up the block coming in their direction.

Dump said, "Where the fuck they at?"

Gonzo said, "Come on, man. Let's go!"

He took out running across the field. Dump followed behind him and hopped a fence into some brick apartments. His shoe string got caught at the top of the gate, so he came down and fell because it was stuck. He got it loose then ran off.

As he looked back, he could see the police swarm the hotel from a distance. A stranger came out of nowhere in the parking lot and asked, "What's up? Do you need a ride?"

It spooked Dump out. He didn't trust him.

"No," he said.

Gonzo said, "You tripping. That's Duck's homie."

Dump said, "I ain't fucking with that. Call us a cab."

So he did. Almost fifteen minutes later, a cab pulled up with an African driver. They hopped in and called Bird.

"Yeah, where y'all at?"

"We're around the corner," she said.

Gonzo said, "Meet us at the gas station on Hillcroft and 6-10."

She said, "Okay," and hung up.

Dump was really fucked up about the fact they left them behind like fuck them. Bird made sure her son, and she got away, but her man and friend were stranded running to get away from the cops.

When the police made it to the hotel room they made the report, but because of the paraphernalia, the officer arrested the victims. Bird pulled up in the gas station and waited for Dump and Gonzo to pull up. When they did, they paid the cab driver then hopped in the car with them. Nobody said a word.

Bird pulled up to an office building. Swerv got out and walked up to a Dumpster. He reached down in it and pulled out the gun case and the garbage bag. Bird popped the trunk, Swerv put it in the trunk, then hopped back in the car. Duck called Gonzo and told him he was at home. They shot over there.

When Bird knocked on the door, he let them in.

"Bruh, why did y'all not tie me up?" Duck asked. "That shit made me look flakey as fuck."

Gonzo looked at Dump.

Swerv said, "My bad."

Bird walked outside and grabbed the bags. When she came back in, they divided the work between them. Dump kept the 223 and, Swerv kept the 9 mm. After they hit that lick, Kash, Swerv, Bird, and Dump moved back to New Orleans. They found an area in the east that was perfect for business.

Two weeks passed by, and they were now settled in their homes. Dump and Bird stayed in one apartment, and Swerv and Kash had their own apartments across the court from them. They were chilling with Swerv at Kash's spot.

Bird heard her phone ringing. When she looked at it, she saw it was Gonzo.

"What's up, baby?" she asked.

Gonzo said, "Duck just got killed. Them niggas said that they knew it was his work."

She said, "That's fucked up."

She looked at Dump. He could tell by her facial expression that whatever she was hearing, she didn't give a fuck.

He asked, "What's up?"

She said, "They just killed Duck."

Dump said, "Damn. We should have tapped him up."

Kash walked out her room wearing a robe with her blonde hair wet from the shower.

She said, "Y'all got too much going on."

She gave Dump a look. Her body language said, "You're stupid from fucking with her."

But he didn't catch on to it. Every time he looked at Kash all he felt was attraction and sometimes fantasized about fucking her. Little did he know, she felt the same way.

One day Bird and Dump were sitting down at the table eating and talking about her mother and father. She spoke about her mother being a loving woman. She told him that her father was a major drug dealer from uptown back in the days that was a voodoo wizard. It made him feel really uncomfortable because he knew how serious voodoo was.

She said, "I learned a lot from him before he committed suicide."

Dump asked, "Why did he commit suicide?"

She said, "I don't know. All I remember is I was eighteen years old walking up the street and some Italian drug dealers kidnapped me. They brought me to a house and beat me then raped me twice. After that, I was tied to a chair with tape over my mouth. They had me in a room so dark I couldn't tell if it was night or day. I was afraid for days. I heard a crashing sound, then a lot of gunshots. The next thing I know, John, my daddy's hit man, walked through the door with a gun in his hand. He walked up and untied me then took the tape off my mouth. I said thank you. He said, 'I'm just doing my job.' I told him if he didn't do his job, I would be dead. It seemed from that day, we never separated. He told me that my dad killed himself in a car that day before he found out where I was. That crushed me. One month later, I found out when I was raped, I got pregnant. That's when I had Kash. After my father died, I started to see spirits a lot. My mother decided to cremate his body, and she kept his ashes in a vase.

"One day, my mother and I were arguing, and I made a mistake and dropped the vase, and red thick blood spilled and splashed everywhere. It was if he was still living through the voodoo after this death."

Dump found that story interesting. It helped him understand why she was on some gangster shit, deep in the drug game. But what he missed was she was telling him she was into voodoo.

The next morning, Bird was on her menstrual cycle. She laid in the bed all morning because she was cramping. Dump gave her a kiss and went outside. She pulled herself out of the bed and walked to the kitchen. It crossed her mind about the conversation her and Dump had. She never wanted him to leave her and the time was perfect to put a voodoo spell on his life involving their relationship. Bird started to cook spaghetti and meat sauce. She put the ground meat in the pan and cooked it brown. After that, she put the tomato paste in a pot, mixed the ground meat into it, and seasoned it as it cooked down. Then Bird grabbed a silver spoon out the drawer and went into the bathroom.

She sat down on the toilet and pulled her tampon out. It was covered in blood. Then she took the spoon and scraped the tampon getting clumps of blood on the spoon. After that, she sat it down on the edge of the sink, opened the cabinet, grabbed another tampon, opened it, then slid it in her pussy. She walked back to the kitchen and put the spoon in the pot and stirred it until the spoon was clean of blood. Then she took a big spoon and stirred the pot.

After that, she let it cook down for two hours, stirring the pot every twenty minutes. Dump walked in the house with Swerv and said, "Damn, you got it smelling good in this, bitch."

As he walked up to her giving her a hug and a kiss, Swerv said, "Look at y'all, all in love," smiling, showing his ten gold teeth.

Dump said, "You just mad I got your mamma nigga."

Swerv was like, "Whatever!"

They had no idea Bird just put a voodoo potion together in the meat sauce to hook Dump to her for life. After he ate the spaghetti, if he wanted to leave her, he couldn't.

Dump said, "I'll be back."

He and Swerv shot to the store, picked up some drinks, and came back. That was when Dump and Bird sat down to eat. They talked for a minute. Once they finished eating, he said, "Damn, that was good."

She said, "I put my ass in it for you."

Then they busted out laughing.

He said, "You ain't lying. That ass do taste good!"

Dump and Bird started spending more time together, learning more about each other. Six months went by, and they started to have problems because they were on two different pages. Dump was in love with her family and progress, but Bird was in love with money, power, and herself.

In the summer of 2007, the Plug came back into play. Bird was the one that was well connected with the Plug. Boo put her back on like he didn't miss a beat. He paid them to go pick up a hundred pounds of weed from Houston every week.

Once they made it back to New Orleans, Bird kept forty of them and fronted the rest out to Calliope P, Big Lips, Short Reg, and Bee. Dump really did his own thing, but his money was nowhere close to hers, and she abused that position.

Dump paid it no mind, because he really loved her. Every two months they had a big fuss, and he left, but he would act under the voodoo spell and come right back to her. She started to clown on him even more because she knew he was under her witchcraft and couldn't stay away, even if he tried.

The way Bird acted made Dump like Kash more. Even her hustle was bringing in more money, plus she took less risk. Dump went by Kash's house one day just to pay attention to what she was doing. Dump and Swerv fixed a couple of drinks and joked around talking shit while she sat at the table printing out fake checks worth thousands of dollars. After she stacked them all up, she looked at Dump and saw he was watching her.

She said in a cute, jazzy voice, "What the fuck you looking at?"

"I'm looking at your duck ass!" Dump said.

She picked up her phone and made a call while she counted the checks.

"Hello, what's up, lil bitch? I need twenty numbers and thirty cards. I'm waiting for you. You know where I'm at."

Kash hung up and looked back at him, but he turned his head before she caught him looking. When she stood up, he looked at her. She was wearing some tight red shorts gripping her pussy, and as she walked away from him, he saw the bottom of her ass cheeks with a gap in between them.

When she walked back in the living room, he looked at her breast sitting upright in a bra top with her pierced nipples poking.

Kash had all her tattoos showing from her feet to her neck. The only ones that were covered was the one on her ass and her breast. Dump's dick started to get hard. He didn't want Swerv to see that through his basketball shorts, so he walked outside and let it go down. When he was walking back to the door, Swerv was walking out. "I'm 'bout to make a run. I'll be right back." Dump went back home.

It was Friday. Boo called Bird and told her it was time for her to come to Houston. Later that evening, Dump booked their flights for 3:15 p.m. Once they got dressed, they let Swerv drop them off at the airport. That was Dump's first time ever catching a flight. He was nervous, but about time they reached the clouds he looked down on the city and loved the view. As soon as the 747 reached the point where it stopped rising higher and leveled itself out, the pilot started descending over Texas to land in Houston. His ears started to pop as he looked down at the sun shining on top of the huge puffy clouds. It was one of the most beautiful scenes he ever seen. Once the plane landed they caught a cab to Calliope P's spot to pick up a rental car he had for them.

After they got the keys from V, they left and headed to Boo's house to pick up the money. As they passed through the suburbs he looked up at the houses with pillars and water fountains standing in front with two and three car garages connected beside them. They pulled up to a two story brick house with two white pillars standing tall at the entrance. Bird hopped out first, walked to the door, and knocked. When Boo opened the door, Dump got out and walked in and saw the walls were painted red trimmed with white base boards he looked up at the high ceilings and saw a huge crystal chandelier hanging down shining clearly. As he walked under it he looked down walking into the living room and saw an all-white pool table with a long white leather sofa sitting up along the wall on top of shinny hard wood floors. He and Bird sat down. Five minutes later Boo walked his short, red, big head ass in wearing Louis Vuitton from head to toe with a bag in his hand.

He said, "Bird lady, what's up?"

She said, "Nothing but the money. What's good?"

He said, "Minus the bullshit, life's great."

He gave her the bag, "That's twenty thousand. Ten for the hundred and ten for the brick."

Bird took it out and counted it up. Dump got up, picked up a pool stick and shot a few balls in.

Boo asked him, "What's up?"

Dump replied, "Shid, out'chea getting to this money."

Bird got up and said, "Let's go. Boo we gone get back with you."

When they went to pick up the work, the Mexican had it wrapped up nice.

Bird passed Paco the money, and they placed the two compressed fifty pound bales on the back seat and tossed the kilo of coke on the floor. Dump dapped Paco off and hopped in. After that Dump and Bird peeled off and hit I-10 East headed back to the city. While they were in Baton Rouge, they got into a little argument. Dump saw Bird was doing sixty miles per hour in a fifty-mile-per-hour-speed-limit zone.

He said, "Slow down. Don't be speeding through this bitch."

She said, "I'm not speeding. Are you driving?"

He said, "No. I ain't driving, but I'm riding hot in this bitch."

"Fuck. If you don't like how I drive, stay home next time?"

He said, "Now you talking my language."

After that, they were quiet for the rest of the ride.

Dump and Bird made it back to the crib at eleven o'clock. They pulled up on the grass and drove up to the door in the courtyard. Bird got out, unlocked the door, and walked in. Dump got out, flipped the seat forward, grabbed the weed, and walked in the spot.

Dump sat it on the floor then went to grab the other. After that, he opened the drawer, grabbed a triple beam scale, and sat it on the dresser. Dump grabbed a razor then busted the bales open. He then went to the kitchen and got a butcher knife. When he made it back to the room, he stabbed the knife in side of the block and pried it apart. He ripped off the first layer then tossed a block on the scale weighing it pound for pound, bagging it up as they go.

Once they finished, Bird called everybody that Boo told her to front the weed to and told them to come pick it up. When they made it, she gave one of them the coke and the rest weed. She had forty pounds left. Dump went took a shower and went to bed.

Early in the morning Bird hooked up with Swerv's girlfriend Shay and made plans to go shopping in Mississippi with bad checks, stolen credit card, and fake IDs.

Dump thought to himself, *All this money and work she got. What the fuck you going shopping with fake checks for?*

But because of their argument last night, Dump ain't tell her nothing. Bird got dressed. That was when Shay and Bird shot out in the rental. Dump kicked back and made a couple of sells, but shit was moving Slow.

The day was almost over, and the sun was setting. Dump was lying in bed watching TV when his phone rung. He looked at it and saw an out of state area code. Dump answered it and heard an automated operator say, "Hello. You have a collect call from Bird at Mississippi Federal Facility. If you consent to this call being recorded and would like to accept this call, press One. To reject this call press, Two, now!"

It fucked his head up. He pressed One. "What's up?" he asked.

She said, "Me and Shay got arrest."

Dump asked, "What happened?"

She answered, "We was driving on the interstate. As soon as we made it to Yazoo Mississippi, the Feds pulled us over. They didn't ask us any questions. Them bitches straight went to searching the trunk. When they couldn't find shit, they popped the hood up. Man, they opened the gas tank. I could tell they thought for sure we had drugs. When they finished looking under the hood, they searched inside of the car. That's when they looked under the seat and found some checks, cards, and IDs. They are not giving us no bonds."

He asked, "What are y'all charged with?"

She said, "Credit card fraud and identity theft."

Dump told her, "I don't know why you went fucked with that shit."

"I don't know either. I should have let Kash do Kash and I do me."

Dump was like, "Real shit. We gone get you a lawyer. Don't trip."

She said, "Okay. Tell Swerv I will call him later."

"Okay, cool."

Bird hung up.

Bird being locked up by the Feds changed the whole game for Dump and Bird's situation. Bird was now absent, and her money stopped flowing. She was stressed out because it was her first time ever being locked up. Every day she told Dump to put some of her money on their phones, and she constantly called all day. Once Dump paid for Bird's lawyer, the money went dry. About a month passed, and he and Bird didn't talk much.

One day Bird called and told him that they were offering her a two-year sentence. Dump told her that was small time.

She said, "My lawyer need to beat this shit. I'm not ready to do that."

He said, "That's understandable."

That night Dump sold some fake drugs to some serious dealers and got some money together fast. Two days passed, and he got a legal job just to keep him off the radar. He felt like the Feds don't do random traffic stops and the only reason they stopped her was because they'd been watching them traffic drugs for months and her going further than normal the day after they came from Houston made the Feds think that they were expanding their operation.

It was Saturday. The whole click was hanging in the courtyard smoking purp. It was Dump, Big Lips, Roy, Geezy, Swerv, Congo, and Ray. Dump lit the gar up.

Roy told him, "Boy, you pulled that act off quick as a motherfucker?"

Dump looked at him and grinned. He expected Dump to say something, but he didn't. Instead he just kept hitting the purp.

Big Lips said, "Yeah. That nigga a fool with it."

Dump obviously made a statement because they wanted him out since Bird was gone, but he bounced back. That night they all decide to hit the club with Shay and Kash, but it had been two months since Bird was locked up and Dump was missing her, so he decided to stay home.

While everyone was enjoying themselves, Dump was watching TV, smoking a couple of gars and making a few calls. A few hours passed by. It was now 4:00 a.m.

Dump heard a knock at the door. When he opened it, he saw it was Kash. She was wearing a buttoned up navel length well fitted black, green, red, and yellow, plaid vest with a very short tennis skirt to match. Kash had on a pair of six-inch heels with some long Oxford golf sox pulled up to the bottom of her thighs. He unlocked the bar door and let her in then locked it back and closed the door.

Dump walked in the room and laid in the bed.

Kash walked in behind him and said, "Let me get something out of the closet."

Dump knew that nothing in the closet belonged to her. She opened the closet as she spread her legs and bent over. As Dump looked at her, her pussy was showing, sitting fat, looking back at him in some beautiful red lace panties. He knew that she was doing it on purpose, letting him know she was ready to let him fuck. All of a sudden, he heard Swerv stick his key in the bar door.

He said to himself, "*Fuck. Here go this nigga.*"

Swerv wasn't stupid. He knew what was up, so he came to put an end to it. As Swerv and Kash were walking out the door, Kash looked at Dump with some horny drunk freaky eyes. What just happened didn't sit right with Swerv at all. He walked her to her Range Rover and watched her pull off. Then he went back inside and went to sleep.

The next day Big Lips came by Swerv's spot, and Dump was there.

He said, "The police have a videotape of Yogie getting killed."

Swerv said, "For real?"

"Fucking right," Big Lips said.

"Them bitches gave Yogie's mamma a copy of it to see if anybody knew the person on the videotape. She let a few of his homies watch it. Picture the pussy bitch Dave told Yogie's mom the person in the video was possibly Dump. They ain't sure because the video ain't clear enough."

That put Dump in a jam because Yogie, his mother, and Bird were close friends. Dave really pissed Dump off, putting his name out there. He asked Roy to take a ride with him around Dave's way.

When they slid through, they saw Dave and his people standing in front of his house. He pulled over and sat his 9 mm on his lap then blew the horn, calling him over.

Dave walked over to the car on Dump's side and said, "What's up?"

Dump said, "I got some purp. Fuck with me."

Dave said, "Let me see it."

Dump gave him a bag. Dave looked at it then smelled it.

Dump said, "Niggas out her putting my name in some fuck shit. I didn't have no beef with dude. I didn't have nothing to do with that shit. Nigga better keep my name out their mouth before I smash their ass," while his hands were on the steering wheel.

Dave felt played, so he leaned over on the open window seal with intentions to grab the gun off his lap and kill Dump and Roy. Dump caught on to that and clutched it with his finger on the trigger. Dave stood up, took a step back, gave him the bag back and said, "I feel you, my nigga."

Dump said, "Dig dat. Fuck with me though."

Then they pulled off.

The day after Dump spoke to Dave the streets started talking. Yogie's mother was furious. She had some young goons put ten thousand dollars on Dump's head to have him murdered. Dump put the word out in the streets that he has fifteen thousand dollars on the head of anyone who take the hit on him.

Bird was green to the situation. One day she called Swerv and told him that Shay, and her have been set for trial. She also told him that they will release them under their lawyer's supervision until the trial is over. When Dump heard about it, he was happy, but it was very strange to him that the Feds let them free because normally they would not arrest anyone unless they had all the evidence needed to convict them. Dump and Swerv rode to Mississippi and picked them up Shay and Bird.

When they made it home Dump took Bird for a ride and told her about what was going on. It had her puzzled. As they pulled up to the apartments, she asked, "Did you kill him?"

He told her, "No. That's not my work."

When they hopped out the car, they saw Dave pulling up in his truck.

He rolled his window down and said, "Welcome home, Bird Lady. Come take a ride with me."

Bird told Dump, "I'll be back."

Dump looked Dave in his eyes, gave her a kiss, and said, "Cool."

Dump walked inside and chilled out for a minute. When Bird came back, she told him what Dave said about the videotape.

Bird called Yogie's mother and told her that she was home from jail and wanted to come by.

Bird told Dump, "I'm going by her house to see that tape."

Dump said, "Okay. Fuck with me when ya get back later."

Bird grabbed her keys, gave him a kiss, and walked out the door.

When she got in the car, she called her friend and said, "I'm on my way love."

After she hung up the phone, she turned on the radio and rushed over there anxious to see the tape, wondering if it was Dump who murdered her friend.

When Bird made it to Pam's house, she saw her standing in the door waiting for her to pull up. Normally every time Pig and Bird came across each other they both had big smiles, but this time was different. She could tell that Pig was full of anger and pain.

Bird parked, got out, walked up to Pig, and said, "I'm sorry for your loss."

As she hugged her, Pig didn't say a word. She turned around and walked in as Bird followed her into the living room. When they both sat down, Pig said, "They are saying your man is the one who killed my son."

Bird said, "Dave came and told me. He said that the police gave you a video of the murder. Can I see it?"

Pig started crying. Bird wrapped her arm around her and reached her some tissue. Pig took the tissue and wiped her tears, and said, "Yes. I want you to tell me if it's him or not."

Once Pig pulled herself together, she grabbed both remote controls off the coffee table and turned on the TV and the DVD player. After the DVD loaded, she pressed play then grabbed the box of tissue. Bird saw a blue car pull up. Then she saw a light-skinned tall dude get out of the passenger side. Bird squinted her eyes to see his face, but it was too blurry, she couldn't tell if it was Dump or not.

The man in the video walked down an alley away from the car and was gone for two minutes then came back out the ally and bent over to the car from the passenger side. She saw the man jerk back then saw the inside of the car flash, and the man ran off.

Bird said, "Oh my god... No."

Pam said, "It's not over."

A few minutes passed, and she saw the man came walking back up to the car on the driver's side and opened the door and started digging inside it. After that he pulled Yogie's body out on the ground then got in the car and pulled off. That's when Pam stopped the video and asked, "What do you think?"

Bird answered, "He don't walk like that."

They sat and talked for a minute then Bird went home.

When Bird made it home, she said, "Boy, that's you on that fucking tape. Why the fuck you killed my friend?"

Dump said, "You fucking tripping, like the rest of them. So you saying you saw my face?"

"No! But I know it was you! Why the fuck you lying?" she asked.

He said, "You know what, Bird? Fuck it. Believe what you want."

Dump walked out the house. By the time he made it to the parking lot, his phone started ringing. Dump looked at it and saw it was a private number. He started not to answer it, but he did.

"Hello."

He heard a female voice say, "Bitch, we know you killed him. You're dead."

Dump said, "Who is this?"

The caller didn't say anything; they just held the phone breathing hard. Dump hung up and lit a cigarette.

Chapter Twenty-Three

Early the next morning Bird dropped Dump off at work. He did his eight hours and came back home. His phone started jumping so, he sold a few pounds of Reggie and some hundred-dollar bags of Grand Daddy purp. Bird couldn't sell nothing no more because she knew the Feds were watching her. She hated the fact that she went to jail with a lot of money, but came home broke. Now Dump was the one with more money. She started back to clowning on him in front of everyone to make him feel small, but he paid her no mind. He just kept getting it. One day he was at work Bubbles gave him a call.

He answered, "Hello."

"Hey, Dump. This is Bubbles."

He said, "What's going on?"

She said, "I had to rush Mom to the hospital. She was diagnosed with cancer in her liver. I think you should come see her."

"Okay. I'll be out there. Text me the address."

Dump hung up the phone. His heart was touched, because Ann *always* gave him her everything. He wasn't ready for her to die. At that moment the conversation he had with the cop on Highway 90 crossed his mind. He remembered telling the officer Ann died, then he remembered hearing a preacher say to him that *life* and *death* is in the power of the tongue. It was as if God was tapping him on the shoulder. When he made it home, he told Bird he had to go to Texas to see his mother in the hospital, so she booked their flights.

When they made it there, they picked up a black Corvette with cherry red guts from Boo and shot to the hospital. When he walked in the room, Ann was in there with another woman. Ann had lost so much hair and weight. He was mentally stumbling as he looked her in her big bubble eyes. Both of their eyes started to water.

Ann was laying on the bed and said, "I'm okay, baby. Don't worry about me. How have you been?"

Dump said, "Everything all right on my end. What are the doctors saying about you?" A tear rolled down his face.

Ann said, "All I know is that I'm not about to die."

Dump asked, "Are you sure?"

"Yes. I'm sure. Have you been talking to your son?" she asked him.

He replied, "No. She been keeping him away from me."

She said, "When you talk to him, tell him I said I love him."

"Okay. Imma do that."

He gave her a kiss and left.

Later that evening Dump and Bird caught their flight back. He just laid low all that week soaking in everything while he prayed for Ann.

Everything was slow motion and it was now the weekend. Dump was downtown in the CBD area two blocks from Canal Street by the Iberville Project in the 4th Ward. Dump felt his phone vibrating in his pocket, so he pulled it out and seen it was an unknown number.

"Hello."

"Yes. Dump, this Aunt Joy. I called to tell you that today Ann passed away."

Dump took the phone away from his ear and looked at it in disbelief. As his mind grabbed on to it, realizing what was just said, he slammed his phone on the ground and it broke into pieces.

He grabbed his head, looked to the sky, and screamed, "*Nooooo! My fucking god! Ughhhhh! Noooooooooooo! This can't be real.*"

It really pulled him out of one box and made it to where he couldn't be put into another one. He wasn't mentally capable of accepting no bullshit from anyone anymore.

Through Ann's death, she broke the voodoo bondage Bird put on Dump. Swerv came and picked him up. When he made it to the house, he told Bird what happened. She told him she was sorry to hear that, but he knew her well, and he could tell that she didn't give a fuck. It made him not give a fuck no more about her either. Dump just went to work every day and would grind out the spot, stacking his bread up.

One night Swerv, Big Lips, Geezy, and Roy went out to the club uptown with Sugar and her new boyfriend Trigga, who used to be friends with her ex-boyfriend. For some reason, Sugar always was able to get the guns in the club. Nobody never knew how she did it; they were just happy to have 'em in there.

When they made it in the club, it was jam-packed and live as fuck. They had their own VIP section and kept the sparkles with the bottles coming. Later on that night Kash noticed her ex in their section booting her up and wilding out. Kash called Trigga over to the couch. When he sat down, she gave him the gun and pointed at dude while he was bucking, but not looking.

Kash ordered another bottle as Trigga got up and walked off through the crowd. Ten minutes went by, and Swerv and Roy were standing with Kash bouncing to the music when the waitress walked over to the table with a bottle; while the sparkles flashed, she looked over to where dude was standing with his click and saw him hitting a gar while Trigga walked up behind him, upping his pistol. Kash heard no more music; she just saw the movement. When the barrel reached Buck's head, she saw his brains get knocked out. As his body fell forward, the club and the music stopped.

Everybody made it to their cars and left. Trigga and Swerv got in the Range Rover with Kash. She dropped Swerv off at Shay's new house, and she and Trigga went to her new secret honeycomb hide-out. It was a two-story brown brick four-bedroom house with six tall white pillars in front of it with a water deck out back sitting on a water channel that separated each neighbor's home from another neighbor. That channel connected to Lake Pontchartrain that is connected to the Gulf of Mexico. It was so ducked off it was like a needle in a hay stack of New Orleans.

Early in the morning Dump got up for work. When Swerv was on his way to drop him off, he told him about what happened last night. It was nothing strange to Dump.

He knew that was always a possibility when they went out since the night he met Bird in Houston. Plus, it was a well-known situation at clubs in the city.

Dump said, "So y'all cut up in that bitch, huh?"

Swerv said, "You know me, bruh. I was chilling. That was Kash's work."

Dump felt him. Kash was young Bird in the streets all over again. When they pulled up to his job, Dump gave Swerv a pound dap and said, "Come scoop me for three."

Dump did some light work and fronted his coworkers a couple of purp bags until payday. Bird heard some shit in these streets about Buck's homies looking for Kash to kill her. She called Kash and told her to lay low.

At 2:45 p.m. Swerv pulled up to pick Dump up. He clocked out at three and walked out and hopped in the car.

Swerv said, "What's up?"

Dump asked, "What's good with it?"

Swerv said, "We about to go by Kash."

Dump said, "Dig that."

They rode all the way to the end of Chef Nature Hug and passed through a secluded area then reached the upscale neighborhood. They drove down until they reached the subdivision and turned left into it. It was Dump's first time going to her new spot. When they pulled up, he looked up to it and thought of it as a palace. They got out the car and walked in. The decorations were top-notch, and the vibe was on some mob shit. When he walked into the den, there was seventy-inch TV hanging over the fire place. There he took a seat. Swerv came downstairs from Kash's room with a long box and said, "Let's go."

They dipped out.

When he made it home, Bird had a shitty-ass attitude. He went to take a shower. When he got out, he overheard Bird on the speaker phone with Kash bucking about the niggas looking for her.

She said, "His pussy-ass shouldn't have been fucking with me in my section! They can look for me all they want! Them bitches don't know where I stay anyway! Fuck 'em!"

Bird said, "Look. Let me call you back."

Dump put on some pajamas, laid down, and said, "What it hitting for?"

She said, "Them lil boys want Kash dead. I told her lie low, but she ready to turn up."

Dump said, "She can only lie low for a second. Fuck letting them catch her slipping. She need to turn up."

Bird didn't like his response because she was so used to being a shot caller. She left and went by Kash's.

Dump chilled until he went to sleep. He had a dream where he was alone in darkness and he felt a bad vibe. He fell down on the ground then he felt something on his back pending him there. No matter how hard he tried to get up, he couldn't move. He felt trapped. He tried to say something, but his tongue was too heavy.

The next morning Dump went to work. That day everything just felt strange. He stocked everything then sat down to eat lunch. It was a beautiful day. Shay was at home getting the children ready to go to a doctor's appointment. After she got the two girls and their newborn baby brother in her arms ready, they walked out the front door. After she took about five steps, she saw two cars pull up, one from the left and the other from the right.

They stopped and hopped out with guns and opened fire on them. Shay grabbed the baby's head and held it against her breast. The two little girls ran and grabbed her legs as bullets missed them, hitting the house and the Rover. Shayla opened the door and ran in with the children. Shay called the police then called Swerv and told him what happened.

It was obvious that since they didn't know where Kash lived but knew where Swerv did, so they came for his head. Dump had just finished his lunch and was talking in front of the building in the driveway with his manager waiting for a delivery truck to pull up.

All of a sudden they saw a black Range Rover Sport followed by a black Volkswagen Jetta and a black Pontiac Grand Prix all with tinted windows pull up in front of them.

Swerv rolled the window down while Dump walked up and said, "Come on. These bitches just shot up my house while Shay was in front with the kids."

Dump walked in the office and told them he had a family emergency, he had to go. They told him okay, so he rolled out. They all went to Kash's house. They sat down and told him how it happened. Dump asked who all was involved in the beef. They told him who they were and where they stayed. Dump and Swerv went to Dump's spot and grabbed 223.

When Bird saw him walk out with it, she asked, "Where you going?"

Dump said, "Take care of a little business. I'll be back."

They went back by Kash's. When they got ready to spin on one of the dudes houses to smash his ass, Dump said, "Its broad daylight. I can't creep with a big motherfucker."

Dump told Kash, "Give me that .40 cal."

She went and got it for him.

Kash, Dump, Swerv, and Trigga hopped in a navy-blue Altima and spent through the New Orleans East neighborhood and parked on a corner from dude's house. They sat behind the tent and waited. About fifteen minutes passed, and a brown SUV turned onto the street two blocks away.

Kash said, "There he go."

Dump got out first then Trigga and Swerv. Dump and Swerv stayed on one side. Trigga crossed the street. When the truck got close, they started busting that bitch up. A bullet went through the driver's arm. He ducked down and smashed the gas as the truck was under a hail of fire. They squeezed their triggers until their clips were empty. The brown truck turned left at the end of the block.

They hopped in the Altima and speed off with their adrenaline pumping.

Dump said, "Fuck, man! Fuck! We were supposed to kill that bitch!"

Trigga said, "We hit him up. Ain't no guarantee that nigga gone survive."

They pulled up by Kash's spot. Big Lips, Bird, Roy, and Geezy came by soon after. It fucked Dump up that Big Lips and Roy didn't show up from the beginning. That was their family, but they were staying out of it to keep their hands clean, but paying close attention to Dump once again.

Kash and Trigga was saluting Dump for his work an attitude. Bird didn't like that at all. She was actually Dump's biggest undercover hater. The sick thing about the situation is that Bird and Dump were principal. The beef had nothing to do with him. He was riding for her kids' life simply because he loved them, and they were true friends. For a woman not to appreciate that made him lose all respect for her to try to match her level of respect for him. Bird, Lips, Roy, and Geeze left to go by Bird's spot.

Kash and Swerv felt the vibe Bird was on with Dump.

Kash said, "I know moms be tripping with you on some dumb shit. I ain't got time for that. She be wanting us to not fuck with you when she be mad, but the way you fucking with us, we fucking with you."

Dump said, "Yeah. She on some other shit."

Swerv said, "With you, always."

Kash said, "If she try to put you out, you can sleep over here."

Dump said, "Cool. Thanks."

They chilled for a little while, waiting for the night to fall, so they could spin on two of the other dudes that was in the club with Buck that night.

When night fell, Big Lips and Geezy showed back up.

Dump asked Swerv, "Where these niggas live at?"

Swerv said, "In the Dead End hood off Nola Avenue. That bitch is only two ways in two ways out."

Dump said, "Okay. Let's rock."

They loaded up. Swerv and Dump rode with Kash. Trigga and Geezy rode with Lips. Lips followed Kash. When Kash made it to the hood, she turned in and drove down the block. They saw dude and two of his homies standing in front of a house. They drove past them then ducked off behind the tinted windows. They went a block down and made a left and then another quick left at the corner. Kash drove down to the corner where dude and his homies were on, but they were just a short block down.

Kash stopped there and said, "Y'all go ahead."

Dump hopped out first, then Swerv got out and ran up the block behind him. When Dump made it to the corner, Dump Slowed down, walked to the side of the house, and peeped around the corner. Dump saw dude standing ten feet away from him on his cell phone with his back toward him. Dump looked back at Swerv then ran around the corner, placed the 223 to dude's back, and pulled the trigger.

When dude heard the first shot, he tried to start running. The third shot to his back made him collapse on his face. When he fell, Dump turned right and saw his homie trying to open the house door, but it was locked. When Dump started to squeeze the trigger, he heard Swerv letting off his whole clip. Dump bent dude up in the door and ran off back to the car.

Once Swerv got in the back seat, Kash pulled off. They all met back up by Bird's house. They all hung in front the apartment in the court way by the cars, Dump stood by the brick wall with the 223 on the side of his leg as he clutched it. Swerv stood on the sidewalk with the 9 mm in his pocket with the extended clip sticking out under his T-shirt. Geezy was standing in between the cars with his .40 caliber. Kash was standing two feet from Dump while Bird and Trigga were sitting on the hood of her Monte Carlo.

Everybody was talking, but Dump didn't say a word. He just kept his finger on the trigger with his eyes wide open scanning every car that passed.

Kash said, "Dump Boy, you cut the fuck up!"

Swerv said, "For real! Man, y'all should have seen that nigga slinging that bitch. When he spent the bend, he cut that bitch loose. I saw the long ass fire jumping out that bitch."

Bird put her hand up to Trigga's ear and whispered in it. He looked at Dump and laughed. Bird was really jealous of Dump because he was now the hot topic, and Kash and Swerv were flexing for him without him saying a word.

Trigga was jealous himself. Bird kept whispering in Trigga's ear, and he kept laughing and looking at Dump.

Kash said, "I'm about to go."

Dump said, "Hold up." He went and got his money, drugs, and clothes and left with her, Swerv, and Trigga.

That shit crushed Bird. She never could imagine him having the strength to make that move after she hexed him with the voodoo. Bird's life took a serious twist. First she went to jail, then money disappeared, now her man left her. She didn't know how to deal with this position.

Dump, Swerv, and Tweety slept at Kash's. The next morning Bird and Shay had to go to trial, so Swerv and Dump rode out there to show support in the Federal courtroom.

When they walked in, it shocked Bird to see Dump. She stared at him, but he never looked at her. The lawyers and the prosecutor pleaded their case for two and a half hours, then the judge called for a thirty-minute recess. Swerv, Bird, and Shay ate lunch in the lunch room. Dump chilled alone in the hall.

After they finished eating, they walked past Dump into the courtroom with Bird looking down at his phone.

Dump called Koonta and told him he would hook up with him when he made it back to the city. He hung up the phone and walked back in the courtroom and took a seat on the back row.

The prosecutor looked at him then looked back at the judge and said, "Your Honor, at this time we would like to call our witness, Lavar Star, to the stand."

Dump thought to himself, *Who the fuck could be a witness on this case?*

The man in a suit walked out to go get the witness.

When the courtroom door opened up again, Calliope P walked in dressed casually and looked around the courtroom. When he made eye contact with Dump, it blew his mind. For Calliope P to be a member of the drug ring and a so-called gangster to be on the stand raising his hand, swearing to tell the whole truth as a witness for the Feds. That fucked Dump up.

166

The prosecutor asked, "Mr. Star, the car rental that is evidence in this case was in your name. Is that correct?"

Calliope P responded, "Yes, sir."

The prosecutor asked, "When you had the vehicle, where there any checks, identification cards, or plastic cards in the vehicle along with you?"

He answered, "No, sir. There were not."

The prosecutor said, "Okay." Then the prosecutor asked, "Who else had the vehicle, Mr. Star?"

Calliope P looked over at Bird and tilted his head down toward her and said, "Bird Blacksmith."

The prosecutor asked, "Did anyone else use the vehicle, Mr. Star?"

He paused then said, "No, sir. She was the only one that I let use the vehicle."

The prosecutor said, "Thank you. No further questions, Your Honor."

He looked at Dump then turned around and sat down.

Shay and Bird's lawyers sat in their seats and said, "No questions, Your Honor."

After that, both sides made their closing statements, and the judge took an hour to make his decision.

The judge came back to the stand and stated that Bird and Shay are guilty of identity theft and credit card fraud. The lawyers scheduled their sentencing for two weeks from then. After the verdict, Dump walked out the courtroom and got on the elevator. When the elevator door opened at floor one, he saw Calliope P walking past.

Dump booted him up and said, "Ratting ass."

V. looked back and kept walking. Dump went to the car and waited for Swerv. When Bird, Shay, and Swerv came out the building, Dump saw Bird crying, talking to Shay. Swerv and Dump pulled out, and Bird and Shay followed them. When they made it back to New Orleans, Bird expected Dump to come home by her, but Swerv dropped him off in the 8th Ward by Koonta. That hurt Bird. It made her want to hurt him. All night long, Bird thought of a way to get him back.

167

The next day Dump was by Kash's house with Swerv when his phone started ringing. He saw it was Bird, so he answered it.

"Hello."

That was when she said, "Bitch, you want leave me and think it's a game. I'm gone set you up hoe. You going to jail."

Dump didn't believe her, so he talked shit, "I don't give a fuck. I'm out here. Do you. Imma do me."

And she hung up the phone. It made him think about it. She was a murderer with a deep-in-the-streets history that followed her. He never would believe that she would play the police on him; because he knew so much of her illegal business, he could tell on her.

Kash's phone rang. She answered it and put Bird on speakerphone. "What's up, Ma?"

Bird answered, "I'm on my way over there."

"Okay, Ma." Kash confirmed then hung up the phone.

Dump said, "I'm about to get the fuck up outta here."

Kash tossed Dump the keys and said, "You can take the rental. I'll call you when she leaves."

He said, "Okay."

And he walked out the door. Chef Mature Highway was Highway 90 with one lane going in each direction to and from Kash's subdivision. Dump saw Bird's car coming up Chef as Bird saw the rental coming down Chef. When they crossed paths, they locked eyes. To see Dump coming from that way riding in Kash's rental made her blood boil.

Dump pulled up by Koonta's and hustled with him on his block. When Bird left, Swerv called Dump and told him, "Don't go to work tomorrow, bruh. I heard Bird on the phone with the police. She is moving on you."

Dump said, "Damn. That's fucked up."

Swerv said, "Dog, I couldn't believe that shit. She tripping."

The next day was Friday. Dump didn't go in to work that morning.

About noon, his coworker called him and said, "Man, two detectives just left this bitch asking questions about you."

Dump asked, "For what?"

Dude said, "I don't know."

Dump told him, "Pick up my check so you can meet me with it when you bring me that other money."

Dump's coworker agrees, "Okay." And he hung up.

Later that day, Dump met him on Chef Mature at the Easy Time convenient store.

When Dump pulled up, homie got in on the passenger side and said, "Boy, you lucky you didn't come in today. Them motherfuckers pulled up and hopped out looking like the Men in Black."

Dump said, "Fuck 'em. Them bitches gone have to find me. Since them ratting bitches tried to make it easy for them."

Dude asked, "What they looking for you for?"

"I don't have no idea," Dump responded.

Homie passed Dump the money he owed, gave him his paycheck, and said, "I'm gone fuck with you. Be easy out here."

"Dig. Fuck with me."

Then Dump dipped. He went back to fuck with Koonta for a minute. After that, he went by Kash's house with the rest of the click. It was Gezzy, Roy, Swerv, Slow, Nell, Big Lips, and Trigga.

Dump asked Swerv, "What's the next move?"

He said, "All them niggas hiding right now."

Kash said, "Them bitches spooked."

Dump was like, "I'm trying to make sure y'all good before I leave. I can feel the heat coming down. Kash book me a bus ticket tonight for Houston."

After he announced that, his phone rang. He picked it up off the table looked at it and saw it was a private number.

"Hello, who is this?" he asked.

"Bitch we gone get you."

Then they hung up. It really started to annoy Dump.

Kash walked back in the room and said, "I booked your ticket. They didn't have none for tomorrow, so you got one for eight o'clock the next morning."

Dump told her, "Cool. Thanks."

She said, "No problem, baby."

He sat back, thinking until he dozed off.

Dump woke up about noon to his phone ringing.

He answered it, "Hello... Hello... Hello!"

Nobody said anything, so he hung up. He looked at the phone and saw it was a private number again. Later that evening Dump figured he would lie low and stay off the radar. He went to the Crystal Inn hotel on Tulane Avenue in Mid-City and hooked up in a room with O-Head and Snick. They caught back up because they hadn't seen each other in a year. While catching up, they heard a knock at the door.

When Dump opened it, Trell walked in and said, "Oh my god. The lucky man. What's up?"

Dump said, "I'd be damned. You done growed all the way up, huh? All thick and shit."

She said, "Yep, you like?"

He said, "What you think? How old are you now?"

Trell answered, "I just made eighteen yesterday."

O-Head said, "Come on, Snick. Let's go get a gar from the store."

As soon as they left out the door, Dump said, "Damn, I don't get no hug?"

Trell sucked her teeth and walked over to him and hugged him around his neck. He put his arms around her waist and slick side grabbed her ass. She looked up at him and didn't say nothing. Before she knew it, he was on top of her in bed, tongue-kissing her. He pulled her shorts to the side between her legs and slid his dick in, making her young, pretty, thick ass moan. It turned both of them on so much, knowing he fucked her mom before. He was actually making love to her. He started digging deep and nutted inside her.

She said, "That nut so warm. Good thing I'm on birth control."

And she started laughing.

"Damn, that pussy way better than Trish shit."

Smiling at Dump, she said, "Duh! Tell me something I don't know?"

She gave him a kiss and left. He laid in the twin bed and turned the TV on. Then his phone rang. He looked at it and saw it was a private number.

He answered it, "What?"

They said, "You dead!"

He said, "Fuck you, bitch. I stay strapped. Come see me!" And he hung up.

Snick and O-Head came back to the room. They didn't have a clue about what Dump had going on. He'd been into so much that he didn't want to sleep in their room in case something happened; he wanted to be alone.

When night fell, he went down to the motel office with clear glass walls all around it and purchased a room. Once they gave him a key, he walked out the office and saw a chick walking carrying a small baby in her arms with a short, slim, red nigga with buku tattoos on his arms, and three teardrop tats under his left eye. He looked at Dump and started singing Solja Slim.

Dump caught the vibe when he heard him say, "It's my duty to serve ya quickly. When I come, my drum gone be holding fifty."

Dump saw his hand in his pocket, so he clutched his gun ready to pull it out if dude made one false move. Dude looked at him with and anxious look on his face, but Dump kept it no secret he was waiting and ready, so the so-called gangsta folded as Dump walked up the stairs to his room.

When he made it to the second floor, his phone started ringing. He looked at it and saw Private, so he didn't answer. He just wanted to make it in his room. When he made it to the third floor, they called again. He just kept moving. He made it to the door, stuck his key in, walked in, and shut the door behind him.

Dump's phone kept blowing up. The whole situation had him on edge. He pulled out the baby 9mm and peeped out the curtain in the window right next to the door. When he looked downstairs by the motel office, he saw Yogie's brother's car with dark tinted windows with his foot on the breaks. Dump's phone would not stop ringing, so he turned the ringer off. Something told him to look out the peephole.

Dump held the nine in his hand and put his other hand to the door and leaned over to the peephole. When he looked, Dump saw a short, light-brown chubby chick walk up to the door and heard her check the door knob to see if the door was locked. He couldn't believe what he was seeing as she walked off. He never left from by the door. Dump leaned over to the window and peeped out it and noticed a video camera up top on the wall facing down toward his room.

Dump stood up and leaned back to the peep hole. Two minutes passed as he was looking out it. He saw a brown skinned dude with a bald high top fade walking up to his door with big diamond earrings in his ears and two diamond chains around his neck putting his ear to the door then checked the knob. That made Dump mad and nervous. When dude walked off, Dump wanted to open the door and kill him, but he thought about the camera. Dump stood by the door the whole night until he dozed off.

When he woke up in the morning, he got O-Head to drop him off at the bus station downtown. He put his bags under the bus and got on it. When the bus pulled out, Dump was now comfortable to get some real rest. By the time he made it to Baton Rouge, he was in a deep sleep.

When he woke up, he had made it to Houston. Dump got off the bus and called Dilland, who was O-Head's big brother, and told him he was at the bus station waiting for him to pick him up. Dilland told Dump he was outside already, so Dump grabbed his bags and went got in the car.

Once in the car, Dilland told Dump, "Long time no see, huh?"

Dump smiled and said, "Yeah, man. I've been in a whole 'nother world."

Dilland said, "Oh well. Welcome back."

They hit Interstate 59 and got off on Hillcroft Street. They made a left turn at the light and drove down to Dilland's apartment. Once they got inside Dilland and Dump talked for a minute, then Dump called Swerv, but his phone went straight to voice mail. He called again, and it did the same thing. Dump hung up and called Kash, and she didn't answer.

He called Tweety's line.

She answered and said, "Hello."

Dump asked, "Are you by Swerv?"

She said, "Yesterday the police ran in Kash's spot. They took everybody to jail. Bird was mad that Kash and Swerv were fucking with you and thought you were over there, so she sent them for you and got them caught up. That hoe sad."

Dump said, "You gotta be fucking lying."

Tweety said, "Nope. This hoe ratted on you and her own children."

Dump said, "Baby, let me call you back."

And he hung up.

Everything was fucked up, but Dump wasn't shocked because he felt the heat coming down. The dream he had about the rain falling on the window and the snakes hissing plus him seeing snake scales all over her body one night finally made sense to him. The dream was a message that his life was about to be upgraded. The king-size bed represented that. The rain up against the window represented the storm in life he was going through, and the snakes hissing represented Bird.

Dump was mentally flat, sitting on the sofa, dazed. It punched him into a depression. He was quiet for the rest of the day. That night Dump called and asked Tweety what was Swerv and Kash charged with. She told him that Swerv was charged with two counts of attempted murder and Kash was charged with murder from the club along with Trigga. Tweety told him that Big Lips and Roy were at the house when the police hit and were arrested for attachments. Dump slept on the couch in Dilland's living room.

The next morning O-Head knocked on the door and woke him up.

When he opened the door, O-Head asked Dump, "Boy, who the fuck did you kill?"

It caught Dump off guard.

He said, "Nobody. What are you talking about?"

O-Head said, "My nigga, your face is all over the news in New Orleans, saying that you're wanted for capital murder."

Dump dropped his head and said, "Bitch!"

O-Head said, "My nigga, you gone have to leave from big brother's house. I'm gone bring you by Nicole."

Dump said, "Who is Nicole?"

"Man, you remember ya girl who stayed next door to me around the corner?" he told Dump.

Dump said, "Okay. Let's go."

O-Head pulled up to Nicole's apartment and walked him through the cut, then through the court, then up the stairs. When he walked in the spot, he saw a little homie from Press Park named Nomak.

He gave Dump dap and smiled. "What's up, big homie?"

Dump said, "Shit, out here trying to get it."

Nomak said, "I can feel that. Nicole not here right now. She be back in a minute."

Dump said, "How she rocking?"

He said, "Fuck, she cool."

Dump responded, "That's what's up. What's been popping with you though?"

"I been chilling. Me and Shorty got our own spot in the back."

O-Head said, "Look. Y'all be cool. I'm gone fuck with y'all."

And he walked out.

An hour blew by, and Nomak and Dump were still running it. Dump was looking through the window and saw a short, bowlegged, chocolate female walking up the stairs.

He said, "Damn, she thick in all the right places."

Nomak said, "I know, right?"

Dump sat down on the couch before Nicole walked in.

When she did, she said, "Hey, Dump. How have you been?"

He said, "I'm good."

He didn't really remember her, but he could tell she remembered him well.

She said, "The last time I saw you, you tried to holler at me on our porch, and I shot you down."

He said, "Oh yeah. Now I remember you." And he smiled. "I was shining hard, and you ain't wanna fuck with ah nigga."

Nicole said, "Man, you were doing too much. I see you chilling. I could fuck with ya nah."

He laughed and said "Oh yeah?"

She looked at Nomak then back at him and said, "Yeah."

Dump was entertaining her at the moment, but the capital murder charge was heavy on his mind. It was his first time being on the run for such a serious crime. He knew that Nicole couldn't know anything about the situation.

He said, "I just came from the city. Is it okay if I stay here until I find me a spot?"

She said, "Sure."

Dump kicked back and paid attention to how things were going in the house and seen she was a natural-born hustler.

A few hours passed, and it got late. Nomak dipped, and Dump went laid at the foot of Nichole's bed. His mind was going one hundred miles per hour. No matter how hard Dump tried, he could not go to sleep. He needed to be to himself and think of his next move. He pretended to be sleep when he heard Nicole walk into the room. She then went into the bathroom and started taking a shower. Dump thought, if she found out that he was on the run for murder, how would she react? Nicole was cool and down to earth, but Dump was operating like he was from another planet. When she finished in the shower, she came out into the dark room and saw him lying on his stomach stretched across her bed. Nicole thought he was sleep, so she didn't ask him to move. She just laid next to him.

Thirty minutes went by, and Dump's mind was still racing. He thought about having sex with Nicole to help him relax. He put his arm around her and waited for her response, but she didn't move, so he scooted over to her and laid on his side. When Nicole felt Dump's dick getting hard, she opened her legs a little.

Dump saw that as an open invitation to play with her pussy, so he slid his hand between her legs and felt her pussy dripping wet. Dump placed his middle finger between her lips and rubbed her clitoris. Dump could tell by the way Nicole was moving that he was doing it perfectly, so he didn't want to stop. Nicole legs opened up a little more as she trembled. Dump could tell she was about to cum. Nicole grabbed Dumps arm and started grinding her body up against his hand.

She started to bounce up and down while she was cumin. After Nicole came, Dump rolled over and went to sleep. That fucked Nicole's head up.

She laid there, thinking, *How could he make me cum and don't want to fuck?*

Form that night on, Nicole was very interested in him. Little did she know, she was in for a surprise.

The next morning Dump woke up, and Nicole was gone.

When he walked out the room and into the living room, he saw Nomak sitting on his couch, rolling a gar, and said, "What's up, nigga? I'm 'bout to blow this shit. What's good?"

Dump said, "Not ah motherfucking thing. Where the Plug at?"

Nomak asked, "What need?"

Dump answered," Two and a quarter of coke."

"Damn round, I don't know a Plug with coke," Nomak told him.

Dump asked, "What Plugs do you know?"

He answered, "That green."

Dump said, "Nicole fucking with that. I ain't gone fuck with her lane."

Nomak said, "Man, she a real bitch. She ain't gone trip." Dump said, "Imma just sit back for a minute and peep the play." That's when Nicole walked in the door and told Nomak, "What's up baby." Then looked at Dump and said, "You slept good last night huh?" He admitted, "Not really. How about you?"

Nicole said, "Yeah. I was comfortable." And she gave him a slick look.

Dump asked, "What's that look for?"

She said, "You know what it's for." And she smiled, showing her two gold teeth on the side of her two front teeth.

Dump looked down to her stomach then to her hips and thighs that was hugging her camel toe.

When he looked back to her eyes, she said, "I told my friend Tina about you. She said she was coming over to meet you. Dump looked at Nomak and said, "Oh yeah?"

As he looked back at Nicole, she said, "Yeah!" She sat next to Dump on the couch. Nomak lit the weed and passed it to Nicole.

She hit it, and as soon as Nicole passed it to Dump, there was a knock at the door. "Come in!" she said.

Two dudes walked in. Dump and the second one made eye contact.

Nicole asked them, "What's going on?"

The first one said, "Give me a dime."

Nicole got up and walked to the back. Nomak passed Dump the gar. When he hit it, Nicole walked back in, took the money, and gave him the bag. As they walked out the door, dude and Dump made eye contact again.

Dump asked, "Who was that?"

Nicole said, "They live in the back by Nomak."

He asked, "Where the store at?"

"You walk to the front of the apartments, and you gone see it right across the street. Bring back a gar."

Dump said, "Cool."

And he walked downstairs. As he walked under the breezeways, he started to notice gang tags spray painted on the walls. Then he saw a few Mexican guys all wearing gray Dickies slacks. Once he got close to the store, he noticed a group of young black guys wearing all black. Dump walked past them and entered the store, got the cigars, and walked out.

Out of the corner of his eye, he saw one of the dudes tuck a Glock under his shirt and heard another one saying, "One pop, all pop, don't pop, get popped."

Another said, "Ya heard me."

Dump kept walking as if he heard or saw nothing. When he made it to the street, he saw a police car approaching, so he stopped to let it pass before he crossed the street and walked back into the apartment. Dump saw two different gangs but didn't know he was sitting in the middle of a gang, drugs, and turf war he could never understand.

When Dump made it to the apartment, he saw Tina sitting on the sofa with Nicole. Tina was a dark brown with a short bob hairstyle. Dump noticed she was much thicker and cuter than Nicole. From the way Tina looked at him, he could tell she liked what she was looking at, so Dump decided to play a game with the two.

Dump flirted with Nicole live and direct and took a few shots at Tina flying over Nicole's head. Tina and Nicole caught on to what he was doing, but they liked the fact that he was doing it smooth.

Tina said, "My girl told me all about you."

He said, "She can't tell you all about me because her sexy ass don't know all about me."

Nicole said, "I know enough about you."

He said, "Real shit, but what she told your thick ass?"

Tina said, "You play your cards right. That's all I'm gone say."

Nicole started laughing and said, "Girl, he bold."

Tina said, "I see."

Dump didn't know, but both of them were fucking Nicole's weed Plug. He was paying Tina's bills and fronting Nicole quarter pounds of weed.

One day Nicole ran out of weed, so she called Butter to bring her a pack. When he made it over, Dump opened the door for him and sat on the couch while Nicole talked to him.

Butter looked at Dump and said, "What's up, bro?"

Dump said, "Cooling. What's good with cha?"

He said, "You must be from New Orleans?"

Dump said, "Yeah."

Butter said, "Bet."

He looked at Nicole and said, "I'll be back."

When he walked out, Dump said, "You saw that look on ya boo's face?"

Nicole said, "Yep. He's jealous. But fuck, he ain't my boyfriend."

"Yeah, but he is your money man," Dump said.

Nicole agreed, "I know, right."

Tina started coming around more because of Dump. Nicole didn't like it. Dump also hooked up with Butter to score a few pounds, but Butter didn't hold any heavy like that, so he only served him a quarter pound here and there.

Dump hooked up with Butter one day and asked, "Who is your Plug. I need three pounds?"

Butter said, "It's dry right now. I'm ah let you know when it's good."

Dump knew he was bullshitting. He said, "Cool." And took the quarter pound.

Later that day Nicole needed some more work. Butter told her he was on his way over, but he never showed up. Nicole didn't understand what was going on, but Dump did. He was in his feelings mad at her and hating on Dump. Dump ain't give a fuck. He fronted her the quarter pound.

By the next day it was all gone. Dump hooked up with Tina to ride around and find a Plug. They stopped by a barbershop on Hillcroft Avenue by O-Head's apartments, and one of the homies gave him the number to a Plug.

As the sun set, Tina and Dump were enjoying being together alone. Dup picked his phone and called the Plug.

The Plug answered, "Hello."

He said, "What's up? This Dump. Big Will told me to hit you up."

The Plug said, "Oh yeah. What's good?"

He said, "I need two Incredible Hulk birthday cakes."

The Plug said, "Okay. I got you. Meet me at Greenspoint Apartments on Airport Street. Call me when you make it."

He said, "Bet," and hung up.

Dump told Tina to shoot by the Greenspoint Apartments. They were only five minutes away. When they pulled up to the gate, Dump called.

"What's up? This Dump."

The Plug said, "Pull up by building G. Come to apartment 32."

Dump said, "Dig."

When they pulled up by the building, he saw a pearl-colored 300 Chrysler sitting on some 84s poking with vogue tires.

Dump thought out loud, "That bitch clean."

Tina said, "That's Butter."

He said, "Oh yeah?" and grinned.

"That nigga didn't want to give me the Plug, and I still got at him."

He hoped out and walked through the cut up to the door and saw Butter walk out with his head down. When he looked up and saw Dump, he was surprised with a dick look on his face.

Dump said, "What's up?"

Butter said, "Nothing much," as Dump walked past him and up to the door.

When Butter made it to the parking lot and saw Tina parked, he felt played, thinking to himself, *Dump got at this Plug and took both of his hoes.*

He and Tina made eye contact, and he gave her a stupid look, shaking his head.

Tina put her head down because she was embarrassed. When Dump walked back to the car with the Foot Locker bag in his hand, he could tell she was feeling funny because of the look on her face.

He got in and asked, "You good?"

She answered, "I'm straight."

"You're sure?"

"Yes."

She put the car in reverse, backed up, and pulled off.

When they pulled up to Nicole's spot, Tina said, "I'll be back."

Dump told her, "Fuck with me," and hopped out.

As soon as he walked in, Nicole said, "Damn, you took long enough. Did you fuck her yet?"

Dump told Nicole, "Stop playing. Did you want me to get the work or not?"

She said, "That's a crazy question."

Dump asked, "Where's the scale at?"

Nicole went grabbed the scale and brought it to him. He weighed the pounds and gave her one. Nicole sat down at the kitchen table and started bagging dime bags. He sat on the couch watching TV, but he was really paying attention to her. Dump noticed Nicole kept sniffing and rubbing her nose and lighting cigarette after cigarette.

Dump came straight out and asked, "You keep sniffing. Where that good at?"

Nicole tried to play it off and said, "What are you talking about?"

Dump said, "Come on, man. I fuck with that. Where it's at?"

"My people got it," She told him.

He said, "I need a gram."

"Okay, let me finish this. I got you."

After Nicole bagged a few ounces, she went and got the coke for him and they both got high as fuck. Once they got on that level, everything took a twist and started moving fast. Every day it was about the money. Dump sat back and watched Nicole pitch a pound of weed all dime bags in one day. He expanded his business by adding coke to the shop. After that played out well, he added ecstasy to the program. After ecstasy, then came Xanax. After Xanax came speed, and after speed, he heard about embalming fluid called wet or water.

One day Dump was sitting on the sofa looking down at the court through the closed blinds. He saw Mike walking up the stairs, so he walked to the door. As Mike raised his hand to knock on it, Dump opened the door, standing behind it with his head sticking around it.

He asked, "What's up?"

Mike said, "Where's Nicole?"

Dump said, "Come in."

When he came in, Nicole said, "This nigga know the Wet Plug."

Dump said "How much for a strack?"

Mike said, "One seventy-five."

Dump said, "I need you to run me over there."

He said, "I got you. Give me a dime, Nicole."

After she gave it to him, Mike said, "I'll be right back," and dipped.

Dump scored two more pounds, one hundred ex pills, a quarter of cocaine and came back to the house. Mike was there waiting for him. Dump walked straight to the room and stashed the work, and he and Mike left. When they made it to the Wet Plug, they walked in the dirty ass low-budget hotel room. Dump stood by the door. He saw a sexy gangster bitch looking at him lying in the bed.

When he looked over to Mike, he and the Wet Plug were talking low for a few seconds.

The Wet Plug said, "I'll be back."

He and Mike walked out the door. The chick got out the bed and smiled at Dump with her one gold on the front tooth as she walked by the counter. There he noticed a Chrome 357. She stood there until Mike and the Wet Plug walked back in. Dump went in his pocket and pulled out a knot, counted out $175 while the Wet Plug pulled out a pack of cigarettes, took one out, dipped it in the little brown bottle, pulled it out, flipped it upside down, stuck it inside his mouth and blew air down, stuck it inside his mouth and blew air down it.

Mike said, "This that guerrilla piss right her my nigga."

Dump said, "Yeah."

Mike said, "You ain't never fucked with it?"

"No. I ain't never fucked with it," Dump said.

The Wet Plug said, "Shit, hit this bitch."

Dump walked over to them. The Wet Plug passed it.

Dump grabbed it then hit it and said, "This shit taste like flowers."

He hit it again and passed it back. It spaced Dump out. He never felt the feeling before. His body felt light as he and Mike walked out to the car. Everything was fussy mentally.

Mike said, "That shit good, huh?"

Dump said, "Fucking right."

As they came up to the red light, Dump saw a gas station at the corner.

He told Mike, "Stop and get some gars."

When they pulled in, Mike said, "Look at that hoe standing over there."

When Dump looked, he saw a short big fine bitch standing in front of a motel.

Mike said, "Man, that hoe selling that pussy. We should go fuck her."

Dump said, "Let's see how much she want."

Mike went in and bought the gars.

When he came back out, he pulled up by the hoe, rolled his window down, and asked, "How much?"

She replied, "Fifty for each."

Mike pulled over and parked. Dump went and got a room. When they got inside, the hoe didn't waste any time. She took of her pants and started sucking Dump's dick.

Mike said, "Dip a cigarette."

So Dump dug in his pockets and got the pack and the strack and dipped it. Mike started fucking the hoe from the back while she sucked Dump's dick some more. Dump took a lite and lit the dipped cigarette whole she slurped on his shit.

Dump passed it to Mike, but Mike said, "Hit it."

So Dump hit it two more times and passed it. Before Dump knew it, he *blacked out.*

When Dump opened his eyes, he was in the room alone with the door open. He pulled up his pants as he walked to the door. Dump saw the hoe pulling off in a car. He looked over to where Mike was parked, and the spot was empty. He patted his pockets and felt the strack, but his money was gone. Dump was so loaded that he closed the door and laid in the bed until he fell asleep.

Chapter Twenty-Four

The next morning when Dump woke up, he felt out of place. He grabbed his pack of cigarettes and lit one up. After he smoked it, his wet high came back. He left the motel and walked back to the apartments. He was thinking about last night. When he did the math, he lost out on $230. It was good that he scored all his work before he was played like a duck.

As Dump walked his mind was wrapped around the thought of killing Mike if he ever saw him again.

Once Dump made it to the spot, Nicole said, "I'm happy you're okay. I've been blowing your phone up."

Dump said, "It went dead, and I didn't have my charger."

She said, "Did you get the water?"

"Yeah. I got it."

He didn't tell her about what happened because it made him feel like shit and thought maybe she would look at him different. A few days passed and the money was coming fast.

Dump was sitting on the steps smoking a cigarette.

A short Mexican standing at five feet four inches, walking like a gangsta, poking his chest out wearing a white T-shirt with some blue Dickies, came walking through the cut up to the stairs and asked, "What's up, homie? You got smoke?"

Dump said, "What chu need?"

He said, "A dove."

Dump told him, "Hold up."

He got up and walked inside, grabbed the bag, and walked back out. When Shorty gave him the cash, he gave him the bag.

The dude said, "Okay, homie. I'll holler at you later."

Dump said, "Fuck with me."

Then he walked back in the house. For some reason, the Mexican's attitude was stuck on his mind. He could tell that he was serious about that gangster shit.

Dump asked Nicole out of the blue, "Do you want to get high?"

She said, "Of course."

He realized that gangster vibe brought the history with Bird and the murder chargeback as a reality check that made him depressed, so he wanted the drugs to take the feeling away. He pulled out two ecstasy pills, and they popped them. Then Dump went to the stash and grabbed a bag of coke and made eight lines on a dinner plate, and they snorted two lines a piece. After that, he went to the freezer and grabbed the strack out.

Dump took a seat at the table, dipped a cigarette, blew air down it, pulled the filter out the back end, and sparked it up. Dump hit it three times then walked over to Nicole on the couch, passed it to her, and sat beside her. Dump watched Nicole while she hit it blowing the smoke out in circles looking back at him.

He said, "That shit make you feel great, but it smell like a funeral."

She said, "I thought I was the only one who thought that."

She got up and grabbed the plate and brought it back to the sofa. Nicole snorted a line and passed it to Dump. He snorted two lines, passed it back to her, and lay back with his body feeling numb. Nicole looked at Dump, sat the plate down on the floor, took his belt loose, unzipped his pants, pulled his dick out, and started beating it. Once it got hard, she started sucking on the head while she continued to beat it slowly. Nicole stopped beating it and grabbed his balls as she deep-throated his dick.

She came up off it and asked, "Is that helping you relax?"

He said, "You must have known I needed that."

She said, "Yeah. I can tell when something is on your mind."

Dump told her, "You're doing a good job easing ah nigga mind."

Nicole went back down to sucking it until he came, and she swallowed. Dump gave Nicole a kiss then asked her to roll a gar. As she rolled it, he started thinking about God. He got up and went to the bathroom. After he used it, he came out and saw Nicole was sleep. Dump sat on the sofa for a minute.

Then he heard a voice in his head say, "Pick up the Bible."

He looked over to the Bible on the shelf, but he didn't move.

The voice told him again, "Pick up that Bible and read it."

That was when Dump got up, walked to the shelf, grabbed the Bible, and sat back down. He opened it up to a random spot in Psalms. When he looked at Psalm6, the letter *O* was huge sitting off the page, and the other words were the regular size. Dump was literally hallucinating, but he read it out loud, "(1) O Lord, do not rebuke me in your anger, Nor chasten me in your hot displeasure. (2) Have mercy on me, O Lord, for I am weak; O Lord, heal me, for my bones are troubled. (3) My soul is greatly troubled; But you, O Lord-how long? (4) Return, O Lord, deliver me! Oh, save me for your mercies' sake! (5) For in death there is no remembrance of you. In this grave who will give you thanks?"

At that moment, Dump stopped and thought to himself. "Those words touched his soul. In his situation it had meaning. He lay on the sofa and sat the Bible on his chest. Dump meditated on what he read until he dozed off.

Nicole woke up early in the morning from a knock on the door. She looked over and saw Dump was sleep, so she got up and answered it. When she opened it she saw the short Mexican with his chest poked out.

She said, "Hey, what's up?"

He asked, "Is homie in?"

She said, "Hold on."

Nicole walked up to Dump ad tapped him on his shoulder and said, "Dump, get up. Somebody want you at the door."

He looked up and said, "Huh?"

"Somebody at the door for you," she repeated.

Dump sat up and said, "Let 'em in."

When she opened the door and told him to come in, Dump saw Shorty walk in and said, "What's going on, homie?"

Dump said, "I'm chilling, what's good?"

He said, "Nothing much. You got smoke, homie?"

Dump said, "Yeah."

He said, "Give me a half."

Dump called Nicole, "Bring me a half."

Nicole brought it to him then went back to the room.

After Dump gave it to him, he passed the money and asked, "Is it cool for me to roll up, homie?"

Dump said, "Do your thing."

Dump got up and walked to the bathroom and took a piss. He walked out, looked in the room, and saw Nicole lying down with her eyes closed.

He walked back into the living room and asked, "Where you from, my nigga?"

He answered, "I'm from Los Angeles, Cali. Where are you from?"

Dump said. "NO."

He said, "I heard that is the murder capital."

Dump said, "Yeah, That bitch wild."

Dump started checking out Shorty's tattoos and saw a *Playboy* bunny on his neck and asked, "You on some *Playboy* shit huh, *Playboy*?"

He said, "Yeah, homie. That's my family in Cali. We're Crips for life. Do you bang?"

Dump said, "No. We don't bang in my city. It's all wards."

He asked, "Wards?"

Dump said, "Yeah, I'm from the 9th Ward. What's your name?"

He looked up at Dump and lit the weed with an evil look in his eyes, "My name is Demon. Don't never tell anybody my name."

Then he hit the weed and said, "It seems like we have a lot in common. I'm out here because I'm on the run for murder in Cali. What about you?"

Dump said, "Yeah, me too."

Dump wanted nothing to do with Demon because the way he carried himself and his name exposed he was evil, but because Dump was ah real nigga, he didn't fold up. Dump had intentions on holding his ground and pivoting his position. Demon went on talking about how he had beef with a gang called MS13 for killing his little nephew. Dump heard of that gang before and knew that they were deadly.

Dump said, "I'm about to make a couple of moves. Imma fuck with you later."

Demon got up, gave Dump a pound dap, and said, "Okay, homie. I'll holler back."

It was about 5:00 p.m., and Dump's phone went to ringing. When he looked at tit he saw it was Swerv.

He answered it, "Hello."

Swerv said, "What's up, my nigga?"

Dump said, "When you got out?"

He answered, "Yesterday."

Dump said, "I felt that heat coming, but I ain't thinking it was gone go down like that."

Swerv said, "She did that bad."

Dump added, "That's an understatement. For a mom to put her children in jail on them charges behind a nigga is unreal. Now you free, Kash locked up, and I'm on the run. Where she at?"

"She at home!" said Swerv.

Dump asked, "When she have to turn herself in?"

He answered, "If they don't catch you, she gotta go in on the eighteenth."

Dump said, "Huh, bruh."

Swerv said, "My nigga when I was on I-10 on my way home, I saw your face on a billboard big as fuck saying you're wanted for murder."

Dump said, "Are you fucking serious?"

Swerv said, "Yeah, not only that, on the news at night they have this criminal wheel of justice where they spin this wheel that has pictures of wanted people on it. Tweety told me that it lands on you every time they spin that bitch. Them motherfuckers making you famous out here."

Dump didn't say anything.

Swerv said, "Hello."

He said, "Yeah. I'm here. Look, let me hit you back."

Swerv hung up.

Dump's head was fucked up. He never could imagine his life being at this level. He lit a cigarette and hit it hard blowing the smoke out his nose. A few days passed. Nicole and Dump were sitting on the couch watching TV as he looked out the blinds down at the court way he saw Demon roll up on an old-school cruiser.

When he reached the steps, he carried it up and put it on the porch then knocked on the door.

Dump yelled, "Come in!"

When he walked in, he said, "I need to holler at you homie."

Dump looked at Nicole then looked at him and told him, "Come on," and walked into the bathroom.

When they got in there, Dump closed the door behind them and asked, "What's up?"

Demon said, "The homies came and talked to me and said that you are selling all these drugs, making all this money, but you're not giving them nothing."

Dump looked down at him in his eyes and said, "Where I'm from, real niggas don't pay no motherfucking draft."

As Dump was pointing his finger at him, he said, "You tell them motherfuckers to come tell me that shit to my face, and *Imma chop 'em dowwwwn!*"

Demon looked at him, not surprised by what he said because he knew Dump was retarded. Demon looked at Dump and smiled with a calm voice and said, "I'll tell them."

Then they both walked out into the living room. Demon looked at Nicole and said, "Be cool, mama." He gave Dump a dap and said, "I'll holler back, homie."

Dump said, "Bet."

Demon went and told the top dogs what Dump said, and now they wanted him dead. Since Dump was comfortable with Demon, they wanted him to take the *hit.*

Dump was living the life of a lost soul, but he was actually chosen by a higher power to make things against him look foolish.

Swerv called Dump and said, "Hurry up and turn the television on that 378 New Orleans channel out there. Hurry up!"

Dump said, "All right."

He looked for the remote, and when he found it, he turned it to 378 and said, "It's a commercial on."

Swerv said, "Hold up. It's coming."

He said, "What's coming?"

Swerv said, "Hold up. You gone see."

So Dump sat down and waited. After the next commercial went off, a bounty hunter show came on with a bounty hunter sitting in a chair, and Dump's picture was on the screen in the top-right corner. Dump's mouth dropped as the bounty hunter said, "Mr. Coleman, we don't know where you're at, but we do know what you look like, and you can't run from us forever. If it's the last thing I do, I'm going to find you."

Swerv said, "Bitch, you on fire."

The bounty hunter said, "Anyone who can help us locate Cage Coleman, we have a $5,000 reward up on his conviction. Contact me at Bulldog Bonds located at 7025 Tulane Avenue."

Dump turned the TV off and said, "My nigga, I don't know how this shit gone turn out."

Swerv said, "They putting a lot of money behind catching you. Yesterday me and Tweety were riding in the car listening to Q93 and heard a commercial about you being wanted for first-degree murder."

Dump said, "This can't be life. I ain't do that bitch nothing. I was riding on niggas behind her children, and she tried to shit on me, so I left. Now she lied to the cops and got these bitches hungry."

Serve said, "You gone beat that shit. Just lie low."

Dump said, "I am low, but fuck, I got to get this money up. What your bread looking like?"

Swerv answered, "My shit fucked up since Mom's played it like that. Boo ain't fucking with me. That nigga ain't even on the radar."

Dump said, "I bet he ain't. Fuck. If somebody I was doing business with exposed their self as a rat, I would be on somewhere's Waldo shit my fucking self."

Swerv said, "Huh, bruh."

He said, "Don't trip. It's gone open up."

Swerv was like, "Bet. I'm gone fuck with you later."

Then he hung up.

Dump sat there for a minute thinking about everything. That's when Nicole and Tina walked in the front door, laughing.

Nicole walked to the back and Tina sat on the sofa and said, "You been acting funny, huh?"

He said, "No. I just been making sure my shit straight."

She said, "That's what's up."

As Nicole walked back in, Tina said, "I just got me a new spot. I'm about to move out my apartment next week."

Dump said, "Is your lease up on that apartment?"

She said, "No."

He said, "Well, I can take over your rent so it don't affect your living arrangements history by breaking the lease.

Tina looked at Nicole and said, "That's a good idea."

He said, "When you get free. I want to go check the apartment out."

Tina said, "Tomorrow is cool. I'll call you when I'm on my way."

Nicole didn't want him to leave, but she couldn't make his decisions.

Nicole came out and said, "Boy, you lucky," being sarcastic.

He caught it, but because of his situation, he paid it no mind. She didn't know it, but he was trying to keep her out of his bullshit, knowing the police could rush her spot any day. Little did he know, she didn't give a fuck. Nicole loved his lifestyle and was willing to ride with him till the wheels fell off.

Later on that night, Nicole and Dump lay in bed talking.

He asked, "Why do you find our friendship so interesting?"

Nicole said, "When I first saw you and you came on to me, the level you were on, you wasn't my type. You were actually out of my range. Plus, I knew you just wanted to fuck. Now it seems as if you humbled yourself, and instead of you being way up and I'm ordinary, we came up together."

That statement made him respect her mind. Dump looked at Nicole totally different. Most females would have fucked him at the drop of a dime, but because she wasn't money hungry, she didn't. For hours they talked.

She hit him from the blind side and said, "I love you."

He said, "You don't mean that."

She said, "You don't have to believe me. I just wanted to tell you how I feel."

Dump got on top of her and kissed her. She started to stick her tongue in his mouth. He spread her legs open, and as he was kissing her, he was playing with her pearl tongue. She started to kiss him more passionately. Dump slid down to her beautiful breast nibbling on her nipples and made them hard as he continued rubbing her pussy.

Nicole arched her back as she stretched her arms out, grabbing the sheets with her hands, and said, "Fuck me."

Dump went down and licked her pretty flat stomach around her navel. He felt her pussy getting wetter.

Nicole begged," Fuck me. Please."

Dump kept going down while he took his wet fingers out of her pussy and rubbed her asshole making it wet. Dump sucked on her pearl tongue and her body jumped. She grabbed his head. He started sticking his middle finger up her ass while he ate her pussy.

Nicole said, "Nobody never ate my pussy like this. Oh my god!"

Dump felt her body shaking as she nutted in his mouth. He licked it as he slurped on her pussy. Nicole just laid there feeling relaxed. Dump stood up, pulling her hand.

She stood up with Dump with a confused look on her face and said, "What chu doing?"

Dump dragged her to the side of the bed and made her face the mirror. When she looked in the mirror at them, he bent her over, grabbed her by the waist with his left hand, and put his dick in with the right, then grabbed the other side of her waist slowly stroking her pretty pink tight pussy.

Nicole was humping her back up from the arch because his dick was touching the bottom wall.

Dump put his hand in the middle lower part of her back pushing it down back into the arch slowly and said, "Relax."

Him being demanding turned Nicole on even more. She spread her legs and arched her back. He felt her insides thumping from her pulse as he pushed in it to the bottom and left it there. He bent her over and kissed then licked her back, feeling goose bumps with his tongue. Dump stood back up and started bouncing her ass back on his dick. He saw she was comfortable so, the longer he went, the harder he bounced it, the louder she moaned. Nicole started to run from him, but he was about to cum, so he refused to let her go anywhere. He pulled out, started beating it, and it skeeted up her back and into her hair. Nicole didn't know it, but after she told Dump what she told him and the sex, he loved her too. Their friendship reached the level of a bond that could never be broken. Nicole laid down and went to sleep, but once again, Dump was lying on his back looking at the ceiling fan spinning, thinking of his life, meditating on his next move.

The next morning Dump woke up early. Nicole was still sleep. For some reason, he couldn't sleep well last night. Every time he dozed off, his body jumped because it felt like he was falling. He sat on the couch with a bag of coke. He put it on the table and smashed it with his cigarette lighter then held it up in his hand plucking the bag with his finger.

After that, he took the small straw out of his pocket and stuck it in the bag, pulled it out, stuck it up his nose, and sniffed it hard. The bump was so strong he went to coughing loud. Nicole screamed out the back, "Are you all right!"

Dump kept coughing, "Yeah. I'm good!"

Dump took another bump and lit a cigarette. As the rush hit him, he opened the door and stood in it. There he saw two lesbians walking up the stairs.

The big fine butch chick with a low cut bald fade asked, "Where is Nicole?"

Dump looked at the beautiful thick fem and said, "She in there."

"Can you call her please?" she asked.

Dump said, "You can come in."

Dump walked in and called Nicole then sat at the kitchen table, stalking the fem on the cool, checking her out from head to toe. He loved how her hair was long and wavy. Plus, she had wide hips, a fat ass, with no stomach. She had on a pair of tight jeans hugging every curve with a pair of black six-inch heels. Her toe nails matched her finger nails. Even though she was a lesbian, the bitch had him mesmerized.

She looked at Dump and caught him staring at her when Nicole walked in and said, "Oh my god! Bitch, where y'all been hiding?"

The fem said, "Girl her gutter ass was in jail. You know she don't want me around no hoes without her."

Nicole said, "T-T, you know I ain't trying to fuck, Yella, if you ain't around. I don't eat pussy anyway. But if I fucked around, it would have to be both of y'all fucking me bitch."

Dump was rocked up siting back imagining fucking Yella and Nicole. He pictured Nicole riding him while Yella was riding his face as they tongue-kissed each other.

T-T said, "I fuck with you girl, but I ain't sharing her yellow ass." And she laughed it off.

Dump's phone started vibrating in his pocket.

He answered it, "Hello."

Tina said, "I'll be over in a little bit."

Dump said, "Okay." And he hung up.

T-T asked, "Where the white girl at?"

Nicole said, "He got it."

She told Dump, "Give me a gram."

Dump walked to the back.

T-T then asked, "Is that your man?"

Nicole said, "No. That's my boy."

When he walked back in, he grabbed the scale out the kitchen drawer and sat it on the table. He pulled a quarter of coke out his pocket, picked up a card, and bagged a 1.4 g.

Yella put the fifty on the table, took the bag and said, "Thank you."

When she looked at the bag, she knew it was over a gram.

She looked at Dump and said, "All right, girl. Y'all be cool. We gone holler."

Nicole said, "Okay, Yella, keep that hoe outta jail."

They all laughed. "Okay."

And they left.

Nomack came up the stairs. Dump was like, "You're right on time, nigga."

"Oh yeah, what's good?" he asked.

Dump said, "Roll up."

Nomak said, "Where the gar at?"

Nicole tossed it to him.

He asked, "Did y'all hear about Butter?"

Dump said, "Nah."

Nomak said, "That nigga was found dead on his couch, shot two times in his chest."

Dump said, "Man, are you serious?"

"Yep."

Dump said, "That had to be somebody he knew."

Nicole said, "I bet one of them fuck niggas robbed him."

Nomak rolled the weed up. They watched TV and blowed. When the weed was gone, they just sat there quiet all looking down in their phones. Nicole heard someone walking up the stairs, so she looked out the window and saw it was Tina. She opened the door.

Tina said, "What's up? Y'all ready?"

Dump said, "Yeah."

Nicole said, "Imma stay here and get this money." Nicole looked at him and said, "Don't be all day."

He said, "Bet."

And they pulled out.

As they pulled up to the apartments, Tina said, "Here we go."

Dump said, "That was quick."

She said, "Yeah, about fifteen minutes."

Then she got out. He got out and followed her up the stairs.

"I already moved everything out, but the living room set. You can have it if you like."

Tina opened the door and they walked into the one bedroom.

Dump checked it out and said, "This is good. I'm ah fuck with it."

She said, "Okay."

He asked, "How much is the rent?"

"Four thirty-five," she answered.

Dump went into his pocket and pulled out the money, counted it out and gave it to her for the first month. Tina grabbed it and put it in her purse. Dump walked out and down the stairs as he lit a cigarette, looking up at Tina, locking the door. When she made it down the stairs, she brushed up against him as she walked by.

Dump grinned and said, "You better watch that shit before you get jammed up."

Tina asked, "Do you want to see my new spot?"

He said, "That's cool."

And they got in the car.

Tina drove down Fondren Road to Beltway 8 and rode along the side of the Beltway a few miles then turned off into a neighborhood. They pulled into a section with trailer homes. Tina pulled to the back and parked by a new white trailer.

"Welcome to my world."

Dump's phone rang. He looked at it and saw it was Nicole.

"Hello."

"Boy, where you at?"

He replied, "On my way back."

She said, "Hurry up."

He said, "Girl, stop. I'll be there."

And he hung up.

They walked up the steps to the door.

When they walked in, Tina said, "Oh. It feels so much better in here. That sun have me sweating?"

Dump said, "Nah, your ass just too thick."

Tina said, "I know, right." As she walked through, she said, "This is the living room… This is the kitchen… And this is my room. You can have a seat. I need to use the bathroom."

Dump said, "Do your thing."

And he lay down on the bed, looking through his phone. Dump heard the shower come on and thought she was serious about her sweating.

When Tina finished taking a shower, she walked out the bathroom in a forest-green Victoria Secret teddy looking sexy.

She walked over to the bed, climbed in on top of him, and said, "Is this too thick for you?"

He said, "You got me fucked up?"

She said "Well, what are you gone do with it?"

He told her, "Rock that bitch up and you gone see."

Dump was nervous because Tina shocked him. He always thought he would have to go at her, but she was at his neck. She pulled his pants down and went to sucking it good. When it got hard she grabbed a condom out her dresser and put it on for him. After that, she hopped on top and started bouncing on his shit like a pogo stick until she came. Dump laid her on her back, folded her legs like a pretzel, then pent them to her breast and pounded her until he came. Once he did, he let her legs down, and they both laid with him on top of her for a minute until she dozed off.

Dump woke her up and said, "Come on. I gotta go."

Tina dropped Dump off.

When he walked inside, Nicole said, "So you playing with me with that hoe?"

"Nicole, what chu talking 'bout?"

"It don't take that long to look at an apartment. That hoe always wanna fuck who I'm fucking."

He asked, "How you know if we fucked?"

She poked her lips out, "I'm not stupid, but fuck all that. Tell me why they saying you killed Butter?"

"What the fuck you mean I killed Butter?"

"I was here with you all night."

She said, "That's what I told them, but they don't believe me."

Dump said, "Fuck 'em. Them bitches can believe whatever they want."

Dump took a seat on the sofa, and Nicole walked to the back.

Dump called her back up front and asked, "What we looking like with the weed?"

She said, "We still got a half ah pound."

"What about the water?"

Nicole answered, "I ain't never touched it."

He said, "Dig."

As Dump looked downstairs through the closed blinds, he saw Demon. His phone rang. He looked and saw it was him calling.

Demon asked, "Are you home, homie?"

Dump said, "Yeah. What's good?"

Demon said, "I need a dove. I'm coming up."

Dump said, "Bet."

And he hung up.

Dump opened the door.

When Demon walked in, he said, "Man, today it's going crazy out there. What's been up?"

Dump said, "Shit, I been cooling."

Then he told Nicole to get a dove. She went got it and gave it to Dump. Demon gave him dap and dipped out.

Dump told her, "I don't trust that motherfucker."

She asked, "Why you say that?"

"I don't know. Something about him just ain't right."

She was like, "He seems pretty cool to me."

Dump said, "You're blind to a lot of shit."

She said, "The only shit I'm blind to is shit that don't have nothing to do with me."

He looked at her and nodded. He and Nicole chilled together the rest of the day, hustling out the spot. When it got late, she fell asleep in bed. Dump was chilling in the living room watching TV. He heard a knock on the door.

He asked, "Who is it?"

"It's me. Demon!"

Dump opened the door and sat back on the couch.

Demon sat on the other couch and asked, "Do you have a cigar, homie?"

Dump went to the room, got it, and tossed it to him. As he was rolling up, he said, "These niggas are back here doing too much."

Dump asked, "What chu mean?"

"These motherfuckers act like they run shit."

Dump asked, "Nigga crossed you?"

He said, "No. I want to kill somebody back here. Are you down?"

Demon really had Dump shook. He asked, "Kill who?"

"Anybody. Are you down?"

Dump wasn't fucking with it, because he didn't know what it was all about, but he threw him for a loop and said, "Yeah. I'll fuck with it. Give me a minute, though. Once I'm finished handling my business, we gone get at that."

Demon looked him in his eyes with that evil look and said, "Okay."

When he lit the weed, Dump said, "It's getting late. I'm about to Z out. Come fuck with me tomorrow, baby."

Demon gave Dump dap and left. Dump locked the door and crashed.

The next day came, and it seemed like Nicole couldn't keep still. Every time she sat down after making a sale, another one came. Late in the evening two big bitches came by. Dump could tell which one was in charge, because Tut was more in control. Rell just followed, looked, and listened. Tut sat down at the table with Nicole and Rell by her side. Dump sat on the couch acting as if he wasn't paying any attention.

Nicole asked, "What's going on, baby?"

Tut said, "I know you be doing your thing heavy. I have ten pounds. I figure I could front them to you."

Then she looked at Dump. Dump saw her out the corner of his eye. When he looked at her, she looked back at Nicole and told her, "I feel you. How much you want off the pounds if I take 'em?"

Tut said, "Three seventy-five."

Nicole looked at Dump. He made a stale face and shook his head, looking like one on the slick.

Nicole looked back at them and said, "I'm good. I already get 'em for three twenty-five."

Tut looked at Dump and resented him because she knew he was the one bringing the work to the table. She knew that if he wasn't in the way, she could have dropped the ten on her easy.

Tut asked, "Are you sure you don't want them?"

Nicole said, "Yes."

Tut said, "If you change your mind, give me a holla."

As she stood up walking to the door with Rell following behind her, Nicole said, "Okay, baby."

When they walked out and Nicole closed it, Dump said, "Them hoes tryin' to tax something."

Nicole said, "I wonder where they got that shit from."

Dump said, "They probably hit a lick."

Nicole was like, "Butter ended up dead. Now these hoes pop up with ten pounds."

He asked, "Them hoes out here wild like that?"

She said, "You never know with them. Tut unpredictable with a puppet like Rell. Plus, Butter was fronting them too."

"Oh yeah?"

"Yeah," Nicole confirmed.

Dump's mind started wondering what could happen next if he didn't pay attention to every person, place, or thing. Dump took a seat. Nicole went in the room.

Thirty minutes passed by. As Dump looked out the window through the closed blinds, he saw Demon walking through the cut into the court up to the stairs. Dump got up, walked to the door, and opened it up, standing behind it with his head sticking around it before Demon could knock on it and said, "What's good?"

Demon asked, "How come you always know when to open up the door before people knock?"

Dump said, "I see everything, my nigga."

Demon walked in and said, "I got somebody last night, homie. They had everything I needed. Check this phone out."

As he reached it to Dump, Dump grabbed it, and as he looked at it, Demon said, "I stole a car too."

Dump said, "This bitch nice."

Demon said, "You can have it."

Dump said, "That's what's up. You turnt the fuck up out here, huh?"

Demon said, "I got to go. I'll see you, though."

Dump gave him dap and walked him to the door. Dump locked the door then sat down on the sofa and said to himself, "I'm gone have to kill this nigga."

Dump heard Nicole call him to the back, so he went.

She said, "T-T about to come for a gram. Big Noop about to come for an ounce, and Pete want ten pills. If I'm asleep, serve 'em."

Dump said, "I got you."

And he walked up front. When they came through, Dump laced them up.

At 4:00 p.m., Demon popped up at the spot, and before he knocked, Dump opened up the door again.

And he said, "What's up, homie?"

Demon walked in and said, "The police just came in my crib, yo. They searched my shit from top to bottom, but ain't find shit. While they were still searching the front rooms, I climbed out the back window and got the fuck."

Dump said, "Them people smoking."

Demon said, "Before I got away, they brought you up."

"What they said?" Dump asked.

Demon said, "The big dog told me, 'Your boy is next.' I asked who, and they didn't know your name, but he described you: the red dude with all the golds. I just came by to tell you, homie. Watch yourself. You're hot."

Dump said, "Dig."

And Demon dipped.

Dump walked in the room and tapped Nicole. "Wake up."

She woke up and said, "What?"

"We gotta pack the work up and get it out. The police ran in Demon's shit. They told him we were next."

Nicole said, "I'm gone bring it by Mr. Bob."

Dump said, "That's cool, but we gotta move fast."

After they got the work together, Nicole moved around with it. When she came back in the spot, Dump put on his shades and walked out to peep the section. When Dump made it through the second cut, he saw an unfamiliar short Mexican guy with a clean shave and a police-style haircut. Dump knew everyone back there. He was sure he was an undercover. Dump was walking past him.

When he got beside him, he said, "Policia."

The Mexican showed no response. He acted as if he heard nothing and kept walking. When Dump made it to the front of the apartments, he saw two more Mexican undercovers on bicycles.

When he passed them, he said, "Policia," and kept walking. He felt like his life was a movie. The feeling was unreal. Dump walked up to the street to cross it. It was as if everything was moving in slow motion. Dump looked to the left and saw an old-school water-wet blue-and-yellow trimmed cherry Blazer with the windows down sitting on chrome rims approaching. When it passed, Dump saw two OG VATOS with long ponytails wearing shades looking directly at him. Dump knew without a doubt they were the dudes that sent Demon with the draft message. When all the cars cleared, he crossed the street and walked into the apartments next to the store. Dump could feel the laws watching, but he kept moving.

It seemed as if he was the hood's hot topic. Dump stayed moving around for thirty minutes then went back to the spot and waited for the pigs to hit, but they never did. Nicole showed up when the sun went down.

She told Dump, "You was tripping. They knew I was ready for 'em, so they didn't hit." Nicole said, "You might be right."

He said, "Ain't no mights. I saw them." He shut the shop down for the night.

Chapter Twenty-Five

Early Tuesday morning, Dump walked outside to check out the section. The sun was shining bright, Dump heard the birds chirping and saw three children running through the court playing tag. He put on his shades, lit a cigarette, and walked downstairs.

When he finished his cigarette, he called Swerv and asked, "Have you been talking to Kash?"

He said, "Yeah."

Dump asked, "How much is her bond?"

He answered, "$250,000."

Dump asked, "What about Trigga?"

Swerv said, "He don't have a bond."

He asked, "Ain't nobody trying to put no money together to get her out?"

Swerv said, "Fuck no. These niggas happy she gone."

He said, "I got five for her."

Swerv said, "Me too. We need ten more. Plus, they told me we have to put up property to make sure she don't take flight or miss court."

Dump said, "Well, I guess she gone have to sit for a minute."

Swerv said, "I'm working on it. What's up with you, though?"

He said, "I'm staying focused and stacking up some paper on their radar."

"What the fuck you mean on the radar? I told you to stay low."

Dump said, "I know. These dicks just on me. I think ah nigga put my name in the wind."

Swerv told him, "All I'm ah say is, I'm ah jose ya, bitch."

203

Dump said, "Bet. Keep it one hundred, hoe. Be cool."

Dump chilled for a minute, then he walked through the cut. Everything was clear. He walked up to the front and saw the young gang member hanging. That let him know the police was out the area, so he walked to the back and opened shop. He told Nicole to go get a lil work from Mr. Bob. When she got back, she called everybody to let them know she was good.

It was about 3:30 p.m., and the spot was jumping. His phone rung. When he looked at it, he saw it was Demon.

He answered it, "Yo."

Demon said, "I need a half."

Dump said, "Okay."

Demon said, "I'm here."

Dump told him, "Okay, come get it."

Demon said, "Bring it down to me."

Dump said, "Come and get it."

He said, "No, homie. Bring it down."

Dump said, "Come on, man. Are you serious?"

He said, "Bring it to me. I ain't coming up."

Dump said, "Okay."

He hung up and grabbed the half.

He called Nicole out the back and said, "I want you to come with me downstairs."

She asked, "Why?"

He looked at her in the eyes and said, "Demon is about to kill me. I want you to see it."

He felt it in his gut, but his life and mind was so twisted he was ready to die.

Nicole was spooked, but she was so down for him when he walked out the door she followed. When they made it downstairs, he put his arm around her shoulders as he smiled talking to her walking toward the cut. When he looked through the cut to the parking lot, he saw a shark-gray two-door Honda pull up and stop.

Demon hopped out the passenger side. A fat white dude pulled off as Demon walked through the cut. He had his hand in the pocket of his basketball shorts. Dump could see the shape of a revolver as the wind blew his shorts up against it. Demon saw him walking toward him, hugging Nicole, and looked surprised.

Demon put one finger up and said, "Hold up."

He turned around, walking back to the parking lot through the cut. The Honda pulled back up, facing the exit direction. Demon hopped in then got back out, walked up to Dump, gave him forty dollars, took the weed, and walked, saying, "I'm ah holler, homie."

He hopped back in, and fat boy pulled off. Dump and Nicole walked back to the spot. Nicole sat down.

Dump called Demon and said, "That was the stolen car, huh?"

He said, "Yeah. That was it."

Dump said, "You know I saw that gun in your pocket, huh?"

Demon said, "I was trying to show it to you, homie."

Dump said, "Why you ain't show it to me?"

Demon replied, "I didn't want your girl to see it."

Dump said, "Yeah, okay. It's all good. I'm ah see you, though."

Then he hung up. Dump was thinking Demon was trying to play it off, but he was actually telling him straight up in his own language that he was about to kill him, but according to his gang laws, it was disrespectful to murder someone in front of their family. It went over Dump's head.

Later on that day, Tina came by and dropped the keys off to him. Tina and Nicole talked for a minute, then she left. Dump went to his apartment that night and slept on the couch. Nicole was so used to lying up under him that she tossed and turned all night, missing him.

When Dump woke up, it was noon.

T-T hit his line up and said, "Good morning. You up?"

He said, "Yeah. What's up?"

She said, "I'm about to come by you and get something."

He asked, "You know where I'm at?"

She said, "Yeah, Nicole just told me."

He said, "So she just gone tell motherfuckers where I'm at without asking me."

She laughed.

Dump said, "It's cool. Come through."

She said, "I'll be there."

Dump hung up then went took a shower and brushed his teeth. After that, he took a gold rag and shinned his golds as he looked in the mirror, evaluated himself, and noticed he lost some weight. The stress, the game, and the drugs were taking a toll on him. His lifestyle was flying by on autopilot, so it didn't register to him. He just went throughout his days, day by day, avoiding getting caught by the cops.

Dump was sitting on the sofa waiting for T-T to show up.

Nicole called and said, "T-T is on her way to you."

He said, "Yeah, I already know. Tel me why would you let a bitch know where I stay without asking me first?"

Nicole said, "You shouldn't be there anyway. You should be here."

He said, "It's a reason why I'm here. I'm looking out for your jazzy ass."

She said, "Boy, bye."

And she hung up.

He didn't like what she did, but he found what she said cute.

He texted her, "I'm digging your attitude. Keep it up. It's gone pay off. LOL."

She texted back, "Fuck you!"

He texted back, "JTFO." And he put his phone down.

About twenty minutes passed. Dump heard someone walking up the stairs. *Ding dong.* The doorbell rang. He got up, walked to the door, looked out the peephole, and saw T-T standing there.

When he opened the door, he saw her wearing a white V-neck T-shirt, red-and-black basketball shorts, sagging off her ass with a fresh pair of black-and-red space jam Jordan's.

T-T walked in, smiling, "What's up with you?"

He said, "I'm chilling. I see you solo, huh?"

She said, "Yeah, bae tripping, so I come to get something from you and chill, if that's cool?"

Since she was one of his loyal customers, plus he wanted to fuck her girl, so he said, "Yeah. You good."

She said, "I'm trying to het high and relax."

He said, "Whatever you buy, I'm ah match it, and we gone get lit."

She said, "Perfect. I want a gram."

She was carrying herself different from all the times he saw her before, but he didn't catch on to it. She normally acted like a dude, but she was talking like a chick at the moment.

She asked, "Do you have any cigars?"

He said, "No, I gotta go to the store to get 'em."

It was only a block away, so they walked to it. They talked along the way. Once they made it to the middle of the block, she came from far left field and said, "Men gone always be men. They gone always fuck who they want to fuck."

He grinned and said, "That's true, but women will always be women."

She said, "That's true, because every once in a while, I have sex with my daughter's father."

Dump felt funny because he didn't understand why a real butch bitch would be telling him that, but his reaction made him respond, "Every woman will always love real dick in their life no matter if they love another woman."

The conversation changed right after that.

Dump and T-T picked up a couple gars and shot back to the house. When they made it, she busted down the cigars and started rolling the weed while he put the coke on a plate and chopped it down with a razor. Dump turned on the radio. That's when T-T lit up the first gar.

As they smoked, they talked.

She brought sex back into the conversation and asked, "What about a woman turns you on?"

He looked at her body and said, "I love a freak."

She said, "Me too."

He said, "It turns me on when she is thick."

She stood up and pulled her basketball shorts up and said, "Like this?"

He looked down at her thighs for the first time and thought to himself, *Damn!* But he said, "Yeah. Just like that."

She always wore baggy clothes, so he never saw her shape.

He said, "I ain't know you was thick like that."

She said, "I know."

As she turned to the side and pulled her shorts down to her thighs, she asked, "Does this turn you on?"

Dump looked at her ass and grabbed it, "This nice."

He pulled her shorts down. T-T came out of them and walked over to the plate and snorted a line. When she bent over in the red lace boy shorts, he came out his pants and started pulling on his dick.

T-T sat down, and Dump grabbed the plate and snorted two lines then sat beside her. She laid back on the couch, cocked her right leg up on it, then opened her legs, and put her other foot on the floor. Dump got on the floor and started eating her pussy. T-T looked down at him as he looked up to her. She grabbed his head and started humping his mouth.

She said, "You're eating good, but you can't make me cum when I'm on that coke."

Dump ate her for a few minutes, then she asked him to lay on the floor.

When he did, she stood up pulled her shirt off over her head and dropped it on the floor. T-T was shaped like a Coke bottle standing over him. She walked up to his head, turned around, kneeled down, and started sucking him while he ate her.

They both enjoyed it until she was ready to fuck.

T-T said, "Come on."

She got up from over him but stayed on her knees. He got up, got behind her, and started pounding her, looking at her fat ass bouncing. When he smacked her ass, he could tell she liked it. He was so into watching her ass that he decided to look up at her. When he saw her bald fade, his dick immediately went soft.

She asked, "What's wrong?"

He blamed it on the coke, but actually, her fade turned him off because from the back, her head looked like he was fucking a man. T-T sucked if for him and got it back hard, but when he started fucking her and looked at her head, he went soft again. She was really disappointed, so she put on her clothes and went home to Yella.

Dump felt bad. On the cool, he was embarrassed for not performing well for her when she chose him. He chilled at his spot all day and isolated himself. Later that night, Dump walked to the store and got a few drinks, two cigars, and a pack of cigarettes. When he was on his way back walking up the sidewalk across the street from a large field, everything started to feel odd.

He felt like someone was watching him. As Dump kept walking, he looked around to make sure he was good, but he saw nothing on the block. Something told him to look across the street at the dark field. He slowed down a little and turned his head left looking at the field.

It was really dark, but when he focused in on it, he saw a black shadow in the middle of the field walking along with him. What was strange is the shadow was built just like Yogie. From the energy, Dump felt he could tell that the dark shadow was actually a spirit stalking him from a distance. Dump kept his eyes on it as he picked up the pace.

When he made it to the spot, he really had to gather his thoughts to understand what just happened.

Chapter Twenty-Six

The next day was July 18. When Dump woke up, the first thought that crossed his mind was, *Bird had to turn herself in to the Feds because they never found Dump.*

He got dressed and went by Nicole's to make sure she was straight. He knocked on the door.

When she opened it, he walked in and said, "Good morning, love."

She said, "What's up?"

He said, "Nothing much."

She said, "Once again, I can tell something is on your mind."

He said, "I'm cool."

And he sat on the couch. All he heard was Swerv's voice on repeat say, "If they don't catch you, she gotta go in on the eighteenth."

Dump sat there talking to Nicole for a minute but agreed to call Bird before she turned herself in continued to grow heavier on him, so he got up and walked out on the porch. He stood there with his phone in his hand mentally battling himself, thinking, *Should I call? I shouldn't... I should... I'm not supposed to.*

Then he said, "Fuck it." And he called.

Dump listened as the phone rang. It kept ringing and ringing. He thought she wouldn't answer.

Then he heard her say, "Hello."

He said, "What's up?"

She started to cry as she said, "Nothing."

Dump told her, "You know it didn't have to be like this."

She said, "I know. I made a mistake."

She cried, saying, "I'm sorry."

He hung up in her face because her apology was unworthy of a response. Dump only called with intentions of making her feel foolish because of her actions. When he hung up in her face, she felt like shit, knowing she dropped from being the cream of the crop to the bottom of the barrel. Even though the phone call served its purpose, it didn't change his situation one bit. It actually dragged him down to being more depressed.

Dump lit a cigarette and sat on the steps smoking it as he watched the clouds blow by while memories flashed in his mind. He hated the memories and thought about committing suicide, but as reality soaked in, he rather made a statement by going out in a blaze of glory.

Nicole didn't know it, but Dump was completely discombobulated flying through life waiting to crash at any given moment. Because of his trials and tribulations, Dump was literally bent to his breaking point. It seemed as if being blessed by God to live breathing another breath only added more pressure. Dump got up, walked back into the spot, and went straight to the back room and laid across the bed.

The rest of the day Nicole took care of all the business. She just walked to the back every so often to check on him as the day went by.

The next morning one of the Mexicans that normally came to score Xanbars knocked on the door.

When Dump opened it, he saw him standing there with a stranger and asked, "What's up?"

The Mexican asked, "Do you have pills?"

Dump said, "You come to my spot with a stranger. We don't sell no drugs out her."

The dude tapped his homie walking off down the stairs with an attitude and said, "Fuck you," under his breath.

That sent Dump into a rage.

Dump asked, "Wha chu said?" as he walked downstairs behind him.

The Mexican looked back at him but kept walking with no response. When Dump reached the bottom of the stairs, he took three big skips to get behind him. That's when Dump cocked back and hit the Mexican with a right blow to the side of his head.

When he didn't stop or drop, Dump cocked back and hit him with another one that made him stumble a lil bit, but he wanted to knock him out, so he did it again, but when he hit him the third time, his knuckles broke. The dude stumbled again, but he kept walking as if nothing ever happened. Dump looked down at his hand and saw it disfigured with his knuckles pushed back. Dump felt pain shooting up his hand through his wrist. At that moment, he turned around holding his wrist as he walked up the stairs back into the apartment.

Nicole was walking out the back and asked, "What happened?"

He told her, and she said, "It's broken. You need to go to the hospital."

"No. I'm not about to go to no fucking hospital."

Dump opened a bag of coke and hit it to kill the pain. Once it went away, he sat down and smoked a cigarette after cigarette as his hand swelled up.

About an hour went by, and he saw a lady officer walk up the stairs, so he walked to the back room and went in the closet.

When he heard Nicole ask, "Yes?" the officer said, "Where is the guy?"

Nicole asked, "What guy?"

Dump covered himself with the ton of clothes that was on the floor as the officer said, "The neighbors called because a guy who lives here assaulted him. Is it okay if I come in and look around?"

Nicole looked to the back, turned back around, and said, "Yes."

Dump looked through a small opening in between the clothes pile and saw the officer walking back toward the room. His heart was in his ass beating fast.

When she made it to the room, she looked around then looked down at the clothes on the floor and said, "Okay, ma'am. You have a nice day."

And she turned around and walked out.

"When he returns, tell him that we want to talk to him."

Nicole replied, "Okay."

Then she closed the door.

Nicole told Dump the cop was gone. He came from under the pile and walked back up in the living room. He told her that he was under the clothes.

She started laughing and said, "Boy, you stupid. I thought you was gone."

"Shit. Me too!"

All that day Dump chilled inside. The next morning, he woke up, washed his face, brushed his teeth, and figured he should walk to the store to get some cigarettes. Dump walked out the door.

As he was walking down the stops, he saw an officer dressed in regular clothes wearing a blue vest with police written in yellow across his chest walking through the breezeway into the cut in his direction, pointing at him, and said, "Hey you! Come here!"

Once he reached him, he grabbed the cigarette out of Dump's mouth, then turned him around then patted him down and asked, "What's your name?"

Dump said, "Derrick Willis."

The officer cuffed him then walked him through the cut out to another officer's unit and said, "This is him."

The officer got out the unit dressed in his uniform and placed him in the back of the vehicle.

Dump had no idea what was going on, so when the officer sat back in the unit, he asked, "What am I being arrested for?"

The officer looked at him through the rearview mirror and said, "You assaulted someone."

Dump dropped his mouth, looked surprised, and said, "Hold up. I was at home all day."

The officer said, "This happened yesterday back here."

Dump said, "I wasn't around here at all yesterday."

The officer asked, "Where were you?"

Dump replied, "I was at work."

The officer got out the car, walked around the front of the unit to the back door, opened it, and said, "Get out."

The weight came off his shoulders.

As he stepped out, the officer said, "Turn around."

When he turned around, the officer released him from the cuffs.

Dump said, "Thank you."

And he walked off through the cut. When he made it through the cut to the breezeway, he saw a neighbor that was a customer, smiling, and said, "They let you go, huh?"

Dump said, "Yeah."

The neighbor said, "When you were sitting in the car, dude walked up to the cut and said, 'Yeah. They got his ass in the car right now. His bitch-ass gone.'"

Dump said, "Oh yeah?"

It pissed him off. Obviously, dude was the one who called the cops on him. They heard someone walking through the breezeway, so they looked and saw dude exit it. Just by seeing Dump pushed him into spazz. Dump charged at him, grabbed him with his left hand by his shirt, and punched him in his nose hard with the right. Dude broke away and asked the people standing by to use their phone to call the police. When dude turned his back, walking through the breezeway, Dump walked with the neighbor in his apartment.

Five minutes passed. As Dump was peeping out the window, he saw six tactical officers wearing bulletproof vest dressed in regular clothes, swarming around, looking for him.

Dude and his girlfriend went paranoid and said, "We're going to leave out."

That was when they heard a knock on the door. Dump dipped into the kitchen as the girlfriend walked to the door and opened it.

"Yes, sir?"

The police asked, "Is Derrick Willis in here?"

"No, sir. I don't know anybody by that name."

The police said, "Okay."

Then she closed the door.

Dump came walking out the kitchen and said, "Don't trip. In order for them to come in, they gone need ah warrant."

Dude said, "Come on, Rocky. We be back."

And they walked out and locked the door. Dump kept peeping out the window as they walked under the breezeway to the front.

When they made it up there, the sergeant called them over to his car and said, "We are sure that he is in your apartment. I'm waiting for the warrant to search for him to come back now. If you make me wait for the warrant to search and we find him in there, we will notify the office, and they will put you out. So I'm going to ask you one time. Is it okay if we search your apartment?"

Dude looked at his girlfriend then back to the sergeant and said, "It's okay if you search."

And he gave him the key. He gave the key to the officers, and they went to the apartment. When Dump heard the walkie-talkie sounds at the door, he rushed to a closet in the hall and pulled all the clothes off the hangers. He lay down on the floor and covered himself with them, hoping it worked like it did before. As he peeped through the clothes, he saw one cop with his Glock drawn walking through the spot. He walked into the kitchen then passed Dump up and walked into the room.

Once he checked the room, he walked up to the closet and looked down at the clothes. He thought that the pile looked strange, so he pulled the jacket off top and seen Dump's leg.

He screamed, "I got him!" as he pulled him out the closet by his legs.

Dump was paranoid, thinking he was about to be killed if he made any moves, so he made sure that he kept his hands open in clear view. The tactical unit reported to the apartment as the officer made him lie on his stomach and cuffed him. Two of them grabbed him by his arms and forced him up, walked him out the door, through the breezeway, then to the front by the sergeant's unit. They opened the door and placed him in the back seat. When they closed the door, Dump looked up to the rearview mirror and saw the sergeant looking him in his eyes through the mirror.

He asked Dump, "Are you wanted for murder?"

Dump knew he was caught but said, "No, sir." And he put his head down.

The sergeant smiled as he called another unit to the scene.

When the other unit arrived on the scene, the sergeant ordered the officer to bring him straight to the jail. He took Dump out of his car and placed him in the other. When they left the scene, Dump tried to talk his way out of the car again.

But the officer told him, "You made a fool out of me the first time."

Then ignored him for the rest of the ride. When they pulled up to the jail, a tear dropped from his eye. He knew it was over. Once Dump was booked and fingerprinted, all his information popped up, and they charged him with assault. After that, they notified NOPD that they had him, but he was praying that he would slip through the cracks.

It took the police four days just to process Dump in the system. He was so mentally drained. He just slept for those days on the cement floor. Once he made it to the back and saw the nurse, she put a cast on his hand then sent him to speak with a psychologist.

After he was reviewed, the psychologist diagnosed Dump with post-traumatic depression and paranoid schizophrenia. He didn't understand any of those illnesses, but from Hurricane Katrina up until now, he was exposed to a lot of situations that mentally affected him in many ways.

When they brought him upstairs, they placed him on a medical dorm where they all took meds. Once Dump settled in, to help ease the pain from the pressure, he popped pill after pill after pill after pill, but once each one wore off he was back at ground zero.

One day Dump pills ran dry, so he couldn't get high. He sat on his bunk all day agitated. A dude walked in the cell with another short cocky dude from Acres Homes and asked Dump where he was from.

Dump stood up and asked, "Why the fuck you want to know where I'm from?"

And Dump rushed him. Dump started swinging on him and hitting him over the head with the cast. It dazed dude up, but he shook it off then grabbed Dump, picked him up off his feet, and slammed him on his head. Dump blacked out as the other dude carried Shorty off Dump and out of the cell.

When Dump came back, he shook it off and looked for dude. When he saw him, he tried to approach him, but all his homies held them back and asked them to squash the beef. Dump played it cool, but he had intentions on getting back at him. Dump ran across a piece of steal that he sharpened down into a shank. When Shorty found out, he checked off the dorm. Dump went back to staying high avoiding reality. No matter how much he got high, he could never shake the facts, so in time he fell back off the pills.

One day Dump saw somebody reading the Bible, and a memory flashed back in is head of him hallucinating when he was high reading the Bible by Nicole. He didn't know it, but him spazzing out and being caught for the charge was actually God's way of sparing his life. He had not one but two hits on his head and three hitmen closer on his tail than he knew.

Chapter Twenty-Seven

Eight months dragged by while Dump did time, reading the Bible, understanding God's Word, and drawing closer to Him. Dump didn't interact with many, but he interacted a lot with the Trinity. It seems as if when he made the choice to dig deep into the Bible he stirred the Holy Spirit up inside himself. Little did he know, his actions would bring forth consequences, repercussions and results that would evolve higher than he could ever expect or imagine. His time continued to drag by.

Dump woke up early one morning for court. When he got in the line with the other inmates, they walked through the long tunnels up one and down the others.

As he walked, he talked to God and said, "Thank you, Lord. Every step that I take is a step closer to my freedom. In Jesus's name."

Every time Dump's current situation crossed his mind, he declared it again. Once he made it to the curt docks, he sat down on a concrete slab and waited for his court appointed lawyer. Two hours passed by, and everyone took care of their business with their lawyers. Dump was the last inmate left on the dock.

When Dump's lawyer walked up to the window and sat down, Dump walked up and took a seat on the other side of the glass and asked, "What are they talking about in there this time?"

The lawyer said, "They're willing to break your charge down to simple assault today and sentence you to one year. If you plead guilty, they will give you credit for time served, and you will be released as soon as they finish processing your paperwork."

As Dump looked own with his finger on his chin, thinking about it, the lawyer asked, "So, Mr. Coleman, what are you going to do? Take it or leave it?"

Dump looked up and said, "I'm ah take it."

The lawyer said, "Okay."

And he slid him two papers under the glass window and said, "Sign those."

After he signed them and slid them back, the lawyer said, "I'll be back to bring you in the courtroom to plead out in a minute."

"Yeah, okay," said Dump.

The only thing on his mind was, *I hope Orleans Parish don't come get me.*

He sat there for twenty minutes talking to God until the deputy came through the door, put handcuffs on him, and said, "Let's go."

After Dump pleaded guilty, he went back through tunnels and shot upstairs to the dorm. He packed all his things and waited for them to call his name. Two days passed, and he was still sitting. He knew for sure he was waiting for Orleans Parish because he had a red flag on him.

It was Thursday morning, 12:01.

He was waking up to hearing the guard say on the intercom, "Cage Coleman, pack your shit. ATW."

Dump grabbed his mattress and bag then exited out the dorm into the hallway with the guard. As the guard led him downstairs, he kept hoping Orleans didn't make it to get him. When he got all his paperwork and walked out the exit doors, two New Orleans police officers greeted him.

"Hello, Mr. Coleman. Can you put your hands behind your back please?"

Dump stopped, put his head down, turned around, and felt like God had let him down as the officer cuffed him.

Because of his lack of knowledge, he didn't understand his journey wasn't over yet. God was still preserving him as he was dealing with him, preparing him for his future.

They put Dump in the back of the SUV and hit the highway going toward New Orleans. As Dump looked out the window, he enjoyed looking at civilization once again that he hadn't seen in nine months. To him, the world looked so different. For three hours they rode I-10 in complete silence. The office exited and pulled into Mickey D's and ordered food.

Once Dump finished eating, the officer sitting on the passenger side offered him a cigarette. After eating free-world food, Dump thought smoking a cigarette was icing on the cake. Dump got out the back of the SUV and smoked the cigarette like it was weed, holding the smoke down in his lungs until he had to release it.

At that moment, Dump acknowledged God for blessing him along the way. After they finished smoking, they hit the highway.

When they arrived in New Orleans, Dump heard the officer say, "Welcome home," as he was looking at the Mississippi River Bridge passing up the Super Dome.

Him being there actually made him feel homesick. To him, the city was a battlefield stained with blood of evil and innocent people.

As they pulled down Tulane Avenue, Dump looked at Bulldog Bonds and saw Bulldog standing in the door looking at them pass wearing a smile on his face as Dump booted him up.

Then he heard his voice reply, "You can't run forever."

Dump turned his head and looked at the courts while they passed Orleans Parish Prison. That was when everything he heard about OPP ran wild through his mind, driving him insane on the cool. They pulled up and parked by intake.

The cop on the passenger side got out and walked Dump in central lock-up, took the cuffs off him, turned his paperwork in, looked at him with a smirk, and said, "Good luck."

Dump said, "I'm blessed."

And he walked into a holding tank overloaded with gangsters, drug dealers, robbers, and killers. He walked over to the phone and called Swerv.

Swerv pressed One and said, "Hello."

Dump said, "I'm down here nah."

Swerv said, "That's what's up. I told you that I got chu, nigga."

He said, "Tell Kash and the hitters I said what's up. I'll hit you when I get upstairs."

Swerv said, "Dig. Don't drop the soap."

Then he laughed it off.

The next day they booked Dump for first-degree murder and gave him a bloodred band around his wrist with no bond. Once again, his current status drained him mentally, so for the next two days, he slept on the cement floor.

On Thursday morning they loaded him and two murderers into a van and transported them across the street to OPP. When they pulled up to the gate on Broad Street, they sat and waited for it to open. Dump's mind was dazed up knowing he was about to enter hell on earth.

After the gate opened, they pulled through the alley between OPP on the left and the courthouse on the right. They pulled to the entrance, stopped them and then unloaded them. The green bar door opened, so they walked in the section then the door closed behind them.

Once that door closed, Dump looked at the black glass wall that officers were watching them from behind. As he stared at it, he heard the other bar door open. When they walked in and the door closed behind him, he felt the spirit of death roaming in the building freely.

He walked to the first holding tank and felt chills as he looked up at the wall and read This Is Prison. Dump looked down at his arms and seen the goose bumps. The environment itself had him tensed. They gave him a mattress, package, and an orange jumper then brought him upstairs to B3 on a tier flooded with killers.

When the door opened, he heard an inmate scream, "Roll in!"

Dump walked in and saw everyone looking at him. His face was tight as he walked through to the back looking for an open bunk. Once he found it and put his mat in it, an OG walked over to him and said, "I'm the tier rep. We're locked down for twenty-four hours a day, six days a week. If you have any issues, come holler at me."

Then he walked off.

Dump fixed his bed then hopped in it. When he dozed off, he woke up to someone screaming from being stabbed up in his face.

Dump rose, looked at them, then turned over because it was none of his business.

He prayed, "Father, in the name of Jesus, walk with me through this valley as I trust in you with all my heart. Protect me from my enemies, and have mercy on them. Amen."

He laid there until he dozed off and faded into a dream. As the smoke cleared, while he stood there, he saw Ann walking up to him.

He started to cry and asked, "Mom, why did you leave me out here alone?"

She said, "You're not alone. God and I am with you all the time."

Dump asked, "Then why I go through all this?"

She answered, "I told you before that you were making foolish choices. You put yourself in this position. Be sure that you pay attention."

Then he woke up feeling lost without his mom. To see Ann in his dreams made him happy, but once the dream was over, her death sat in on him heavy. He overheard two young bucks fussing up front for a minute, then it got quiet. One of the dudes walked past Dump's bunk to the back while the other one started back talking shit. Dump seen the dude walk past his bunk back up to the front with a blade in his hand.

Then he heard him say, "Bitch, you doing all that bucking! What's up?"

"What's up!"

The other dude said, "It's cool, my nigga. You got that."

Then turned his back and walked off. That was when dude stabbed him from behind in his neck with the knife then pushed him down and got on top of him, poking the shit out of him. Dump saw another dude run to the front and pulled him off top of him and said, "Here they come," as both of them walked to the back and got in their bunk under the covers.

Dump heard the keys twist in the door and saw the guards walk in and asked, "Which one of you motherfuckers got him leaking?"

One of the guards walked dude out covered in blood while he held a bloodied white towel on his neck, while the other guard walked through the tier looking for anyone looking suspicious. Dump put his cover over his head as he left.

The next day Dump called Swerv and told him his inmate number and his location. He asked Swerv for Kash's information so he could write her. Swerv gave it to him and told him to stay focused. He asked Swerv to find him a lawyer. Swerv told him that his money was still tied up with Kash.

Dump said, "I understand." After that, the call ended.

A few months blew by, and Dump was called out for court. The judge appointed him a state lawyer named Peter Mavrik.

After the session, Peter came to jail to visit Dump.

He asked Peter, "What am I facing on this charge?"

Peter replied, "With first-degree murder, here in the State of Louisiana, if you're found guilty, a life sentence is mandatory. On the other hand, you are eligible for the death penalty by lethal injection."

Dump said, "I didn't commit any murder."

Peter said, "Mr. Coleman, I understand that, but this is a process. Do you know that they're saying that they have a witness?"

Dump said, "I don't know what they have as far as a witness. All I know is, I'm innocent."

Pete asked, "Are you willing to take a lie detector test?"

Dump was like, "Yes. But I don't trust lie detector test. If it is wrong and they say I failed, I'm gone forever."

Peter looked at Dump as if he felt as though he was avoiding the test for a reason. Dump didn't give two fucks about how the lawyer felt; he just wanted to get out of jail.

Dump asked Peter, "Can you bring me a copy of my police report when you come to visit me next time?"

Peter said, "I'm going to file a motion for evidence. After I do that, I'll bring it to you."

Dump said, "Okay."

Peter replied, "While you're back there, stay out of trouble. If you have to go to trial, it will help you out a lot."

Then he gave Dump a hand shake and left out the room. Dump was escorted back to the tier. He looked out the window and saw B1 out on the yard. When Dump went to checking the inmates out, he saw Da-Da on the side of the basketball court. Because of the fact that they grew up together, he was happy to see him, but the thought of him murdering Nelly and Marsha produced the feeling of resentment toward him. Dump banged on the window and hollered at him, but after that, they never interacted again.

Two months came and went as Dump studied the Bible and prayed to God in Jesus's name on a regular basis as majority of the other inmates were jacked, jumped, stabbed, roped, or convicted. He continued to isolate himself from every negative person, conversation, or thought. Dump actually began to trust nobody but God. Other inmates hated him because he stayed in that Book every day. Not only that, they had no opportunity to cross him or involve him in their ignorant bullshit.

On the third month, Pee came to visit Dump and gave him the police report.

Dump sat down and asked, "What's our next move?"

Peter asked, "Do you have any prior convictions?"

He answered, "No. I don't."

Peter said, "Okay. That helps. I am going to have my private investigator go to the Federal facility to question their so-called witness to see where she stands. She is a convicted felon so that can be used to discredit her testimony."

Dump said, "When the murder happened, she was locked up. How in the hell could she be a witness?"

Peter said, "The report will break it down to you, but we're going to get to the bottom of it."

Dump said, "Okay. I'm waiting on y'all."

Peter gave him a handshake and said, "I'll be back."

Dump went back to the tier. Later that night he wrote Kash a letter letting her how he felt about her and their situations and sent it to her wondering what her response would be.

Four days later Kash was on her tier, and they called her name for mail. When she looked at the envelope and saw it was from Dump, she smiled from ear to ear and told the other female inmates all about how he was coming out there heavy behind her and Swerv and how Bird play it.

She walked to her cell, laid on her bunk with one of her home girls, and read the letter.

When she finished reading it, she looked at her girl and said, "Girl, that nigga solid."

"Bitch, why would your mom play it like that?"

Kash said, "She cutthroat. If it wasn't for her, we would both be fucking free."

Later on that night when Kash was in her bed alone, she read it again and caught something he was pitching in between the lines. When she wrote him back, she touched every base he had been waiting for. She held back no secrets and sent him a picture along with it.

Back in OPP, Dump was on the tier in his bunk going over his police report. He found out that Bird called the police and used the information that she got from watching Yogi's murder on the videotape to lie to the laws and said that he told her exactly what he did and how he did it. They had no idea that she watched the video, so they figured the only way she could know so much intel was the suspect had to tell her. Therefore, they issued a warrant.

Five months passed by, and Dump was still trusting God to give him another chance at being free, but with everything stacked against him, it wasn't looking good. He knew that he was fighting against a life sentence, so he made sure his faith in God outweighed it.

He received a letter from Kash. When he sat back and read it, it shined light on his situation. By him sitting in jail, he used to think that he made a mistake going dumb for her, but obviously, the letter proved him wrong.

As he looked at her pictures, he heard the guard say, "Cage Coleman, get dressed, you have a visit!"

When he walked in the visitation room, Peter was sitting there. When he sat down, Peter said, "How has everything been?"

He said, "Tell me something good."

"Well, my private investigator went to Mississippi and spoken with Ms. Bird. The story she told him does not match what she told the detective. She also said that she will not testify. Now one of our only problems is the videotape.

Dump said, "That videotape is blurry. They can't see the guy's face, but it resembles me, they say. Will that hurt me or help me?"

Peter said, "I'm not sure if they will use it. We will handle that when we get to it. Did you know that she wore a wire to try to bust you with using the rule 35?"

He said, "You serious? A wire? And what the hell is a rule 35?"

Peter said, "Never mind it. I'll see you at court next week. She's supposed to be down here. If she's not, they will set your court date back."

Dump said, "Okay."

Then he stood up and walked out.

On the court date, Swerv told Dump that Bird was in the New Orleans jail, but she refused to testify for them. He sat on the docks for five hours, but they never called him in. They just reset his court date and sent him back to OPP.

That night Dump got on his knees to pray and made a covenant with God.

He said, "God, in the name of your darling son, Jesus Christ, forgive me for my sins. By his blood, I ask you, Lord, to free me from this place. If you free me Father, I will not hurt innocent people, I won't sell drugs anymore, and I will find a woman, marry her, and have children. I will forever praise your name."

Two weeks after that he received a letter from Bird saying that she was sorry and she still love him. She also asked him to forgive her. She also asked him to forgive her. He didn't really want to write her back, but because of his situation and her actions, he did. He let her know that he forgave her and love her as well.

Dump started paying more attention to everything like Ann told him in his dream. He knew one guy that was fighting a murder charge for four years, another one been fighting for five years and another for eight. He wasn't built for that process. When Peter came to visit him, he sat down and got straight to the point.

"Look, Mr. Maverick, I'm not waiting for them to prolong this situation. Either they have me, or they don't."

Peter asked, "Hold up. What do you mean?"

Dump said, "File for a speedy trial."

Peter said, "Cage, that is not a good idea. You're not ready for trial."

He said, "Peter, I don't work for you. You work for me. *File for a speedy trial now!*"

Peter looked at him with an impressed look and said, "Okay, Mr. Coleman."

Dump said, "Thank you. I appreciate it."

Then he walked out.

Two months later Dump went to court for a speedy trial, and the district attorney, Leon Canahoe, wasn't prepared, so they had no choice but to release him from OPP. Peter was shocked because not many inmates in his position took that route. Dump wasn't surprised, because he trusted God. He realized that even though he believed in Him, God showed him. He was real and more powerful than any situation he ever dealt with. When he made it back to B3, he packed his shit up and played his bunk until they called his name at 12:01 a.m.

"Cage Coleman, ATW! ATW!"

He grabbed the mat and bag then dipped out, feeling brand-new.

Chapter Twenty-Eight

Dump walked out the building, looked up to the stars, and said, "Thank you, Lord."

Then he started walking up to the dark street. He looked around to make sure nobody was lurking waiting to move one him. He noticed a black Grand Am behind him approaching slowly with dark tinted windows. Dump's heart was pounding. A part of him was ready to run. The other half made him keep it cool as he kept strolling. After the car passed him, Dump picked up his pace to make it to a well-lit area. When he made it to Tulane and Broad Street, he walked in the corner store, bought a pack of cigarettes, then called Swerv.

"Hello."

Dump said, "What's up, ya pussy bitch?"

Swerv asked, "What's up?"

He said, "I'm out the hole. Come scoop me."

Swerv said, "I'm on my way."

Swerv pulled up on Dump, sitting down, smoking a cigarette.

He rolled the tinted windows down and said, "Come on!"

Dump hopped up, smiling, bucking, and said, "Yo, I told you them bitches can't hold me forever, nigga!"

Swerv grinned and said, "Hurry up, bitch. You know it's hot around here."

Dump said, "Fuck all that! I'm back like cooked crack! What's up?"

Swerv said, "I'm chilling. Welcome home. I told ya you were gone beat it."

Dump said, "Thank God."

Swerv said, "Now you're speaking my language."

He said, "What you mean?"

Swerv answered, "I'm not fucking with these streets no more. I read the Word, go to church, and take care of my family."

Dump looked at him with a serious face and said, "That's a big step for you round."

Swerv said, "You need to join me."

Dump looked out the window at the city and said, "Bet."

Swerv turned up the radio and jumped on I-10 East. Dump continued to look out the window as his mind drifted back into his old ways thinking about how he needed fast money since he was free. He didn't realize the devil was tempting him to pull him away from under the wings of an angel who has been protecting him.

As they pulled up to the apartments, memories of him and Bird's relationship flashed in his mind, and it made him sick to his stomach. Swerv parked and looked over at him. He could tell something was on Dump's mind, but he didn't ask any questions. They got out and went into the spot.

Swerv tossed Dump a comforter and a pillow then said, "I'm ah fuck with you in the morning."

He said, "Dig."

Once again he was free, lying on his back, looking at the ceiling, thinking about his next move.

As the days went by, he started running into the old click. He and Swerv were at a car wash on Chef Mature Highway talking to Geezy when Big Lips and Roy pulled up in a cherry-red Corvette and hopped out.

Big Lips said, "Oh shit. I heard you was home."

Dump said, "What's good?"

Roy said, "Real niggas back!"

Big Lips said, "It's going down tonight. My birthday party is at the Chocolate Bar. If y'all not in the building, y'all dead out here."

Swerv asked Dump, "You fucking with that?"

Dump said, "I'm fucking with that."

They all burned out.

It was 9:30 p.m., and Swerv was in his room, getting ready for the club. Dump and Geezy was in the living room talking about his Jose in OPP.

Geezy asked, "You ain't have to poke nothing in that place?"

"Yeah. I had to touch one, but I was on some other shit."

Geezy asked, "Other shit?"

Dump said, "Yeah. Learning about God. He the reason I'm free."

Geezy said, "Yeah, I feel that, but these streets missed you, my nigga."

Dump looked at him and said, "The streets don't miss shit but blood when it ain't spilled."

Geezy said, "Real... Realla shit!"

Swerv walked out and asked, "How this look?"

They busted out laughing.

Dump said, "If you don't sit cho duck ass down boy."

Geezy said, "You straight."

They heard a knock at the door.

"Who's that?" Geezy asked.

"Roy!" Dump opened the door.

Big Lips walked in with Roy behind him and asked, "Y'all ready?"

Swerv said, "Yeah. Let's go."

They all shot to Mid-City to meet with the rest of the click at the club and went dumb in the VIP section. Dump walked through the club on his way to the restroom and saw a tall, slim, super sexy yellow bone standing by the bar with a gap between her legs like parentheses in a pair of red six-inch stilettos matching her skin tight dress.

When he made eye contact with her hazel-brown eyes, he knew he had to have her. After he used the restroom, he walked up to the bar and ordered a drink as he waited to make eye contact with her again, but she never looked. She and her girls started to walk toward him.

When they were walking past, he said, "Excuse me, baby."

She stopped and told her girls to hold up.

He asked, "What's your name?"

She looked Dump up and down then said, "Ra-Ra. And you are?

"Dump," he replied then asked, "You want a drink?"

She said, "No. I'm good. What's up?"

"You—shit, you smoking in this bitch. Ya hair like yeah. Face beat right like ah nigga like."

She started blushing as she smiled.

He asked, "What's ya number so I can get at cha?"

She held her hand out and asked, "Where's ya phone?"

He gave it to her; she put it in his phone and saved it, then leaned over, putting her hand on his shoulder and kissed him on his cheek as his hand was on her side, then they walked of.

Dump walked in the VIP section by Swerv and asked Dump, "Damn, where my drink at?"

Dump said, "At the bar."

Swerv leaned over, squinting his eyes at him, and said, "You got lipstick on your face, huh. Who kissed on your ass?"

Dump took a paper towel, wiping it off as he said, "A bad bitch."

Big Lips said, "Oh yeee?"

Dump looked through the club and pointed her out.

Roy said, "Yeah, she hot."

They kicked back, ordered some more drinks, and blew gar after gar. Dump was twisted, so he sat on the couch. Roy, Swerv, and Big Lips were lit bouncing to the DJ doing his thing. As Dump sat back checking everything out, he saw Ra-Ra on the dance floor with her girls winding her body.

He could tell by her motion that she could ride him right. She looked up and saw him staring at her, so she thought she would give him a show. She turned around and bounced that ass to the beat, dropped it down low, then she stood up and made that ass clap for him.

Swerv looked at Dump then pointed his finger at her and said, "Oh boy!"

Dump stood up and said, "I'm gone bend her ass up."

Big Lips said, "If I was you, I would too."

It was no secret; she was on Dump's list to fuck, and it was almost obvious that she was willing. He just had to play it right. Once the night was over, the click split up.

When Dump made it to the apartment, he crashed. When he was deep in his sleep, he began to dream that he was at a dice game with Turtle, O-Head, Willie, and Big Homie in an unfamiliar living room. They all had a fistful of hundreds.

Dump bent over, picked up the dice, and said, "One hunnit on sixes, two hunnit eights."

As he shook them, Big Homie said, "Don't shot the dice."

Dump said, "Fuck all that. Put cha money up."

All of them dropped a grip, and he rolled the dice. After they hit the wall and stopped flipping, Turtle looked at them and said, "Snake eyes!"

Dump said, "Ain't that some shit," and dropped his cash.

Knock, knock, knock!

Dump walked to the door and opened it. There he saw a triangle barrel blaze in his face."

Dump was spooked out of his dream. He sat up on the sofa and lit a cigarette as he gathered his thoughts; he couldn't understand the dream. After he finished smoking the joe, he lay back down and fell back asleep, but he slept light like walking on eggshells.

Things started to move fast in Dump's life again. He kind of lost focus since he was released from OPP. In Orleans Parish Prison, he was secluded from the world and its activities, so he didn't have many distractions from his relationship with Jesus, but he knew because of the homies, women, needs, and streets, he was beginning to stumble. He remembered his covenant with God at the moment. On the other hand, Dump foolishly began to relapse into his old ways without noticing it.

One day Dump hooked up with Ra-Ra, and they went by Swerv to kick it. She was enjoying their conversation smiling as he kept cracking jokes. Deep inside, she knew that his plan was to have sex, but that didn't bother her because she was used to getting that from guys.

As they sat on the couch, Dump asked, "Are you hungry?"

She replied, "Yes."

He called Swerv and said, "Come here!"

Swerv walked over, "What's up?"

Dump said, "Shorty hungry. She want a plate."

Swerv looked at her, smiling, showing his ten golds, and asked, "What kind do you want?"

She asked, "What kind do you have?"

"Um…hot sausage with fries, hamburger, chicken wings, and chili and cheese nachos."

She replied, "Give me the chicken with fries."

He told Dump, "That's $4.50," and walked to the kitchen.

Dump busted out laughing and said, "Dig! Put it on my tab!"

Swerv said, "Oh no, boy, gimme!"

And they both laughed while she looked at them, smiling.

She asked Dump, "How old are you?"

Dump said, "Old enough to be ya daddy."

As he put his arm around her, she smacked him on his chest, laughed, and said, "Boy, don't play with me."

As they continued to communicate, Dump started to rub on her legs. Her face froze stale.

"So I see you're getting too comfortable."

Dump was like, "I be on some real shit. If I'm feeling you, I don't hold back."

She said, "Me either, but we just met?"

He said, "That's true. But is it wrong for me to be into you?"

Ra-Ra answered, "No."

"Well, let's move forward without boundaries," Dump suggested.

She said, "I don't know."

Swerv walked in with the plate and said, "Four fifty."

Dump went in his pocket, peeled off five, and as he handed it to him, he told him, "Keep the change, woa."

Swerv said, "Fifty cent. Oh, thank you," being sarcastic.

When Ra-Ra finished eating her plate, Dump got up and said, "Come on. Let's go in the room."

She stood up and followed him to the back. They walked in and he closed the door behind them.

Dump laid in the bed and said, "Come here."

She got in the bed and lay in his arms. Dump grabbed the remote and turned the TV on and told her how he liked what she was wearing in the club. Ra-Ra told him that she always switched her style because she was a model.

He said "Yeah. In those heels, I could tell you walk like a model."

She grinned and said, "Practice makes perfect."

He said, "That's how I became perfect with my tongue, practice."

It caught her off guard. Ra-Ra said nothing because she didn't know how to respond.

He looked at her and asked, "Are you perfect with your tongue?"

She looked shocked. He could tell she was in a jam and didn't know how to answer, so he just kept quiet, looking at her, applying pressure for her to answer.

She knew the correct answer would open up a door she wasn't ready to open, but she couldn't lie.

"Yes. I'm a pro with it," she replied.

Dump said, "With those lips, you look like it."

She said, "You pay attention to everything."

"I do, but you should pay attention to this," he said as he kissed her on the neck, slightly biting on her jugular vein, sending chills down her spine to her toes.

Dump looked at her nipples poking through her shirt and slid his hand under it playing with them as he climbed on top sliding down to her stomach. Dump put his face between her legs as he opened his mouth on her pants by her pussy and blew his hot breath on it through the material twice making it warm.

After that, he unbuttoned her pants as she was attempting to refuse him; he was persistent with it. That turned her on even more, making her want it.

Dump got up on his knees and pulled her pants off, looking at her lace rose-colored boy shorts wet by the split.

He said, "Damn, you're dripping."

Then he pulled them to the side and licked his tongue between the lips up against her clit. He started making love to the pussy with his mouth. It started to get so good she couldn't take it. She began to try to crawl away from him, but he had both legs interlocked with his arms. Dump began to apply pressure that she had no choice but to enjoy.

After she nutted in his mouth, he came up and tried to put his dick in.

She stopped him, pushed him back off her, and said, "Wait. No... What are you doing?"

He answered, "What?"

She said, "Put a condom on."

He said, "I just ate you. What sense it makes to put a rubber on?"

She said, "Because I said so."

He saw that she was serious, so he got up, grabbed one out the drawer, and asked, "Suck it for me to rock it up."

Once she did, he put it on then got on top. Once he worked it in and she loosened up, he pinned her legs back, looking her in her beautiful eyes as he pounded her perfectly while she bit her bottom lip, grabbing the sheets. Dump was about to cum, so he stopped. After the feeling of the nut went away, he charged back up.

He let her legs down and laid her on her side. Dump then laid behind her, stroking her slow for a second. Then he saw she was enjoying it, so he lifted her right leg in the air and started back-pounding it. When she started feeling Dump getting harder, she knew he was about to cum. He started hitting it faster as she moaned.

She told him, "Don't stop."

That turned him on, making him skeet. When he pulled out, she turned over and tongue-kissed him, then they laid there, replaying it in their minds.

About an hour had passed, and they ended up having a brief conversation. He told her that he had just come home from jail. She told him that she had a boyfriend and she was attending college. She also told him that she worked for the city. He told her that he used to be heavy in the streets and stayed into ill shit.

She asked, "Would you like to go with me to get a tattoo?"

He said, "That's cool. Just let me know when you ready."

She said, "Okay. I got to pick up my daughter. I'll give you a call."

"Okay."

She got up, put on her clothes, and dipped out.

The next day Dump woke up with money on his mind. He saw that his money was getting lower and lower each day. He decided to go for a ride to clear his mind, so he asked Swerv for the ride.

When he gave him the keys, he told him to be careful.

Dump said, "Okay," and burned out on the east side.

He drove down Lakeforest and turned right on Crowder then pulled into the gas station and parked by the pump, counted his money, then hopped out. When he looked up to the sky, he realized it was a beautiful day. The sun was beaming over the puffy bright-white clouds. The breeze was perfect as the birds were chirping. He walked into the spot, paid for gas, and walked out to the car. When he popped open the gas cap and put the nozzle in, a black range Rover Sport pulled up to the pump behind him with the music beating hard. It sat there for a minute until he finished pumping his gas.

When he closed the tank and put the handle back on the rack, he heard the music beat louder and a voice say, "What's up, lil homie?"

Dump turned around and saw Big Homie getting out the truck dressed in all black with diamonds shinning from his ears to his neck down to his wrist.

He said, "Damn, Big Homie, where the fuck you been hiding?"

Big Homie chuckled and said, "I just got out the Feds, nigga."

Then Dump asked, "How long you been down?"

Big Home replied, "Ten years."

Dump said, "Welcome home. What's been up wit' cha?"

"Shit. You know me, lil homie. I'm out here baking a cake."

Dump said, "Dig."

Big Homie said, "Don't nothing move but the money. How you living?"

Dump said, "I just got out OPP a few weeks ago. Right now, I need to get my bread up."

Big Homie said, "I got something for ya."

Dump said, "Oh yeah?"

He told him, "When I come out this bitch, follow me."

Dump was like, "Bet."

Then he hopped in the Monte Carlo and cranked it back up. Big Homie walked in the gas station and walked back out. A passenger got out the Rover, pumped the gas, then hopped back in, and the Rover swerved from behind him, exiting the gas station as Dump followed them.

Big Homie turned right onto Crowder, went through the light under the bridge, then turned right on the service road. He drove a half a mile down then made a left into the Dead End hood. They pulled up to a white brick house in front of the garage and got out the truck.

Dump parked, walked over to them, and gave Big Homie dap. As they walked up the door, Dump looked, and he saw a camera on the neighbor's house pointing in their direction.

He didn't know if Big Homie ever noticed it so when they sat down at the table, he brought it up. "My nigga, did you know the camera on the house next door is pointing over here."

Big Homie answered, "Yeah. That bitch nosy."

Dump said, "That shit illegal."

"Three months ago we had a shootout on the block with some niggas, and a couple of bullets hit her house, so she put cameras up on some snitch shit," he said.

Dump asked, "You cool with that?"

He chuckled and said, "Be honest."

Then he got up, opened the kitchen cabinet, pulled out a black bag, then sat it on the table. At that point all Dump saw was a money bag. He forgot about the covenant he made with God that actually was the reason that he was free.

Big Homie asked, "Do you know anything about heroin?"

Dump said, "Not really."

Big Homie looked at O-Head then looked back at Dump and said, "Well, this what it's hitting for."

He opened the bag. He pulled out a bundle.

"This that dog food. If they fuck with it, they need it early in the morning as soon as they wake up. If they don't get it, they'll be sick and unable to operate. The first bag won't get 'em high. It only kills the sickness. Their next move is to get their money up to get another bag for the fix."

Big Homie held the bundle up in his hand and said, "This raw shit have them motherfuckers hitting ya line all day."

Big Homie opened the pack and pulled out a gram as Turtle walked in the kitchen and said, "A gram go for a hundred."

He gave it to Dump and said, "See what you can do with that. Bring me back fifty."

Dump said, "I got cha."

Turtle asked Dump, "What's up?"

"I'm cooling. What's happening with you?" Dump asked as Turtle dug in his pocket and pulled out a shitload of cash and said, "Out here grinding to get it, my nigga."

He went to counting the twenties and sitting them on the table. After every stack, Big Homie picked it up and counted it. After Big Homie counted the six thousand, he put rubber bands on each stack and placed the money in the bag. Then pulled out four ounces, handed them to Turtle, and said, "Bring me back twelve."

Turtle gave him dap, looked at Dump, and told him, "I'm ah fuck wit' cha, nigga. Be easy."

Dump said, "Dig. Fuck with me."

And Turtle walked out. Big Homie gave O-Head the bag and told him to put it up.

Dump stood up. "I'm about to dip. I'm ah holla back at ya."

He gave O-Head dap and Big Homie a fist pound then left.

Dump hopped in the car and stashed the dope in the ceiling and peeled out. He drove to the end of the street and turned left. There he saw a guy pull out a gun on another and open fire as the other dude tried to run, but his legs gave out. Dump made a right and got out the area quick. It was actually a message he needed to pay attention to, but he paid it no mind. All Dump seen was an opportunity.

O-Head sat down with Big Homie and said, "I know you fuck with hood, but I heard some shit about Dump. You need to watch that nigga."

Big Homie asked, "What chu mean?"

O-Head replied, "He's unstoppable. Ain't no telling what he'll do."

"Oh yeah?" Big Homie said. "When homie was growing up, he wasn't on that type of time."

O-Head said, "Yeah, I know, but when your ass was locked up, he started robbing motherfuckers, snorting coke, popping pills, and murking shit. When he was growing up, we was crossing him every chance we got, so I don't trust him. And I don't think you should either."

Big Homie said, "All right." Then he thought to himself, *The sickest mind games win.*

Willie walked in the front door.

O-Head yelled, "Who dat?"

Willie said, "Woop."

O-Head said, "Lock that door!"

Willie locked it then walked in the kitchen and asked, "What's going down?"

Big Homie said, "I don't know, but the money going up. What cha look like?"

Willie dug in his pockets and said, "My shit right."

And he pulled out two knots in rubber bands then tossed them on the table.

Big Homie chuckled and said, "Double up."

Willie went in his back pocket, pulled out another knot, and said, "This all me right here, homie."

Big Homie counted the money and went to the back. He come back to the kitchen with three ounces, gave them to Willie, and said, "Bring me nine."

Willie went back in his pocket, tossed Big Homie the knot, and said, "That's three, so I owe you six."

Big Homie thought to himself, *You would be doing much better if you bought your own work and didn't owe me shit.* And he smiled.

Willie said, "What's funny?"

Big Homie said, "Nothing. I'm 'bout to make a few runs. I'm ah fuck wit' cha later."

Willie said, "Get at me."

Chapter Twenty-Nine

Dump was cruising on Lake Pontchichrain as the sun was setting while it was glistening off the water under the burnt orange sky without a cloud in sight. Dump pulled into the parking lot and hopped out to enjoy the view. His mind started to wonder while he was sitting on the trunk. He looked back at his life and realized how far he came through a struggle. He knew since he was a teenager he always wanted to be a gangster. The older he got the wilder he became. Once the city thought, saw, and heard about him on the news finally stamped him as a gangster. When he realized he had reached that level, he paid more attention to the game and recognized that most of the dudes he thought were gangsters were actually great pretenders selling dreams to anybody that would buy them.

It made his blood start to boil, then his phone rang.

He answered it, "Ra-Ra, tell me something good."

She said, "My pussy."

He laughed.

She said, "I'm just playing. I'm going to the tattoo shop tonight. Are you coming?"

"Yeah."

She said, "I'll call you after I get ready."

Dump said, "Okay."

Then he got in the car, backed out, and pulled off.

Later on that night when Dump was back at the crib Ra-Ra called and asked, "Are you ready?"

He said, "I stay ready."

"Do you want to meet me up there or do I have to come pick you up?" Ra-Ra asked.

He said, "Come slid through."

She said, "Okay. I'll be there."

Dump told her, "All right." And he hung up.

Swerv walked in the apartment and asked him for the keys.

When he gave them to him, Dump said, "Picture I seen a nigga get hit up in Dead End."

Swerv said, "That's why I told you to be careful man. Every day niggas getting killed out here. I'm going to church tomorrow. You should come."

Dump replied, "I'm in there."

Swerv said, "Cool." And he left.

He sat on the sofa and waited for Ra-Ra to call.

Fifteen minutes later, she hit the line, "What are you doing?"

He responded, "I'm waiting for you."

She said, "I'm out front."

"Okay. I'll be out there."

Dump took the dope out his pocket, stashed it in one of his shoes, and walked out. When he got in the car, she was cheesed up smiling from ear to ear.

He asked, "What's good?"

She said, "This mouth. No, I'm just playing."

"No. You ain't playing. Ya shit is off the chain."

She asked, "You ready?"

He said, "Yeah. Let's roll."

She turned the radio up and shot straight to the spot.

"Damn, this bitch packed." Dump noticed as soon as he and Ra-Ra walked into the tattoo shop.

Ra-Ra said, "It's always packed."

He asked, "What chu getting?"

"Something on my lower back."

He said, "That's a perfect spot for my name."

She laughed at him and said, "We must be getting married."

He asked, "You think your man gone be cool with that?"

"Oh, you got jokes."

He told her, "Nah. I'm really fucking with cha."

Ra-Ra was like, "I don't know. I've been thinking about ending that relationship. I just want to be sure I make the right choice."

"Why you been thinking of ending it?"

He said, "I don't trust him."

Dump thought to himself, *Shit, from the looks of it, he shouldn't be trusting you.*

And he said, "I feel that."

She was so beautiful, sexy, and cool to him. Dump was willing to start a relationship with her even though she was cheating on her man.

She asked, "Are you getting something?"

He said, "I might."

She rubbed his fore arm and said, "My name ah be good right here."

He said, "Girl, stop."

She asked, "What?"

"You got jokes." He laughed it off then said, "We must be getting married."

She busted out laughing and said, "If you play your cards right."

He said, "Royal flush over here."

Ra-Ra's phone rung. She looked at it and saw it was her man, so she held up her index finger to Dump then stood up and walked off with the phone to her ear. Dump got up and started looking at the artwork thinking about what he could get tatted on him. He looked to the left and saw nothing that he liked. Then he looked up and still seen nothing interesting. When he looked to the right, he saw a section with any crosses with different designs that caught his attention.

What God did for him crossed his mind. He realized that all his tattoos told true stories that represented his character and situation he dealt with. Dump wasn't proud of his history, so he figured he would get a tattoo of something that was worth representing. He had remembered hearing a preacher say that there would come a point in time where people would ask others if they believed in Christ, and if they'd say yes, they would kill them. He appreciated what God did for him releasing him from jail on the first-degree murder charge he decided to get two crosses one on each temple with the color red on the tips of the crosses to represent His Blood.

That way his purpose for the tattoo was to ask them not to have to ask him do he believed. When they saw his face, they would see Christ. At that moment, his spirit was connected to His Spirit, but his flesh was back bound in lust for sex, drugs, and money taking him from under His umbrella. It was sad to say it, but he didn't even know it. The tattoo artist called Ra-Ra. Dump walked to the door and stuck his head out looking for her. He saw she was fussing on her phone. He waved his hand and caught her attention letting her know it was her turn. She nodded. He walked back to the back and told them that she was coming in. Then he walked to the front desk and told them he wanted to be tatted.

While Ra-Ra was sitting in the chair with the back of it between her legs busted open Dump was sitting in a chair across from her watching her face frown up from the pain looking at him as he smiled. When they finished, he told her to go to Lake Pontchatrain.

She took the back way to duck her man. Dump caught on to it but didn't say nothing. She pulled up to the lake, and they both hopped out.

Dump sat on the hood. She walked over to him and stood between his legs. They were the only two in the area. Dump put his arms around her as they looked up to the moon and stars.

She said, "The moon is beautiful."

He asked, "Do you understand why our city is nicknamed Crescent City, after that moon?"

She replied, "No. Why?"

He said, "The moon which is one of the brightest lights in the world is covered with 90 percent of darkness. Only left with 10 percent of the light shining. That represent the city. Good people are rare to find, while evil people, place, and things flourish, stamping New Orleans as the murder capital."

She said, "Wow, I never thought of it that way. You're smarter that I thought."

She turned around and kissed him. He stood up as he tongued her down. She grabbed his dick and made it hard. He made her face the car and got behind her. That was when he raised her skirt.

She stopped him from putting his dick in and said, "Put on a condom," so he did.

After that, he bent her over and fucked her as they heard the waves splashing on the concrete stairs while he looked at the stars twinkle.

He said, "I'm about to cum."

She said, "Me too, daddy."

He waited for her to nut, and when she did, he skeeted too and said, "I wanted to bust inside of you."

She took her wet panties off then gave them to him and said, "Happy birthday."

He laughed and smelled them then put them in his pocket. After that moment, he fell in love with her. The only thing Ra-Ra loved about their situation was the rush she felt from cheating with him.

Three weeks later Dump met Big Homie at his ducked off spot.

When he walked in, Big Homie hollered from the living room, "Lock the door, son!"

Dump did that then walked in on Big Homie, sitting in front of his fireplace on white leather couch with stacks of fifties and hundreds by his side.

He asked Dump, "The game treating you good, huh?"

Dump said, "Yeah. That dog food got them itching."

Big Homie said, "The streets talking nigga. I think you should slow down a lil bit. Nigga seen you serving dope fiends downtown then turn around and see you uptown doing the same shit. I'm gone need you to park that ride and chill for a minute."

It made Dump a little uncomfortable to know that someone was watching him and reporting how he moved.

He said, "I got cha."

Then he gave Big Homie three thousand dollars and said, "I need an ounce."

Big Homie counted the money then gave him two. He didn't want to take the front, but out of respect for Big Homie, he did.

When he made it back by Swerv, he did the math off his ounce; he cleared six thousand off the ounce Big Homie gave him he would clear three thousand and owe him three thousand. He went and laid up in the bed and watched television.

Dump heard Swerv's phone ringing. He grabbed the remote and started flicking through the channels. Swerv walked in the room, handing him the phone.

He asked, "Who's dat."

When he grabbed it, Swerv didn't respond; he just walked out.

Dump put the phone to his ear and said, "Hello."

Bird said, "Hey, baby!"

He said, "What's up, luv?"

She said, "I see you made it home, huh."

Dump said, "Yeah. Quicker than I thought."

She said, "They bought me down there to testify, but I killed that."

Dump thought, *You shouldn't have put me in that situation in the first place.* Then he said, "I appreciate that."

She said, "No problem."

Dump asked, "So when you get out?"

"In four months."

He thought to himself, *I need to be far away from here when she gets out.*

She asked, "Do you still love me?"

He lied and said, "Yes," just to keep her in her place.

She said, "I love you too." Then she asked, "Where Swerv at?"

He yelled, "Oh, Swerv!"

When he walked in the room, smiling, Dump hit him with a stale face, passing him the phone, poking his lips out. Swerv knew that Dump had no respect for her and had no plans on dealing with her because of her actions. He put the phone to his ear, walked out, and said, "Hello."

She asked, "How long he been out?"

He said, "He been out here a lil minute."

She asked, "Why do you have him there?"

Swerv said, "What you mean?"

She said, "Never mind. Just watch him."

He said, "He never did me shit. But okay."

Bird said, "I'll call you back."

She felt resentful because of the fact Swerv wasn't mindful of her intentions. Swerv walked in the room and was like, "You know I fucks wit' cha, my nigga. She still on some other shit asking me why are you over here."

Dump said, "I already know how she coming. I'm ah dip before she touch down. I don't trust her one bit."

Swerv shook his head and walked out.

Dump thought to himself, *That bitch set me up to go to jail, but she went to jail before me, and I got out before her.*

Then he smiled and said, "Stupid bitch."

Swerv said, "Huh?"

Dump replied, "Nothing?"

He positioned himself on his back and looked at ceiling and felt the room get colder.

Dump phone rang. When he looked, he saw it was Big Homie. He just let it ring because his mind was twisted at the moment. When he calmed down he hit him back.

"Hello."

Dump responded, "What's up, Big Homie?"

"Come swing on me."

He said, "Give me a sec. I'm ah slide through."

Big Homie said, "Bet."

Swerv and Dump were in the living room for a minute, talking. Dump had been keeping him selling dope a secret. A part of him wanted to tell him, but he knew Swerv didn't want nothing to do with the game. Swerv never brought it up, but he knew he was into something because he was always pulling out knots of cash. Dump told him that he was about to start looking for a spot of his own. Swerv told him he understood.

Dump said, "I'm about to make a run. I'll fuck with you when I get back."

Swerv said, "Cool. Be careful."

Dump walked out the door to the crib, called Big Homie, and asked, "Are you still at the spot?"

"Yeah. I'm here."

Dump said, "I'm on my way."

Big Homie told him, "Alright."

He got in the car, stashed his dope, and made a few dope sales on his way to the spot. It seemed like after every drop, he ran across the cops in the areas. That didn't even spook him. He was so addicted to making money that he didn't give a fuck about the police being hot. He pulled up to Big Homie's spot, parked, then walked up to the door and knocked.

Big Homie hollered, "It's open."

When he walked in, he locked the door behind himself then took a seat in the living room in front of the flat screen television.

About ten minutes passed, then he heard Big Homie coming down the stairs. When he walked in the living room, he asked Dump, "What's up, lil nigga?"

Dump said, "You know what it is. Same shit just a different day. What's up with chu?"

Big Homie said, "I'm about to slide the long way and make a couple of plays. I'm ah be gone for a few days. Do you want me to leave you with something in case you be done before I get back or what?"

Dump dope was moving fast, so he said, "Yeah."

Big Homie said, "Hold up."

Then he walked in the kitchen, opened the cabinet, pulled out a block of heroin, pulled up a stool to the counter, sat down, opened the drawer, pulled out a scale, weighed a few ounces then brought Dump two. Dump gave him fifteen hundred of the three thousand he owed him and said, "I owe you seven five."

Big Homie said, "Yes."

They talked for a minute then Dump tucked the dope in the trunk under the spare tire and left.

Dump decided to pass through Dead End and spin by to see if O-Head and the other homies from Press Park was around. When he pulled up he saw a couple of whips parked in the driveway, so he stopped, got out and walked through the cut to the side door.

When he made it through, the cut he saw O-Head, M5, Willie, Turtle, Joey, and O-Shay, talking ill shit shooting dice while Little Bee, Young Shaq, and Lil Dee smoke weed and watched them.

Turtle looked up and saw Dump then said, "Look who den popped up."

O'Shay said, "What's up, nigga?" as he bent over and rolled the dice.

Dump said, "What it do?"

Willie gave him dap and said, "You know we out her getting it. I heard you out here in these streets trapping."

Dump told him, "Don't nothing move but the money, baby." Dump looked at the money on the ground and in their hands and said, "Fuck, I see y'all niggas out here getting it."

O'Shay hit his point and said, "Blows."

Turtle said, "Fuck them tens. Shoot twenty, bet twenty."

Young Shaq and the lil homies started laughing. O'Shay felt played and dropped some more cash. Turtle dropped his bread. Then O'Shay rolled a hard four then bet twenty more. Turtle dropped his. O'Shay rolled then crapped out.

He said, "Fuck, man!"

Turtle picked up the money. As they kept shooting dice, Dump and O-Head went in the house and talked. Dump told O-Head what was going on with Bird and asked could he chill over there until he found his own spot.

O-Head said, "Shit. You good over here nigga."

Dump said, "Bet!"

Then they walked out to Willie and O'Shay arguing about O'Shay's point.

Willie said, "Your fucking point eight!"

O'Shay said, "My motherfucking point was six!"

Turtle looked at Dump smiling as he pointed at them.

O'Shay walked off and said, "Fuck it. You can keep ya money."

Dump walked through the cut and told them, "I'm ah fuck with y'all later."

Turtle asked him, "You don't want to shoot?"

Dump told him, "I'll be back."

He shot by Swerv and told him he was moving out. After he packed his things, he chilled for a minute and ran it with Swerv then went outside to make a few sells until the sun went down.

Back at the house in Dead End, O-Head and the rest of the crew were hustling on the block. They chilled in the cut and called the dope fiends to the back; when they came, they served them. They didn't know it, but some niggas they had beef with from the project were camped out at the end block, watching and waiting for them to come out.

O'Shay, Turtle, Willie, O-Head, and his nephew Swally were sitting in the living room talking about Dump.

Swally said, "That nigga came home and getting it, but he barely come round this bitch."

O'Shay said, "Shit, he doing him, and we be doing us."

Turtle butted in and said, "Man, fuck all that. I don't know why Big Homie giving him that shit anyway. We can pitch it all without him."

Swally told him. "I feel you, but he spends his own money every time he go and Uncle still front him."

O'Shay said, "I feel like it's enough drugs and money for all of us."

Willie just sat, looked, and listened.

Turtle asked him, "How you feel about it?"

He replied, "I don't know. He ain't been around for a few years."

Swally stood up and said, "It is what it is. I'm gone with my Shorty to make a run. I'm ah fuck with y'all later."

Swally called his girlfriend out the back, and they walked out. When the rival dudes seen them getting in the car, they clutched and cocked their Glocks with extended clips and got out the ride dressed in all black.

Swally asked Jazz to go inside to get his phone because he left it on the kitchen table. After she went and got it and hopped back in they pulled off. As Swally made it to the corner, he noticed two niggas standing in the middle of the street upping their guns when he turned. His eyes got big. He smashed the breaks, and they opened fire while they ran down the car with hollow points flying through the windshield.

Jazz ducked down, and Swally dove on top of her, getting hit with bullets in his back as she screamed. The dudes unloaded their clips on them then hopped in their car and screeched off. Jazz was terrified. She balled up on the floor crying while he was laying on top of her gasping for air. She called his name twice, but he didn't respond. When she heard him stop breathing, she went into a panic and got from under him. She got out the car in shock covered in blood. People started coming to the scene. When they realized who Swally was, they went to the house and called the homies to the scene. Seeing Swally bent up in the car dead it made O-Head feel like he lost his own life. It made Turtle feel like it was meant for him and not Swally. Willie heart was broken, because he and Swally were the closest. O'Shay was in disbelief as he held Jazz in his arms, crying.

Dump left from Swerv's spot and went by O-Head. He had no idea of what had happened back there. When he pulled up to the street, he saw yellow tape blocking off a section while a couple of detectives were asking people questions by the patrol cars with the red and blue lights flashing.

Dump pulled up to the house and parked. When he walked through the cut, the door was wide open, so he walked in.

He hollered, "Yo!"

But nobody responded. He walked through the house and saw no one was there. Then he walked back to the front and saw Willie walking in the door.

Dump said, "What's up?"

Willie said, "Nigga just killed Swally."

"You serious? Fuck! Who killed him?" Dump asked.

Willie said, "It had to be them pussy niggas from the Florida project."

Dump asked, "What's the beef 'bout?"

"A whole lot of shit been going down since you were locked up, my nigga."

"Shit, like what?" Dump asked.

Willie said, "We robbed a couple of them, and after that, we been at war. We gone ride on 'em heavy behind Swally, woah."

Dump looked at him and realized that he was back deep in the streets again, but he wasn't wise enough to understand; he was now out of position to continue to receive the favor God was providing for him.

The week after Swally's death, everybody's minds were twisted. They weren't doing much moving or hustling, but Dump operated differently. He hadn't been around in years, so he and Swally weren't that close, but he did feel the void in the clique.

Big Homie called a meeting with all the homies at the house after Swally's funeral and told who to go and who to chill. Later that evening, they took three cars, four deep in each with assault rifles, and spent on The Strip. They saw six dudes from the project hanging on the porch. One of them noticed the same cars spend back around the second time.

He said, "Say, man, check these niggas out."

One of the dudes stood up and clutched his Glock as the homies pulled to the side and hopped out with the Choppas. The dude on the porch started busting, but when the Park Boys started plucking at 'em, they applied too much pressure, hitting a couple of them up while the rest of them ran off. The homies jumped back in the rides and dipped out with two left lying dead on the porch.

Back in the east Dump was riding around making dope drops. All day his phone rung nonstop, so he made pop after pop. He chilled at the crib after he made a few thousand and sat on the couch counting his cash. Willie and Turtle walked in the door.

Dump said, "What's happening?"

Willie said, "We just touched them bitches."

Dump said, "Dig."

Turtle looked at Dump then looked at the stacks on the coffee table. It made him jealous. He hated the fact Dump was growing large as him in the game. While Willie and Dump talked, Turtle walked straight to the back. Dump packed up his money and put rubber bands around it then stuffed it in his pockets. Turtle went in one of the rooms and sat down on the bed. As he looked through his trap phone, he went to his contacts and reviewed all the customers that stopped scoring dope from him since Dump been around.

Turtle called a few of them and asked what had been up. One of them told him that they quit using, but the other two told him that they'd been dealing with Dump, because his dope was better.

They told him that to make him put less cut on his dope. The truth was, overall Dump had a better attitude and showed them more love giving them extra bags here and there.

Willie walked to the back and asked Turtle, "What's good, baby?"

"Say, bruh, y'all niggas think I'm tripping. This nigga stealing our motherfucking pops."

Willie asked, "How he stealing?"

Turtle said, "I think that bitch went through my phone."

Willie said, "Come on. Are you serious?"

"You fucking right I'm serious."

Willie was like, "I don't know dat. Turtle asked, "You really fuck with that nigga?"

"My nigga, I fucks with you, but we all boys. You act like we ain't grow up together." Turtle looked at him with a foolish look then shook his head.

Dump was in the living room on the phone with Ra-Ra talking about his family reunion he had to go to on the weekend across the river. She told him that one of her friend's husband was taking her friend and her daughters to a reunion across the river as well. He told her that it may be the same reunion. They talked for a minute while Lil Dee, Turtle, and Willie started a dice game in front the door.

After he got off the phone, he walked out there.

He pulled out his money and said, "Let me get on the dice next."

While Turtle was shooting, he said, "We shooting twenty bet twenty."

Dump asked, "What's ya point?"

He said, "Five!" Dump told him, "Bet."

And dropped twenty.

Turtle said, "Bet," and dropped his money.

Willie told Dump "I'm going him."

And he passed Dump twenty.

Dump grabbed it then dropped it on the ground. Turtle kept rolling then dropped twenty more and said, "Twenty on sixes and eight."

Lil Dee told Dump, "I'm going with him on the sixes and eights then dropped his cash."

Dump dropped his forty then Turtle rolled a seven and crapped out. Dump picked up all the cash and grabbed the dice, grinning.

Turtle dropped his money and said, "I got my back." Dump rolled the dice and hit a nine and said, "9th Ward scared." All three of them said, "Bet." Reaching their money to Dump. As he was shaking the dice, he said, "Damn. Everybody against me, huh?" Then rolled them after he dropped the Bets for all. He didn't hit his point, so he kept rolling 'em. They wanted to bet more.

When he took the extra bets, he said, "Six three."

And he rolled 'em up against the brick wall and hit the nine and said, "Add it up!" picking up his money.

Turtle and Willie really ain't like it, because they wanted to win his bread. Dump felt the envious vibe. His next point was ten. He bet them all then crapped out quick. Lil Dee got the dice, and Dump caught his back. The dream crossed his mind about shooting dice with them and under his breath said, "This déjà vu."

After Dee crapped out he quit and walked to the front of the house.

Dump sat in a chair and thought to himself, *What the hell am I doing?* He knew that he promised God that he wouldn't go back to hustling in the streets if He let him out of jail. As bad as he wanted to quit, he was addicted to making money. He started paying attention to every car that passed up the block. Dump began feeling paranoid. He heard Willie talking loud in the cut.

"Dump ran from back here on some shit!"

Turtle yelled, "*Bring your ass back her with that money!*"

While Lil Dee was laughing, Dump got up and walked to the back.

Dump said, "Y'all bitches playing. Give me the dice." He picked them up off the ground and said, "Let's bet forty on fours and tens."

Lil Dee said, "That's the hardest points. You can only hit 'em two ways."

"I know," Dump responded.

Lil Dee replied, "I ain't fucking with it."

Dump asked, "You scared?"

Turtle dropped his money. "Shoot 'em."

Dump put his money down, "I'm shooting for a ten."

Then he rolled them. Dump hit an eleven, then a nine, then crapped out with a seven.

Turtle got on the dice, "I'm shooting a four."

He rolled a six then a hard four.

After he picked up his money and said, "This a ten right here."

He rolled a seven out the door, and Dump laughed at him then grabbed the dice. He cut up on him, and Willie and won $720. When they noticed he was way up, Turtle quit, and Willie followed him in the crib.

Dump shot by Big Homie and scored a quarter of dope with their money. When Big Homie was weighing the dope up, he said, "I been paying attention to you out her in the streets, and so has everybody else."

Dump didn't respond.

Big Homie said, "The word is you're my hit man."

Dump told him, "Let them motherfuckers keep talking. That's why I stay strapped."

Big Homie chuckled and said, "You doing too much. On the real, you need to turn down a lil bit."

Dump said, "Turn down for what?"

He didn't know it, but God was using Big Homie as a messenger to send him back in the right direction.

Big Homie asked, "Why are you fucking with this shit, man? You don't even have to do this. You straight out chea."

Dump didn't even understand why Big Homie was asking him that question, because he was all about selling and fronting him the work.

Dump said, "I feel you, Big Homie, but ain't nobody out here taking care of me but me."

That statement touched God's heart because He had been taking care of him every step of the way.

Big Homie said, "Okay. Keep doing ya thing, homie."

And he gave him the quarter. Then he left out up the block. He went back to the house and chilled in the back room until he dozed off.

The next day was Saturday, and Dump woke up, took a hot shower, and brushed his teeth, getting ready for the family reunion. He hadn't seen many of his family in years since his mother passed away, so he was excited about going. Dump got fresh to death and shot across the river at noon. When he made it there, everyone was happy to see him."

Uncle G got his DJ equipment set up and had the park jumping playing old school jams whole aunt Jessie was handling all the food tasting like she was fresh out the kitchen with the gumbo, BBQ burgers, red beans and rice, crawfish, corn on the cob, potatoes, and crabs. After he greeted all his family and settled down, his cousin Kewone called him over to him and said, "Diggy Dump. What's up, cuz?"

"What's up, cousin?" he asked.

Kewone replied, "You know me, boy. I'm cooling." He turned to his girl and said, "Baby, this my cuz I been telling you about."

She shook Dump's hand. "Hi, my name is Brook. And these are my daughters Mary and Mia." Kewone always talking about you!"

Dump said, "I bet he do, huh?" as he looked at Kewone, grinning, and he told them, "It's nice to meet y'all."

They all smiled, then Kewone and Dump walked off, talking about memories.

Dump was sitting at the table eating alone with his face in the plate. Something told him to look up, so he did, and he saw Mia and Mary staring at him with a funny look on their faces, thinking to themselves, "Yeah, he is Ra-Ra's type."

He turned his head for a sec then looked back, and they were still looking dead at him. He figured they were the girls Ra-Ra was talking about. About an hour passed, and Dump saw Kewone walking up to him, looking puzzled.

Dump asked him, "What's wrong?"

Kewone told him, "Come walk with me. I need to speak with you."

Dump stood up and followed him to the parking lot.

"Do you know a lil chick named Ra-Ra?"

Dump said, "Yeah, that's my baby. Why, what's up?"

He asked Dump, "Did you fuck her?" with a serious face.

He responded, "Come on, cuz, you know me."

Kewone went, "Spishhhh," and put his head down.

Dump asked, "What?"

Kewone looked up and asked, "Tell me that you wore a rubber when you hit that?"

"Of course, nigga. Why you asked that?"

Dump looked at him, looking shaken.

Kewone said, "Man, that bitch got HIV."

Dump's heart dropped. "You gotta be fucking kidding?"

"Do I look like I'm kidding?"

He answered, "No."

Kewone told him, "I'm not. Cuz, don't fuck with that, bruh. She all bad."

That left him speechless. His life had just took a dramatic twist."

Chapter Thirty

The next day Dump life was in a position that he could never imagine. He was living life on the edge. His own friends were ganging up against him. Also, he was unsure about his next move, and a woman he was involved with was known to be HIV positive. He didn't know if it was a rumor or reality. He had no choice but to ask her if it was true. Dump just didn't know how to ask. The thought ran through his mind that she always demanded him to put on a condom every time he attempted to go in raw. It hurt him that if she was HIV positive and kept it a secret. Every hour it embedded itself deeper in his mind riving him crazy. It made him more paranoid as he recognized his current trails in life. It seemed as if he had one foot on solid ground while the other dangled over an empty grave. Just as the world was spinning, so was his thoughts.

Later in the evening the hood was crazy. Two shootings took place that made the police hot from block to block. Dump was lying low. He made a few sells, but he avoided interacting with others. What was strange about the situation with the click was that he actually had love for them, but the feelings weren't mutual, and he knew it. What was more fucked up was that he couldn't do anything about it other than hold his own.

O'Shay started coming to the trap every day with his ass on his shoulders because of problems he had going on in his own house. He couldn't control his wife, so he used his connection with Big Homie as leverage against the younger homies in which Dump was one of them. The problem with that was, Dump had grown to be mentally deranged. Lil Dee, O-Head, Turtle, and Willie normally took what O'Shay issued out as being petty.

One day, O'Shay was sitting in front the trap with Dump. A couple of white girls pulled up, and O'Shay walked up to the car and served them.

When he walked back, Dump said, "You popping, huh, lil bitch?"

O'Shay told him, "You already know, baby."

Dump was like, "Dig that," while he watched the cop car pass with the police looking at them.

O'Shay said, "Damn, them hoes hot."

Dump looked at him and was like, "I wonder why."

He looked at Dump, "What?"

"Nothing," Dump answered then looked up at the camera next door and said, "Cheese," throwing out subliminal message at him on the cool, but O'Shay didn't catch on.

He told Dump that Big Homie had another house around the corner that was almost finished being worked on.

Dump said, "Oh yeah?"

O'Shay said, "Yeah. That's where we gone have to start stashing our shit."

Dump's phone rung. He looked at it and told O'Shay, "No doubt."

Noticing that it was Ra-Ra, Dump was hesitant to answer because of what Kewone told him. It was as if all love was lost on his end.

After the phone stopped ringing, the emotions started to grab ahold of him. Dump got up, called her back, and walked in the house.

She answered, "Hello."

Dump told her, "Hold on," as he walked through the spot to the back room.

When he made it in the room, he closed the door behind him, and said, "Hello."

"Hey, baby! What's going on?" she asked.

"Nothing."

"What's up with you?" she said, "I miss you. Where you at?"

He told her, "Look, I ain't gone bullshit. I seen your home girl at the reunion, and her daughter was looking at me sideways. I didn't know what that was 'bout. A lil bit after that, my cousin came and asked me about you. Then he told me that you are HIV positive. Is that true? Don't lie."

Ra-Ra was in shock. She just held the phone in silence.

Dump said, "Hello?"

She answered, "Hello?"

He asked, "Is it true or not?"

Ra-Ra broke down, crying, and said "Yes. It's true. I wanted to tell you, but the time was never right."

She couldn't believe that he found out the way he did.

He asked, "How can you keep that a secret. If you really gave a fuck about me, you could have told me and gave me the option of making a choice to deal with you or not."

She said, "I do care about you. It's not something easy to tell a person. We started having sex as soon as we met. You didn't allow me to become comfortable enough to tell you."

Dump cut her off. "That's bullshit, Ra'. As cool as you are, I probably would have fucked with you anyway, but the way you played it... I don't know."

"Let me explain," she requested.

Dump shut her down. "Look, I'm ah call you back."

And he hung up in her face.

Ra-Ra balled up in her bed, feeling embarrassed.

Dump was pissed off, sitting on the foot of the bed with his head down in his hands, thinking even though he wore rubbers every time they had sex, he could have caught it from her sucking on him as much as she did. He didn't know if he would continue to be friends with her, but it was obvious that sex was off limits.

After Dump talked to Ra-Ra, he was so depressed he locked himself in the room and stayed there for an hour.

While he lay in the bed, feeling like shit, his phone rang.

He answered it, "What's up?"

And he heard, "What's up, cuz?"

He asked, "Who's this?"

"This E."

He said, "What's up, cousin?"

E said, "I just got released last week, cuz. I need to holler at you. Where you at?"

"I'm on the east. Where you at?" Dump asked.

E said, "I'm out here. Meet me by Swerv."

He said, "I'll be there in thirty minutes."

E told him, "Cool."

Then he hung up.

E was ten minutes away from Swerv, so he pulled up there to wait for him and saw Swerv standing outside.

When he hopped out, Swerv gave him dap and said, "You back out here, huh?"

E said, "Yeah. When the Bird lady coming home though?"

Swerv told him, "Man, she short as fuck."

E said, "That's what's up, but look, you know Yogie was my dog. They still telling me my cousin the one that wacked him."

"That nigga got locked up behind that, but they couldn't prove it, so he got out," said Swerv.

E opened his truck door and got out his pistol from under the seat and said, "That nigga on his way around here. We gone find out." That made Swerv feel uneasy because he knew E was a cold blooded killer. Not only that, it was a fact that in this case he also knew that Dump and E both felt like blood was never thicker than water.

He told E, "I don't know what's going on, but I fuck with both of y'all."

Swerv saw Dump pulling through the gates into the driveway. Swerv felt butterflies in his guts wondering what was about to happen. Dump parked next to them and hopped out and put his .45 caliber in his back pocket.

Swerv said, "Y'all fucking twin boys."

Dump said, "I know," giving him dap, then dapped E and said, "Welcome home, nigga."

E said, "Real shit."

Dump asked, "What chu was locked up for?"

"Them bitches hit me for fifty pounds."

Dump was like, "Damn. What was on ya mind though, cousin?"

E answered, "When I was locked up, I heard about what happened to Yogie, and it fucked me up to know that you were caught up in that mix."

That hit Dump from the blind side.

He said, "Yeah, that shit had me fucked up too."

E asked, "Did you do it?"

Dump said, "No. Me and dude ain't have no beef."

E said, "That nigga got robbed. That ain't have shit to do with beef."

Dump replied, "My nigga, I was caked the fuck up. What I needed to rob a nigga for?"

E looked at Swerv. Swerv nodded. E looked back at Dump and said, "That's what's up. Watch yourself out here. Shit ain't sweet." E gave them dap then burned out as the sun was setting.

To E, something just wasn't sitting right about the situation. After that conversation, Dump didn't trust E at all.

Swerv asked him, "What it's looking like on your end?"

He answered, "Right now, I'm just trying to stay focused in these streets."

"Look, Dump, I know you back in the game, but that shit ain't worth it. I don't want you to get killed, and I have to wear you on a Rest in Peace T-shirt."

Dump told him, "My world don't move without money."

Dump pulled his Desert Eagle out and said, "You tripping, nigga. I stay ready. You ain't gone never have to wear me on a shirt."

Swerv said, "Okay," in a sarcastic way as Dump put his gun back in his pocket.

He told Swerv, "I'm about to move around. I love you, my nigga."

"I love you too, bro. Fuck with me."

Dump said, "Dig."

And he hopped in the FX35 and pulled off, heading back to the Dead End.

When Dump made it two blocks down, he saw a police car turn behind him and hit the lights.

"Fuck, man!" He opened the glove compartment, put the gun in it, then locked it. The cops got from behind him and blew by. He unlocked it, then took the pistol out, and sat it on his lap.

As he made his way back to the spot, it was as if his eyes were glued to the rearview mirror to see if anyone was following him. His mind was so warped every pair of headlights he seen approaching from behind were suspect, so as they passed on the side he clutched with his finger hugging the trigger, waiting for any unusual moves. Dump was really experiencing his life on the edge feeling like he was at the point of no return Swerv was his way out of it, but the enemy used Bird to push him in the opposite direction and he went willingly feeling like he was out of options. If he had paid attention, he would've seen that he had more avenues that he could have taken his life down to avoid dealing with any of his present issues. Once Dump made it home, he went to sleep, contemplating the thought of him against the world with God obviously being on his side along for the ride. It would have been better if he was along for the ride while God was doing the driving.

The next day, Turtle came woke Dump up and said, "Them pigs raided Lil Dee's spot this morning and found the dope."

Dump said, "I seen that boy in a nigga paperwork when I was locked up. He ah rat."

Turtle said, "We need to get that dog food out this bitch ASAP."

Dump got out the bed and called Willie, O'Shay, and O-Head to tell them what was up. When they all came through, they moved their dope to the spot on the back street then went back to the trap. They started a dice game and ganged up against Dump again. He started winning all their money, so they quit. They joked about it for a few minutes then he went inside to use the bathroom. He put his trap phone on the sink to sit down and take a dump. Once he finished he washed his hands then rode to the gas station to get a pack of cigarettes.

After Dump bought his cigarettes, he realized that he left his phone in the bathroom, so he shot back to get it. Everybody had moved around before he got back. When he checked the bathroom, his phone was gone. It pissed him off that one of his friends pulled off a pussy move stealing, knowing that it was his.

Dump dipped straight to the phone store, bought a new phone, and reported the other one stolen, so they canceled the other and gave his new phone the same number.

As soon as he left the store, his trap phone rang.

He answered it, "Hello."

Pam asked, "What the hell was that you gave me?"

Dump said, "Hold up. What you talking about?"

"I didn't come see you," she said. "I thought you sent them around here."

He said, "Sent who?"

She said, "Some short big head motherfucker with the big beard and the tall slim black one."

She had just described Turtle and Willie to the T.

He said, "No. Them niggas stole my phone. Don't trip. I'm on my way around there."

And he hung up.

Dump pulled up to Pam's apartment and called, "Hello."

He said, "I'm downstairs."

She said, "Okay."

And she hung up.

Dump lit his cigarette as Pam was walking down the stairs, looking bad as hell. He could tell she was sick and needed dope.

She got in the truck and said, "The dope they gave me clogged up on the spoon."

With spit in the corners of her mouth.

He said, "Don't trip, I told ya."

And he gave her a fifty-dollar bag to kill her sickness.

"Call me when you ready for another one, baby. I'm ah fuck with cha."

Pam told him, "Thank you, son."

And she got out. When he made it back to the crib, the homies were there.

263

He said, "Ya lil bitches stole my shit, but cha can't stop me with those pussy games."

Turtle wanted to say something, but because of Dump's size, he was afraid of him.

He just laughed it off and said, "Stole what?"

Dump said, "Don't worry about it."

And Dump went down on the couch, counting his cash up. Willie felt bad about it, but he just went along with it because Turtle was manipulating him to roll with him. Not only that, Turtle was so convincing he feared him on the slick. Turtle used that to his advantage on a day to day basis.

Dump was running the streets making sells all day. Turtle and Willie just watched him as Turtle shit was moving Slow. Later that day Turtle's girl called him and told him that their spot got broken into.

When he made it home, he found out all his money and dope was gone. That rally put him in a bind, because he owed Big Homie twelve grand. All he was left with was the one thousand in his pocket. What he didn't know his friend CB4 was the one that hit the lick on him.

Back in the East, Dump was posted at the daiquiri shop on Crowder Boulevard, where a lot of dealers used the parking lot to distribute their drugs. Dump bought a drink and took a seat on a stool out front. The parking lot was popping with hood niggas and females chilling and talking while they sipped on something. Across the boulevard, narcotic force detectives were sitting there, watching the shop.

Dump had his pops to meet him there when they called. Every time they pulled up, he walked in to the bathroom, and they followed behind. The cops started to notice that the people who walked in behind him didn't walk out with a drink and left. They watched him until he left and when he did; they followed him from a distance.

Dump pulled out right on Crowder, drove two lights down, then made a right onto the Service Road on the side of I-10. There, he made a left into Dead End. When they saw him pull into the driveway, they parked at the end of the block.

Big Homie called Dump and asked, "Where you at, lil nigga?"

"I'm at the spot," Dump said.

Big Homie told him, "I'm on my way around there."

Dump said, "All right,"

Dump and Willie chilled up front. Turtle pulled up with Lil Shaq and hopped out looking pissed.

Dump asked, "What's wrong, son?"

Turtle said, "When they hit my house, them niggas got all my shit."

Willie asked, "Everything?"

"Man, what the fuck I said? Everything."

Dump said, "That was somebody you know."

Turtle said, "It probably was you."

Dump said, "You got jokes, huh?"

M5 pulled up in a Lexus truck and hopped out, blowing on some granddaddy purp with his long dreads breaded to the back. He walked up to Dump and gave him dap while the NARCS took their picture.

Five minutes later while Dump and M5 were talking numbers, Big Homie pulled up in a burnt-orange Infiniti M37. He parked and sat there for a minute on his phone.

When he got out, the Narcs took his picture and ran his license plate to find out who he was. When they ran his name, they saw that he had a federal history. He gave M5 dap and told the rest of the lil homies, "What's up?"

M5 told Big Homie, "Give me some of that money."

"Shit, you the one holding. Dump, come holler at me."

And he walked in the spot.

He went in the kitchen and took a seat. Dump sat down across from him and slid him the seventy-five hundred he owed.

Big Homie said, "I just got the word that the hoe that sent you to jail is about to come home. She talking about when she come, she putting some of your other business out her in the streets to get you hit."

Dump asked, "When you heard that?"

"That ain't what you need to be worried about, lil homie. What you need to do is handle that."

Dump couldn't imagine taking Kash and Swerv's mother away from them because he knew how it felt to lose your mother. Maybe if he wasn't their friend, Bird's life would only be a memory to her family and friends.

Dump said, "I got it."

"You would want to."

And Big Homie got up.

When they walked out, M5 said, "Y'all ain't see them niggas sitting in that car on the corner."

Big Homie asked, "On what corner?"

M5 tilted his head in their direction. "Right there."

Big Homie asked, "Y'all strapped?"

Dump said, "Always."

He said, "Fuck 'em then."

He and M5 pulled out while the click went in the house. The Narcs felt like they were on to them, so they left.

As the homies were talking, Willie said, "Them boys sitting down there. We should spin on 'em."

Dump said, "That might be the police, son. That shit happened to me before. We thought it was niggas. It turned out to be them people. One of my niggas fucked around and caught sixty years behind that shit."

Turtle asked, "So you want us to just let a nigga sit on us?"

Dump replied, "No. We just need to make sure it ain't them dicks we spinning on. That's what I'm saying."

Willie told them, "Okay. Let's go see."

They all walked out and saw the car was gone. They got in the Altima and pulled off. Dump went back inside and watched TV until he fell asleep.

At about 11:00 p.m., Dump's phone rung and woke him up. He saw that it was Ra-Ra calling, so he muted the ringer, turned over, and went back to sleep.

When Ra-Ra caught the answering machine, she said, "I see that you haven't been calling me at all. I'm really sorry about what happened with us. Give me a call when you can, friend. I miss you." Then she hung up.

The next morning Dump was sleeping late. O-Head and his wife were home at their other apartment on Haynes Boulevard. One of her friends came over to pop pills with Booty. O-Head didn't know it, but she and Booty shot each other up with dope every once in a while, when he wasn't around because they loved downers.

O-Head told Booty, "I'm about to go to the store. Do you need anything?"

"No, baby. I'm good."

As soon as he walked out the door, she hit his stash for a bag, grabbed a spoon from the kitchen, while her girl got the syringe out her purse. Then she tied Booty's arm up with a shoe string, put the dope on the spoon, and lit it up with the lighter to cook it.

After it burned down, she sucked it up into the needle, found her vein, then poked her. Booty inhaled a deep breath then she laid herself back on the couch.

Katy said, "Don't lay back, bitch. Get up and give me a shot before his ass come back."

Booty got up, "Okay. Come on."

After she tied her up, she fixed the dope then shot the dope in her arm.

Katy said, "This food so good." Her speech slurred.

Her eyes rolled to the back of her head, then her body crouched over. Booty washed the spoon then got rid of the rig.

When she came back to the living room, Katy was stretched out on the floor foaming from the mouth. Booty ran to her hollering her name. She dropped to her knees, tapping and shaking her back, but she got no response. She was so green to the game. She didn't know what to do. The mixture of the pain pills and heroin sent her into an overdose. O-Head walked in the door and saw Booty over her, crying.

He asked, "What the hell's wrong with her?"

Booty looked up at him and said, "She took too many pills?"

He told her to move and tried to bring her back, but she was gone.

He checked her pulse and said, "She's dead."

Booty took a seat on the sofa chair, crying, while Katy lay at her feet with her eyes and mouth wide open, lifeless.

O-Head knew Booty was lying because he had seen so many dope fiends overdosed before and could tell how she was foaming from the mouth it was from dope, but he said nothing. He stashed the package in his car and called the cops.

Dump woke up then went to the living room.

Thirty minutes later Turtle and Lil Shaq walked in and asked, "Did you hear about what happened by O-Head?"

He said, "No. What?"

"A chick OD'd over there. They just took her body."

Dump said, "That's crazy."

Turtle pulled out a stack of money and said, "Bitch, I done came up. Lil Dee Ol' Lady want to score a half."

Dump said, "That nigga in jail for dope and sent his girl to score. Man, that nigga a rat. Don't sell her shit."

Turtle said, "I'm not. I'm ah keep her shit, flip it a couple times, then give her the money back."

All Dump was focused on was keeping the police off their trail, and he knew that any type of action with Lil Dee and his girl would give them more ground to move on them, so he told him, "Dog, I'm telling you, don't fuck with that."

Turtle thought Dump was hating, but his intentions were to save the while click from getting busted.

Turtle and Shaq dipped out. Dump went by Big Homie's to pick up some more dope.

After he got it, he asked, "Do you hear what happened by O-Head?"

Big Homie said, "No."

Dump told him, "It's too much going on out here right now."

"Shit, like what?" he asked.

"You know Lil Dee a rat and got popped for dope. He sent his girl to score from Turtle. I told him not to serve her. This nigga said he gone keep the hoe money. That's still gone put the dicks on us. Plus, a bitch done OD'd by Head's house this morning."

That shook Big Homie.

He said, "Give me that dope to stash."

Once he tucked it, he said, "Bring me to meet up with O-Head."

Dump called O-Head and told him to meet him and Big Homie a block away from his apartment. When they pulled up, they saw O-Head standing in front of his van.

Dump stayed in his SUV, and Big Homie got out and talked to him for a minute. He watched O-Head explain what happened whole Big Homie got on his ass. Big Homie got back in the SUV and called Turtle.

"Meet me by the daiquiri shop."

Then he hung up.

They slid straight to the shop and waited. When Turtle pulled up with Lil Shaq, Big Homie got out, but Dump stayed in.

Turtle talked with Big Homie for a minute and made him call Lil Dee's girl to come get her money. While they were waiting for her, Dump hopped out and was walking past them talking.

Turtle looked at Dump and said, "This not my fucking daddy!"

Dump stopped and amped up on him. "I don't give ah fuck, nigga! That's on you!" with a mean look in his eyes.

Turtle bitched up and nodded. He didn't expect Dump to buck and definitely wasn't ready for it. Dump walked off to the restroom.

After Dump walked out the restroom, Turtle was walking pass him to it and said, "My bad, dog. I'm tripping."

Dump said, "You good." And he kept walking back to his ride.

When Lil Dee's girl pulled up, Big Homie gave her the money and told her that the work was dry right now. She was disappointed and asked him to call her when it was good. Dump looked over to Lil Shaq standing in the car door looking at him. Big Homie told Turtle to holler at him later.

Turtle said, "I got cha." That's when they all dipped out.

Dump dropped Big Homie off and picked up his dope. Everything felt out of place, so he decided to take a trip to Houston to lie low for a couple of days with a chick he dealt with on the Northside. Dump was riding on I-10 in Orange County, Texas at 1:15 a.m., feeling strange, so he turned the radio off to ride in silence.

The road was clear in front of him. He looked up to the rear-view mirror and saw that he was all alone. Something deep inside him told him to pray. Dump started praying the "Our Father" as he looked to the sky. He felt God's presence with him for the first time in his life that he was able to acknowledge it.

Midway in the prayer, he switched and started speaking a language he didn't understand, but he couldn't stop speaking it. When he did stop, he was in a silent spiritual trance. It was like a dream to him. He drove for another hour in the same mind frame. Once his mind settled down, he turned the music on. Dump couldn't explain to himself what just happened. His spirit actually prayed for him in a language that God understood. He had plans to shield Dump from the situations. When he made it to Houston, it was 3:45 a.m. He and Lisa talked for a minute, then they crashed. He held her in his arms as she laid on his chest listening to his heart beat.

The next day back in New Orleans Turtle, and Lil Shaq was chilling in the 7th Ward with some other lil homies from the hood that never hung with the OGs. They were talking about what happened with Big Homie and Dump.

Lil Skeet said, "Don' let that nigga keep putting his hand in your mix. I got some dope fiends that ah kill that shit."

Turtle asked, "Who?"

"Chris and Tucker, that be by the car shop on Chef Highway. Them bitches ah pluck him for that pluck, ya heard me."

Turtle said, "Tell them boys hit me up."

Lil Skeet told him, "I'm about to call 'em right nah."

And he pulled out his phone.

Lil Shaq was paying close attention.

Lil Skeet said, "Hello. What's good with ya?"

Chris said, "Shit, I'm out chea with that pressure. What's up?"

"I got something fo' ya."

Chris told him, "Oh yea?"

Lil Skeet said, "Spin round here."

"I'm on my way." Turtle was nervous about pulling off the move because he didn't want the other homies to know he had plans on sending hitters at Dump, but he felt like he had to get him out the way.

In Houston, Dump was enjoying life with Lisa away from all the bullshit. They were sitting down eating dinner at Hooter's choosing the waitressed to see which one was the best to have a threesome with.

Back in the 7th Ward, Tucker and Chris pulled up on the block by Turtle, Will, Lil Shaq, and Lil Skeet.

When they got out the car, Lil Skeet asked, "What's cracking?"

Chris said, "You already know."

"Look, Turtle want to holler at cha."

Chris looked at Turtle and asked, "What cha got?"

"I got a lick for ya."

Tucker asked, "Who? When? And where at?"

Turtle told them everything about Dump and said, "I'll call you to tell you when. He gave Dump's phone number and said, "When I call you, call him."

Chris said, "Fasho." And dipped out.

Turtle and Lil Shaq shot back to Dead End to scope Dump out, but he never showed up. They didn't know he was out of town. The next day everyone was thinking he got locked up because when they called his phone it was going straight to voice mail.

Sunday evening Dump took Lisa to the movies then left back for New Orleans.

Lisa was surprised that he didn't have sex with her, so when he was on the road, she called him and asked, "I really enjoyed seeing you, but why didn't we do our thing?"

"Don't get me wrong, baby. I wanted to, but I got a lot of shit on my mind right now. If you wanted it, you should have took it," said Dump.

She said, "I should have. Just know next time I will."

Dump bust out laughing.

She told him, "I ain't playing."

He said, "I know."

Lisa said, "Be careful on that road, baby."

"I will."

Then he hung up.

Dump coasted on I-10 for five hours then hit the crib at 11:30 p.m. The only one there was O-Head.

He was like, "Damn, nigga, you been MIA. Like ah motherfucker. We thought you was locked up."

Dump said, "Nah, I was laid up for a minute."

O-Head said, "Them laws been hot as fuck and that same car that was parked on the corner that day been parked in that same spot every night."

He said, "I told 'em that probably was them people."

"I don't know, but I ain't been serving shit," said O-Head.

Dump told him, "After I finish with this pack, I ain't fucking with it no more."

O-Head left. Dump got up and locked the door behind him. After that, he went in the room, put his gun under the pillow, and lay down in the bed and prayed, "Our Father, who art in heaven, hollowed be thy name, thy kingdom come, thy will be done on earth as it is in heaven. Give us this day our daily bread and forgive me for my sins as I forgive those who sin against me, and lead me not into temptations, but deliver me from all evil. For thine is the kingdom, the power, and the glory forever and ever. In Jesus's name. Amen." Then he lay there until he dozed off peacefully.

At 6:40 a.m. his trap phone woke him up for an eight ball of dope. He told them they could meet him at seven thirty on the back street. Dump got up washed his face then brushed his teeth. After that, he went around the corner and got some dope out his stash spot then went back to the house to weigh up some bags.

Once he finished, he went and met the white girl to serve her 3.5g. All that morning his phone was going dumb with sells. The police kept passing the house, so about noon he stated to have his pops to meet him in Swerv's parking lot. He respected Swerv, so he didn't tell him that he made sells in front of his apartment, but he always did when the cops were smoking because there he can see from a distance if they were coming.

Dump made a few thousand dollars and went back to the house to count up. All together he had five grand on him. He called Swerv to tell him that he was on his way over. When he got in the car and pulled off, he saw Turtle pulling up in a car with his phone to his ear smiling.

Dump honked his horn, and Turtle did the same then parked. When Dump made it back by Swerv, they talked for a sec then his phone rung.

He answered, "Hello."

Lil Shaq said, "What's up, fam?"

"I'm chilling. What's good with cha?" asked Dump.

"I need a ride from school."

Dump told him, "I'll be there." He pulled his money out of his pocket and told Swerv, "Hey, homie, hold this thirty-five for me." Swerv took two rubber bands and wrapped it around it then stashed it in the attic.

When he came back down, Dump said, "I'm ah fuck with chu late, nigga."

Swerv gave him dap, and he left. He drove down the Service Road then hopped on I-10 West, drove down then exited on Louisa, turned left, then made a quick right on to Almonaster. When he pulled up to Carver Senior High, Shaq jumped in. The road back to the east without saying a word to each other. Nothing about it was odd to him because they never talked much anyway.

When they made it back to Dead End, Dump's trap phone went to ringing back to meet him by Swerv's apartments in thirty minutes. After he bagged up a quarter, he went there and served four of them, then moved around.

As soon as Dump made it back to the crib, one of his most loyal customers named Stephanie called and said, "Hey, daddy. I need you."

"What's up, baby?"

She said, "I have a hundred for you."

"Okay. Meet me by the same spot we always go."

She asked, "By the apartments?"

"Yep," said Dump.

After he hung up, his phone rang again.

"Hello?"

"Hey, I need a gram."

Dump asked, "Who's this?"

They said, "This Black."

Dump said, "I don't know no Black."

He said, "You always deal with me. Man, you gone know me when you see me."

Everything was moving so fast with Dump getting money.

He said, "Meet me by the Bundy Apartments."

Dude said, "Cool."

Dump pulled back up by Swerv's spot, got out, and waited for them both.

Ten minutes passed as he smoked a cigarette watching the young boys play football in the court way. When he looked to the street, he saw two dudes in a red Q50 Infiniti looking at him. Dump pointed to a parking spot, and they pulled up in it. Dump hopped in the back seat and gave Chris two fifty-dollar bags.

Chris looked at the bags and said, "What the hell is this?"

Dump said, "That's that pop. Both of those equal a gram."

Chris was looking at the bags like he didn't like the size.

Dump said, "You know what? Just give me eighty." And he looked down at his phone.

When he looked back up, Tucker and Chris turned around in the front seats, pointing two pistols in his face.

Chris said, "Come out cho motherfucking pockets, nigga."

This was his first time ever being in a situation like this, but since he did it to so many others, he was calm—so calm it surprised them.

He dug in his pocket and said, "Here is fifteen hundred. That's all I got."

Chris grabbed the cash while Tucker kept the gun pointed at him. Chris was counting the cash looking stupid because Turtle told him that he would have way more than that on him.

Dump said, "Here, you want the dope?" And Dump gave him the small pack. "I have some more in the car. You can have that."

Dump was trying to give them everything, so they could get what they came for and get the fuck. Chris looked at Tucker and told him to go check the Altima that Dump was in for the drugs. When Tucker got out and checked the car, he found nothing. He walked back to the car and signaled Chris to let Dump out.

Chris told him, "Okay. Get out."

Dump said, "Shit, all right."

Then Dump opened the door and stepped out. Once he closed the door, he saw Tucker walking up to him, raising the gun to his head. Dump's reflexes made him reach for the gun, trying to take it from him. Tucker's eyes grew wide. He was afraid that if Dump got the gun, he was gonna die. Chris looked at them as they struggled with the gun. Dump tried hard as he could to stop him, but before he knew it, the barrel was looking him in the eye with the flame spitting out. When the bullet entered and exited Dump's head, his body dropped. Tucker got in Dump's car and followed Chris out the parking lot as the kids walked over to his body lying on the ground with blood skeeting from his head. Dump never saw this coming. If he had remembered his promise to God and kept his covenant with Him, this would've never happened. His breath was fading as his life flashed before his eyes.

To be continued.

About the Author

Gwalla was born in New Orleans, Louisiana, a city with a very great history with many historical events like Mardi Gras, where second line brass bands joined with Indian tribes parading through the streets on the regular. By the age of nine, he began to gravitate toward the music industry, being inspired by hip-hop groups and artist such as Run DMC, Ghetto Boys, Too Short, and Tupac Shakur being played by the DJs at the block parties in the projects. He grew up in the 7th Ward St. Bernard Project, which was one of the most crime-infested neighborhoods in the area.

As he grew up, he started to learn a lot about the streets and involved himself in many situations with other children who were on the wrong path in life leading to destruction. At the age of twelve, he moved to the 9th Ward, living in a single-parent home, feeling a void.

To avoid the pain, he started to write music with dreams of becoming a successful artist in the entertainment business. His music was considered different to others because he didn't copy styles from other artist whom the people loved, so they didn't support his dreams, but he never stopped working on his craft and continued improving his music with a passion.

While living in the 9th Ward, his life became more graphical living in the bricks. He had no brothers; therefore, he had to learn the way to survive in the neighborhood all alone.

By the age of sixteen, he started selling drugs as the murder rate in New Orleans kept rising. He continued to dig deeper in the drug ring, and by the age of seventeen, he was arrested for drug trafficking. Upon his release, he realized how much his life changed. He wanted to find his way out the streets, but it seemed as if the only way out was his music.

By the age of twenty-three, he started his own label and produced his first mixtape titled "Bombing on the Game." The title was inspired by no one recognized how talented he appeared to himself. Without hesitation, he put all his money behind the project and pushed it as he sold and gave away free disc if people didn't have money to buy it. It reached a point where the people started to certify his music, but he was still engraved in the streets in the murder capital of the United States.

In 2005, New Orleans was hit by a category 5 storm named Hurricane Katrina, and the 9th Ward was the hardest-hit location in the country. He watched the winds blow 150 mph before his eyes as dead bodies floated by.

There he almost lost his life twice, swimming through waters that ranged from eight- to twenty-one-feet floods. In 2010, Gwalla received a management deal to help his career take off. When he was put into position to work harder and get his music to be released to the industry, he was set up by some people in 2014 to be murdered because of their envy of his momentum in the music business.

He shot his first video to be released, but before it was, he was shot in is head at point-blank range in broad daylight. People marveled that he survived. It also piqued their interest when his image changed because of the fact he started to wear and eyepatch.

Once he recovered, his level evolved, and he had more access to network nationwide artists such as 2 Chainz, OG Maco, Young Greatness, Lil Scrappy, Rick Ross, Migos, Quavo, Take Off, Offset, Juvenile, and more. He began to build his brand and became more recognized as a well-known upcoming artist in the industry.

Sponsored By:
C-Reality Music Chief Executive Officer C-Jones an independent artist who is the designer for "See Me Doing Good" Apparel Based In Houston, Texas
#Instagram @creality5658

Sponsored By:
Contact us : email penelopej13productionsllc@gmail.com #IG
@Penelopej13productionsllc #weliveindatrap

This Book Is Dedicated To
"Mrs. Beverly Coleman Evans"

CPSIA information can be obtained
at www.ICGtesting.com
Printed in the USA
FSHW021518260420
69446FS